CONTENTS

Helion & Company Limited
Unit 8 Amherst Business Centre
Budbrooke Road
Warwick
CV34 5WE
England
Tel. 01926 499 619
Email: info@helion.co.uk
Website: www.helion.co.uk
Twitter: @helionbooks
Visit our blog http://blog.helion.co.uk/

Published by Helion & Company 2021
Designed and typeset by Farr out Publications, Wokingham, Berkshire
Cover designed by Paul Hewitt, Battlefield Design (www.battlefield-design.co.uk)

ISBN 978-1-913336-37-0

British Library Cataloguing-in-Publication Data
A catalogue record for this book is available from the British Library

We always welcome receiving book proposals from prospective authors.

ABBREVIATIONS

AA	anti-aircraft
BC	Batalhão de Caçadores (Light Infantry Battalion, literally 'Hunters Battalion')
BCP	Batalhão de Caçadores Paulistas (Light Infantry Paulistas Battalion)
BCR	Batalhão de Caçadores de Reserva (Light Infantry Reserve Battalion)
BE	Batalhão de Engheneiros (Engineers Battalion)
BI	Batalhão de Infanteria (Infantry Battalion)
BMCP	Batalhão de Milicia Civica Paulista (Civic Militia Paulista)
BRE	Batalhão Reserva de Engheneiros (Engineers Reserve Battalion)
CA	Corpo Auxiliar (Auxiliary Corps, battalion-type unit from Rio Grande do Sul)
CR	Corpo de Reserva (Reserve unit, battalion-type unit from Rio Grande do Sul)
El.	elements
FP	Força Publica (State Military Police or State Militia units)
FPM	Força Publica Mineira (Minas Gerais State Military Police)
FPP	Força Publica Paulista (São Paulo State Military Police)
GAC	Grupo Artilleria de Costa (Coastal Artillery Group)
GAM	Grupo Artilleria Montada (Mounted Artillery Group)
GAMTH	Grupo Artilleria de Montanha (Mountain Artillery Group)
GAP	Grupo Artilleria Pesada (GIAP) (Heavy Artillery Group)
GIAP	Grupo Independente Artilleria Pesada (Independent Heavy Artillery Group)
MG	machine gun
RAM	Regimento Artilleria Montada (Mounted Artillery Regiment)
RCD	Regimento de Cavalleria Divisionaria (Divisional Cavalry Regiment)
RCI	Regimento de Cavalleria Independiente (Independent Cavalry Regiment)
RGS	Rio Grande do Sul
RGN	Rio Grande do Norte
RI	Regimento de Infanteria (Infantry Regiment)
Sqn	Squadron

ACKNOWLEDGEMENTS

I would like to extend thanks in the first place to my Brazilian friends who helped me to carry out this work: to André Naves, the first person who talked to me about this war; to Luiz Fernando de Mello Camargo, who selflessly sent me the first books I had about this topic directly from Brazil; to 1st Lieutenant Ana Izabel, who provided me with remote access to some of the works placed in the ECEME library; to Luiz Eduardo Silva Parreira, who provided me with his unpublished work; and to Eric Lucian Apolinário and Carlos Daróz, who delivered or gave me access to their excellent books, for free, and later sent me several posters, including the one shown on the cover. Also, I would like to especially thank Tom Cooper, who from the first believed in me, gave me his truly valid assessment and endured the hard task of cleaning up my English draft.

But above all, I want to dedicate this work to my mother-in-law, Chitina Zamora, who assisted me in writing this book in her wonderful country house in El Puerto, Sierra Espuña, Murcia, during August 2018; and also to my wife, Carolina Martínez Zamora, for encouraging me to create this document of the Paulista War, and for her patience, enduring my hours of absence during the holidays to complete this piece of work.

INTRODUCTION AND ERRATA TO VOLUME 1

As related in the previous volume, on 9 July 1932, part of the Brazilian Army, mainly the 2nd Infantry Division based in São Paulo and half of the Mixed Brigade located in what is nowadays Mato Grosso do Sul (then the southern part on Mato Grosso), rose up against the dictatorship of Getúlio Vargas to reinstate democracy and the constitution in Brazil. As the rebellion failed in Minas Gerais, Rio Grande do Sul and the rest of Mato Grosso, the Paulistas were faced by five infantry and three cavalry divisions, and half a brigade of the Brazilian Army, so their chances were slim. These troops were reinforced with the local State Military Police or Força Publica (FP, a kind of army belonging to each state in Brazil) and with local recruits that made a large number of volunteer battalions. Nevertheless, the rebels – or Constitutionalists – were at least half as many in number as the government or Federal armies. The composition, organisation and strength of all these units were narrated in detail in the previous volume.

The Federal Army Aviation Service had six Potez Po-25 TOE and four Waco CSO/225 fighter-bombers, two Amiot 123 BP bombers and two Nid-72 fighters operative at the beginning of the war. On top of that, the Naval Aviation could reinforce the Federals with two Martin PM-1 and three (later six) Savoia SM.55 floatplane bombers, plus four O2U-2 Corsair fighters. The Paulistas had only two Potez Po-25s and two Waco CSO/225s (the latter without machine guns, being armed only bombs and hand weapons), but these were later reinforced by an armed Federal Waco (the C-3 'Waco Verde', or Green Waco) and a Nid-72, which defected to the Paulista side on 14

A public demonstration held on 23 May 1932 in São Paulo's Sé Square, calling for the return of democracy in Brazil. (Unknown author, Abril, Nosso Século, Paulo Florençano collection, via Catalogo)

Students at the public demonstrations held on 23 May 1932 in São Paulo's Patriarca Square, calling for the end of the Vargas dictatorship. Note the black and white Paulista flag and the suits of the students, representative of the Brazilian middle and upper class. (Unknown author, Abril, Nosso Século, Paulo Florençano collection, via Catalogo)

July and 20 August 1932 respectively. Thus, during July and August the Federals had up to 26 aircraft (two of which would defect); 24 armed combat aircraft versus just four to six Paulista ones. Any eventual reinforcements were not enough to change the tide for the rebels, as despite the Paulistas being able to buy up to 10 Curtiss Falcon OU1-Es from Chile from 25 August, only four of these were able to fly during the war. On top of that, the Federals also imported a larger number of Wacos from the United States from 24 August, 15 of them being able to participate in the conflict. The details of these events were narrated in Volume 1.

Returning to the main operations of the war, the major front was in the Paraíba Valley, where the attack of the rebel 2nd Infantry Division towards Rio de Janeiro (then the capital of Brazil), to the east, was very slow and hesitant, and was finally blocked by the 1st Federal Division. Trench warfare then erupted in the high mountain ranges, reminiscent of the Italo-Austrian front during the First World War. Further south, the Varguistas blocked the coast to impede any importation of weapons by the rebels, and a landing there was defeated by the Paulistas at Cunha, in one of their rare victories, evidence of what the Paulistas could achieve by using their interior lines to reinforce each sector attacked by the surrounding Federal troops. Eventually, the Government Army Detachment of the East, under General Góis Monteiro, using massive artillery and aviation support and with 20,000 soldiers (double the number of the rebels), was able to make a breach in the Paulistas' lines, forcing the coastal troops to retreat to the north to reinforce the near-collapsing rebel forces. Góis then launched a cavalry column in this abandoned sector to envelop, in a kind of blitzkrieg, the whole right/southern flank of the rebel front in the Paraíba Valley, but the war came to an end in early October before this pocket was closed and a battle of annihilation could happen.

This set of events were narrated in Volume 1, and now in Volume 2 we will return to 9 July 1932 to narrate in detail the fighting on the other fronts of the war, which was mainly a war of movement. On the Southern Front, from the Paraná State frontier through southern São Paulo, the Federals had to force three or four lines of major rivers that crossed this sector, creating several pockets in the most successful manoeuvres of the conflict. But the decisive theatre of the war, due to its closeness to the main Paulista metropolis and the Mogi Mirim–Campinas railway lines, was the area bordering Minas Gerais State to the north-east of São Paulo city. Paradoxically, this important sector was near dormant until 2 August. There was also some large-scale fighting in Mato Grosso do Sul, following the path of the Paraná and Paraguay rivers; isolated actions in the Amazonas River (Manaus); and guerrilla activities in Rio Grande do Sul.

Middle class volunteers enlisting in the Constitutionalist or Paulista Army in the Derecho (Law) School. (Unknown author, Abril, Nosso Século, Paulo Florençano collection, via Catalogo)

A public demonstration on 11 July 1932, perhaps in São Paulo Cathedral, supporting the rebellion against Getúlio Vargas. Note the little Paulista flags on the left and the Pharmacy and Odontology School supporters on the right. (Unknown author, Abril, Nosso Século, Paulo Florençano collection, via Catalogo)

Finally, this work will narrate the end of the war and, briefly, the political consequences for Brazil.

Some Notes about the Colour Markings of the aircraft and the Flamethrower Vehicle

In the short time between the publication of Volume 1 and the completion of Volume 2, the author had the opportunity to gain access to further sources of information, mainly additional pictures of the time and the autobiography of Major Lysias Rodrigues, narrating his experiences as the commander of the Paulista aviation. These sources included additional reports about the air forces' colours during the war.

For example, despite the fact that nearly all other sources and pictures show that the defecting Paulista Nid-72 aircraft was painted in white overall (or silver), there are some photos showing it painted in green, like the Federal aircraft, but with a white band hiding the serial number, and the nose and propeller painted entirely in white. These were probably the initial colours of this aircraft at the end of August, until the arrival of the Paulista Falcons in early September. Then, to be consistent with the colours of its aviation, the Paulistas probably painted the Nid-72 entirely in white with black bands, as they did with the previously mentioned Falcons.[1]

The Paulistas' Potezs (according to modern reconstructions and some old pictures) were entirely painted in green, with some white bands, but there is a picture showing at least one of them with its upper wing painted in white with some white bands.[2] This was probably done at the beginning of September, as an effort to standardise the Paulista colours, making it at least partially similar to the Falcons. Finally, Lysias states that the destroyed Potez A-116 had its rudder in yellow and green, different to the official markings in which the rudder would be painted in blue, yellow and green (or all in green for the Paulistas). Rodrigues seems to state that at least until the beginning of August, the Paulistas' Potezs still retained their plate numbers. Later, they would hide them under a white band.[3]

Concerning the Federal Corsairs, it was noticed in the pictures that some of them had a blue band on the fuselage. I thought that this band was used later, after the war (see Volume 1), but it is now believed that the band was painted on the aircraft of the leaders of each section, before, during and after the conflict.[4]

Finally, in Volume 1 we mentioned the Paulista flamethrower armoured vehicle, stating that it saw no action, which is not correct.

Some good examples of the Paulista colour markings. The first, fourth and sixth pictures show a Paulista Waco, number C2, which was unarmed, as it shows both pilot seats (when armed, the Waco used the first seat to install a machine gun). Note that it is painted in red, like the famous Federal Wacos called *vermelinhos* ('little reds'). The fifth picture shows the Nid-72 that defected to the Paulista side, totally painted in green (instead of the more well-known white, in which it would probably be painted in September), with its nose in white. The seventh picture shows the Potez A-212, with its rudder in yellow and another colour (green or blue), showing the white Paulista bands over the top wing. Finally, the eighth picture shows a Moth reconnaissance aircraft, totally painted in white, as was the case with nearly all the Paulista aircraft in September, such as the Falcons or the Nid. (via Oliveira Melo)

The *Gazeta* newspaper dated 10 September showed an aerial exhibition of the Paulista Moth in the hands of Adherbal de Oliveira, flying at an altitude of 200 metres. The short officer in the third picture is General Klinger, commander of the Paulista forces, and the taller one is Colonel Herculano de Carvalho e Silva, commander of the Campinas defences at the end of the war, who negotiated a separate armistice with the Federals and was the author of one of the main works about the war. In the fourth picture, the colours and black bands of the Moth are clearly shown. These were the official colours for the Paulista aviation from September 1932. (via Oliveira Melo)

Despite most pictures and modern reconstructions of the Paulista Potezs show them entirely painted in green, this atypical image shows the top wing of the aircraft painted in white with black bands. (via Oliveira Melo)

Paulista flamethrower armoured Caterpillar 22 vehicle built in 1931, which saw action in Cruceiro, in the Paraíba Valley. This vehicle stopped dead the Federal attackers trying to cross the bridge over the river, due to the fire of its four Hotchkiss machine guns and the 100-metre-long streams of flame. (Higuchi)

Exultant Paulista troops departing for the front, in São Paulo, at the beginning of the war. (Museu da Imagem e do Som de São Paulo)

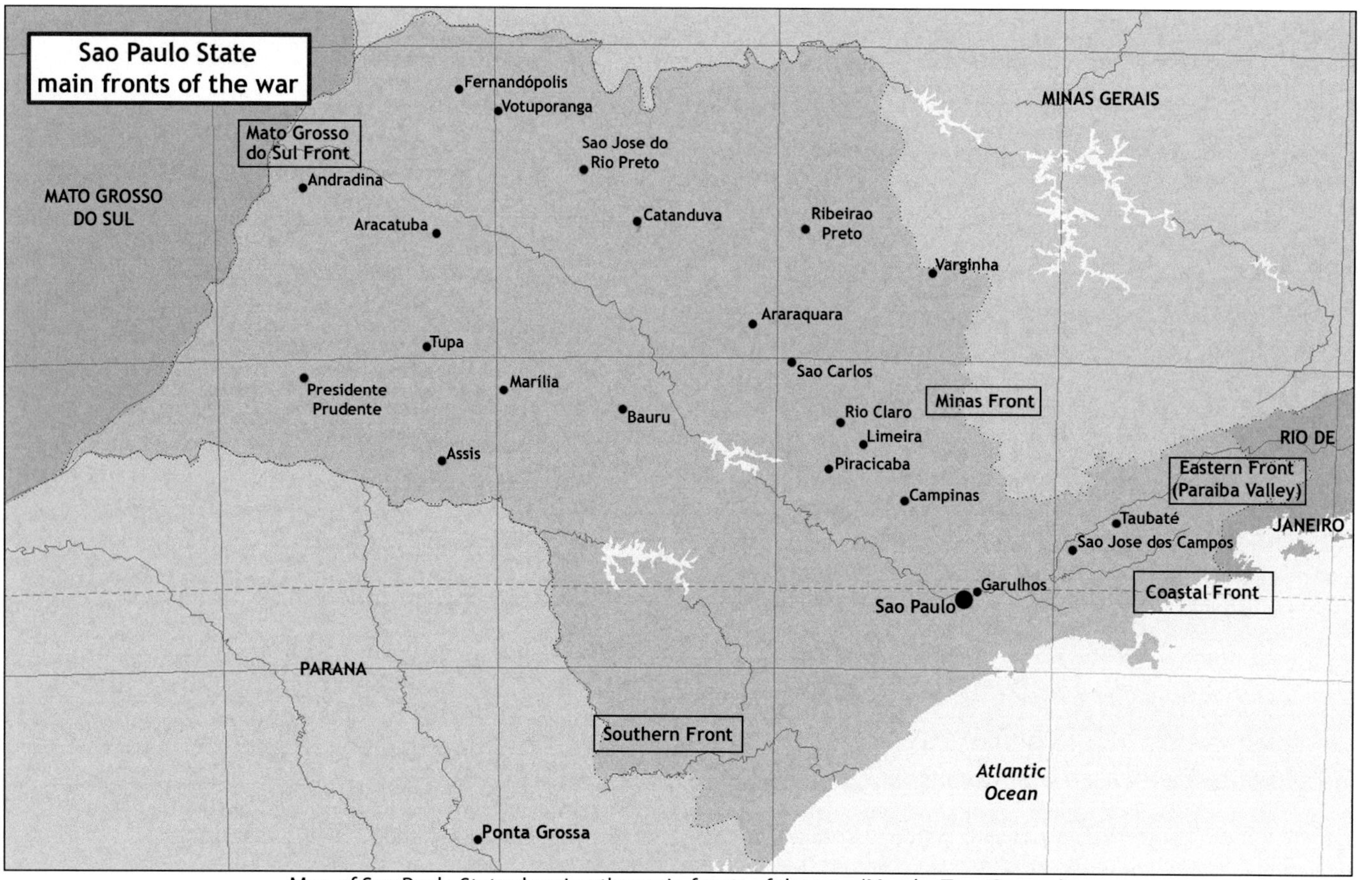

Map of Sao Paulo State showing the main fronts of the war. (Map by Tom Cooper)

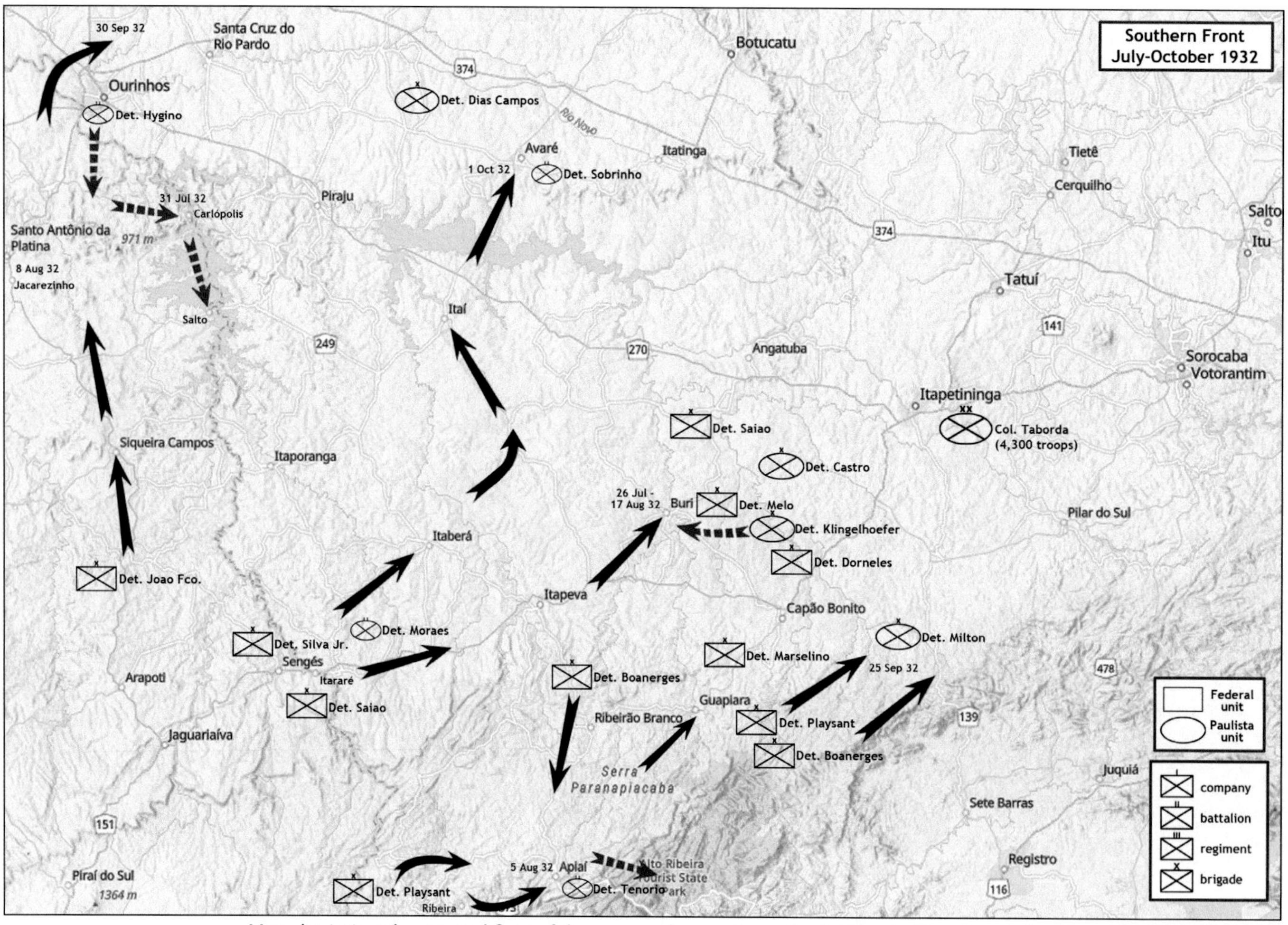

Map depicting the general flow of the war on the southern front. (Map by Tom Cooper)

This vehicle actually blocked the advance of the Federal troops in Cruzeiro, in the Paraíba Valley, panicking the enemy troops due to its machine gun and flame fire.[5] Indeed, the action of this tank covering the Paulista retreat was probably a decisive factor in the exceptionally rapid and well-executed withdrawal made by Colonel Figueiredo from Cruzeiro to Gauratinguetá on 13-14 September (see Volume 1, p.51).

1
THE SOUTHERN FRONT

The Southern Front of the war began on the border between the loyal state of Paraná and the rebel São Paulo. This frontier was established along the Paranapanema River, which in its northern section flowed west to east, forming the frontier with Paraná, then penetrating deep into Paulista territory up to the city that gave its name to the river, Paranapanema, before turning sharply to the south. Before making that turn, there are numerous tributaries running north to south, more or less parallel to the Paraná State frontier, albeit with numerous meanders. These were strong natural defensive positions for the rebels, that the Federal troops had to negotiate one by one. The front, despite being located on a plain, was limited to the north by the Paranapanema River, and to the south by the Sierra Paraná Piaçaba, that rises parallel to the coast in a south-west to north-east direction. Consequently, the Federals were forced to attack frontally, but having a large numerical superiority and the front being rather wide, as we will see, they were able to outflank the rebels several times. The Paulistas were only able to compensate for their lack of soldiers and near total absence of artillery in this sector by concentrating most of their aviation. Hence, the Federals, uniquely in this war, were forced to fight with the sky raining bombs upon them, until, step-by-step, they created the Southern Air Detachment between 26 July and 10 August, which managed to gain control of the air.

A Constitutionalist trench defended by machine guns. These automatic weapons acted as a substitute for artillery on nearly all the fronts for the rebels, except in the Paraíba Valley. Note the Mark I helmet of one of the troopers. (Higuchi)

Due to the theatre's geography, there were two main axes of possible penetration: one located in the central part, with the Sorocabana railway, which linked Paraná State with São Paulo State through Sorocaba, running diagonally from south-west to north-east; and the other running parallel, further south, using the road crossing the Sierra Paraná Piaçaba, then marching towards the north-east to reach the railroad in the city of Itapetininga, deep in the Paulistas' rear. The Federals, by choosing these two lines of advance, could fix the rebels in the sector of the railway line, while by using the southern road, to the right, they could converge in the rebels' rear, which would gradually lead to an encirclement of the enemy from the south. However, as the Federals were advancing, the front would become progressively narrower, allowing the rebels to concentrate their troops and defend less space. The loyalist offensive here began as an authentic blitzkrieg operation, which contrasted sharply with events in the Paraíba Valley sector, but it then turned into a war of position as the front become shorter and more Paulistas arrived as reinforcements, until the front collapsed at the beginning of October.

The aristocratic Major Lysias Rodrigues, who escaped in a fishing boat from Rio de Janeiro at the end of July to assume command of the Paulista aviation. An excellent pilot, he or his gunner had the only confirmed 'kill' of the war. Lysias wrote of his colourful memories as a pilot in his book *Gavioês de Penacho*. (Wiki commons)

Federal General Valdomiro Castilho Lima, commander in chief of the Federal Southern Army Detachment, who began operations very rapidly, breaking the Paulista front and advancing until reaching Buri. (Instituto Histórico e Geográfico de São Paulo, via Donato)

Troops and Aircraft in the Main (Central) Sector (11-18 July)

The Paulista Southern Front was practically undefended on 11 July. The Constitutionalists had expected that Rio Grande do Sul would join the rebellion and that its forces would keep the Federal deployment in Paraná distracted, but as we have seen, this was not the case. In the central sector of the front, on the axis of the railroad to São Paulo, there were no Paulista troops except for the 8th BCP light infantry unit in Itapetininga, deep in the rear, while the Federals concentrated the bulk of their troops here. When the government took Itararé, a town bordering Paraná State through which passes the Sorocabana railway route to São Paulo city, with a cavalry squadron of the 5th RCD (part of the 5th Division), the rebels sent Major Garcia with 203 soldiers of the 8th BCP that forced the loyalists to retreat to Sengés. All 150 riders from the squadron of the 5th RCD defected to the rebels on 13 July, swelling the strength of the defending forces in the area. By 17 July, the Paulistas had elements of the 8th BCP, the Battalion 14 de Julho (armed with 500 old rifles from the Fire Department), two FP squadrons of cavalry, one artillery battery that had arrived from Mato Grosso and even an aircraft.[1] These totalled about 950 soldiers and four guns,[2] deployed in Itararé and commanded by Colonel Pedro Moraes Pinto.

Regarding aviation, it should be recalled that from 16 July, all the rebel combat aircraft were moved to the southern sector to the Itapetininga airfield, from Campo de Marte and the Paraíba Valley (see Volume 1). Major Lysias Rodrigues, who had just escaped in a fishing boat from Rio de Janeiro a couple of days before, arrived at the airfield on the morning of 28 July, assuming command of the rebel aviation and the 1st Constitutionalist Figher Aviation Group. This unit had two Potez (numbers A-116 and A-212) and three Waco (plates C-2, C-3 and C-5) aircraft.[3] However, the Paulista aviation had a shortage of combat pilots, so until the defection of several Federal pilots on 14 July (with the armed Waco C-3) and 25 July (Major Ivo Borges and Lysias Rodrigues),[4] it is likely that these were gradually redeployed to the south. Only at a later date were all the Paulista aircraft manned, which would explain the existence of only a single aircraft and not all the available aviation on 17 July. Nevertheless, Paulista aircraft began bombing enemy units until the end of the month to compensate for the absence of troops in the area, aided by there then being no Federal aircraft in this sector. The rebels generally carried out missions with only a single airframe, and occasionally with two, but these had an extraordinary duration of four or five hours each, sometimes with three or more sorties per aircraft every day.[5]

Returning to the land forces, the Federals had the Southern Army Detachment, led by General Valdomiro Castilho Lima, who had two groups to attack Itararé in the central part of the Southern Front. The Colonel Saião Detachment, in Morungava, Paraná, on the railway line, could attack the Paulistas frontally with artillery support from the heights overlooking the Itararé River, but could not cross it. Saião had about 1,900 soldiers and some 16 artillery pieces (the 13th RI, 5th GAMTH and 1st Artillery Group/9th RAM,[6] all elements of the 5th Infantry Division based in Paraná).[7] Further behind, in Sengés, was the Detachment Silva Junior, which, hidden from the view of the Paulistas, was to march north and cross the Itararé upstream in Passo Cipriano, to fall on the Paulista right flank by surprise. Silva Junior had 2,150 fighters and two artillery pieces

Table 1: The Southern Front (17 July): Central Sector			
Paulistas			
Detachments	**Location**	**Composition**	**Strength**
Moraes Pinto	Itararé	El. 8th BCP, Battalion 14 de Julho, one FP Cavalry Squadron, one squadron/5th RCD Cavalry, one Mato Grosso artillery battery	950 soldiers, four cannons
Federals			
Southern Army Detachment			
General Valdomiro Castilho Lima			
Detachments	**Location**	**Composition**	**Strength**
Saio	South/Left flank: on the railway, Morungava, Paraná,	13th RI, 5th GAMTH, 1st Artillery Group/9th RAM	1,900 soldiers, 16 cannons
Silva Jr	North/Right flank: Sengés	3rd RC/Rio Grande do Sul Military Brigade, 2nd RC/ Military Brigade, 14th and 13th BC, 1st Company/15th BC, one section/3rd GAMTH	2,150 soldiers, two cannons
Total: 4,050 soldiers, 18 cannons			

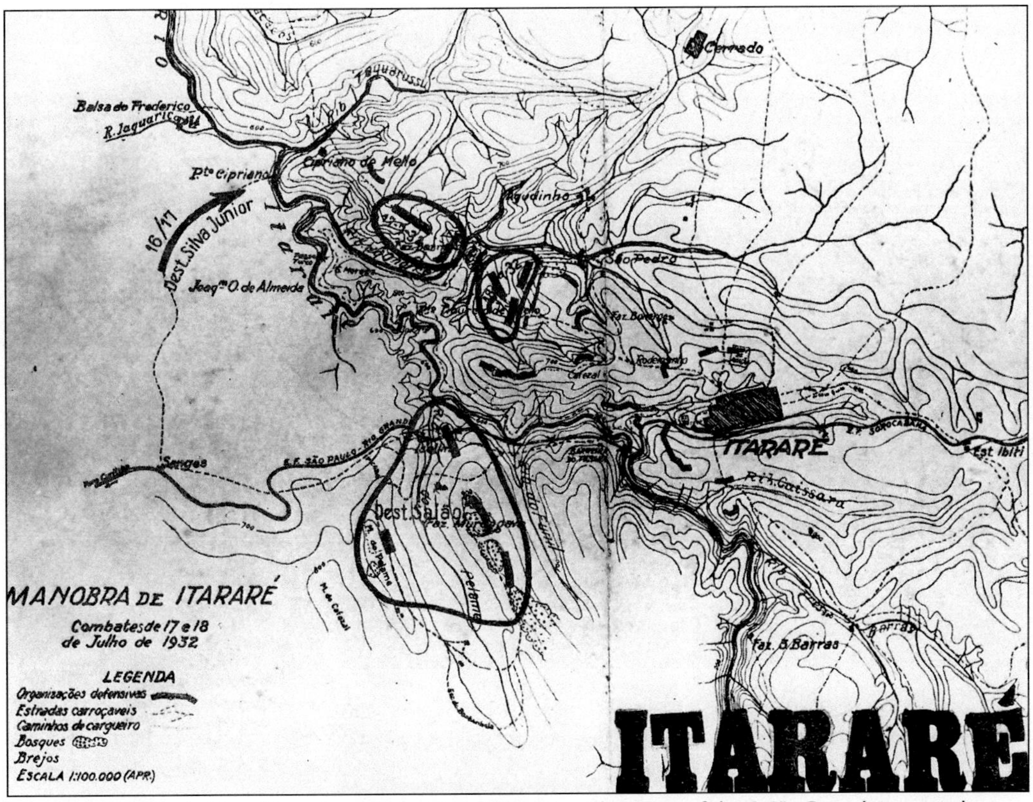

Sketch of the Battle of Itararé made by Jorge Mancini, with troops of the Saião Detachment at the bottom, and above them those of Silva Junior crossing the Itararé River. (Jorge Mancini, via Donato)

(the 3rd RC/Rio Grande do Sul Military Brigade, 2nd RC/ Military Brigade,[8] 13th and 14th BC, 1st Company/15th BC – these last three being elements of the 5th Division – and only one artillery section/3rd GAMTH).[9] My calculations of effectives compare with the official figures of some 4,050 Federal soldiers under Lima during 16 and 17 July, having Silva Junior and Saião with 2,450 fighters on the front line and 700 more in reserve.[10] The Federals thus had a four-to-one advantage in infantry and artillery, something that could only be compensated for by the Paulista aviation and the natural obstacle of crossing the Itararé River.

Blitzkrieg in Itararé (18-22 July)

The government offensive began on 18 July at 0800 hours. After an artillery preparation brilliantly planned by General Lima, the Detachment Saião advanced to occupy the heights overlooking the town, shooting and distracting the rebels, while Silva Junior crossed the river farther north and fell on the Paulista right flank. The crossing was initiated by probably the dismounted riders from the vanguard of the 3rd RC/Military Brigade. The rebel aircraft flown by Lieutenant João Silvio Hoeltz surprisingly failed to detect the loyalist movements in the area, and the rebel right flank fell back and forced the centre to withdraw at 1600 hours. The Paulistas also made the mistake of deploying only troops on the railway line and major roads, with no patrols in the intermediate zones, so they were caught completely by surprise. The rebel commander of the sector, Moraes Pinto, was directing his forces from the rear, having his command post in Faxina (nowadays Itapeva), and therefore he could not be made

Paulista volunteers from the Universitário Battalion in Itararé. Note the white handkerchiefs. (Coleção Dorothy Moretti, photo taken by Claro Gustavo Jansson, via Donato)

Federal troops embarking at Itararé station. Note the absence of helmets. (Coleção Dorothy Moretti, photo taken by Claro Gustavo Jansson, via Donato)

Colonel Christiano Klingelhoefer, of German ancestry, led the Southern Front until the arrival of Colonel Taborda and fought three hotly contested battles at Buri. He then led his own detachment under Taborda. (Wiki commons)

Constitutionalist troopers with a machine gun. Note the steel Adrian 1915 helmets that identify them as Paulistas. (Higuchi)

A 75mm Paulista Krupp 75/L28 Model 1908 gun at Fazenda Bom Retiro, behind the Das Almas River, in September 1932. All the Paulista artillery was deployed in the Paraíba Valley, except a single battery from Mato Grosso that was deployed in the Southern Front. (Museu da Imagen e do Som, São Paulo, via Donato)

rapidly aware of the evolution of the fighting and the deployment of his troops. In addition, the '14 Julio' Battalion, for example, had only 50 cartridges per soldier, and this was further reduced to only just 16 or 17 rounds they found that two-thirds of the ammunition was unusable with the old firefighter rifles they carried. After a fight at bayonet-point, the rebels suffered 11 dead, 20 wounded and 45 prisoners, and their positions were abandoned at 2200 hours.[11]

In the meantime, Moraes Pinto tried to form a new line further back in Ibití, but Colonel Klingelhoefer, who assumed command of the sector, ordered another retreat to Faxina (today Itapeva), several kilometres further back but still protecting the São Paulo railroad.[12] Even the Faxina position did not last long, as, taking advantage of their earlier success, the Federal 2nd RC/Military Brigade and the 3rd Battalion (perhaps from the same FP unit)[13] pushed on and reached the town on 22 July, from which the Paulistas fled almost without a fight. The rebels received orders to fall further back to Buri, still on the Sorocabana railway.[14] Lima now had 5,000 fighters in Faxina, that number being reinforced up to 7,000 in the next few days.[15] In just four days, Valdomiro Lima's troops had advanced 56km and crossed three waterways: the Itararé, Pirituba and Taguarí rivers.

The fall of Buri (26 July)

The rebel troops rested in Buri and dug in from 23-25 July to prepare new defensive positions. The Paulista Detachment Moraes Pinto was established in south-eastern Buri, at Capão Bonito, while to defend Buri, Klingelhoefer had his own detachment and a few outposts, located 2km outside the village, which were reinforced by two battalions (the 'Marcilio Franco' and 'Floriano Peixoto') and an artillery battery. They appeared just in time, as the Federals arrived on 26 July and started shooting across the front line.[16] These attacking troops were formed by the 1st and 2nd Battalions/Military Brigade and a two-piece section of the 5th GAMTH. They first pressed the Paulista outposts on both sides of the railway, the 'Franco' to the north or right and the 'Peixoto' in the south or left. Although the 'Peixoto' more or less held the line, the 'Franco' was dispersed, so the entire rebel position had to go back almost as far as Buri.[17] The Riograndenses (troops from the Military Brigade of Rio Grande do Sul State) again attacked the Paulistas there, the defenders being located on the heights behind the town cemetery, and from there they spread out to their flanks. The rebels' left flank artillery was attacked by surprise and enveloped, their accompanying infantry retreating so that the guns and their gunners were left alone, fearing capture. However, they lowered their guns' elevation and bombarded the loyalists with shrapnel to eject them. The gunners suffered one dead and three wounded in this action.

At 1000 hours, Klingelhoefer ordered Moraes Pinto in Capão Bonito, in the south-east, to launch a counterattack on the Federal right flank, but Pinto was unable to do so because his position was being threatened by a new Federal detachment under Colonel Boanerges. While the fighting continued, the Paulistas began to

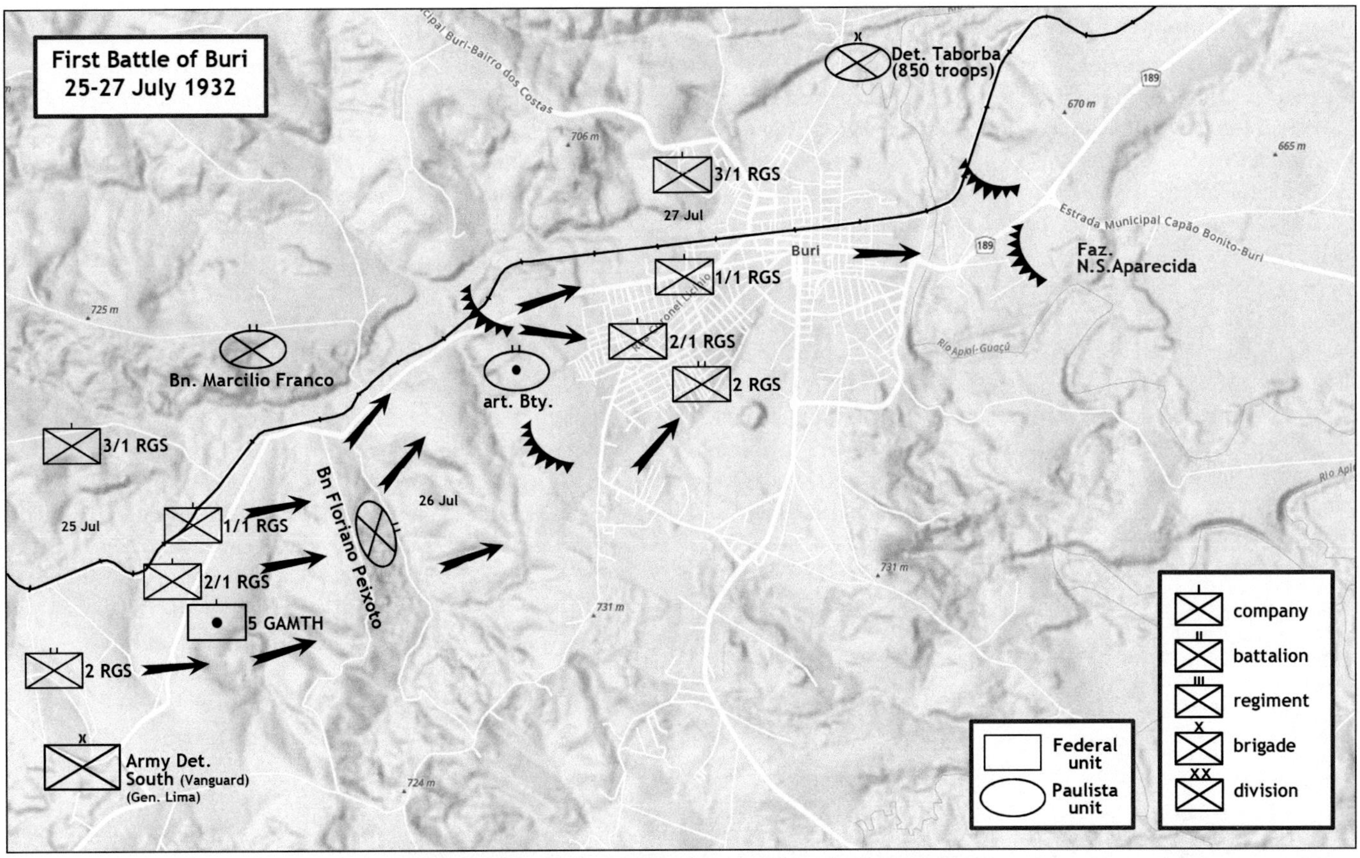

The First Battle of Buri (25-27 July 1932). (Map by Tom Cooper)

Table 2: The 1st Battle of Buri (26 July)		
Paulistas		
Colonel Basilio Taborda		
Detachment	**Composition**	
Klingelhoefer	'Marcilio Franco' and 'Floriano Peixoto' Battalions, one artillery battery	
Total:		**850 men, four cannons**
Note: The Moraes Pinto Detachment, in Capão Bonito, did not take part in the battle.		
Federals		
General Valdomiro Lima		
Detachment	**Composition**	
Vanguard	1st and 2nd Battalions/Military Brigade, a section/5th GAMTH	
Total: 1,050 men, two cannons		

run low on ammunition. Furthermore, no hot meal was prepared or distributed for the under pressure defenders, so several soldiers defected and fled to the station, where a train housing the Paulista staff of the sector came under fire from them. Colonel Basilio Taborda, who had just arrived in a fishing boat from Rio de Janeiro with some Paulista pilots, then took command of the front from Klingelhoefer, who retained control of his own detachment. Taborda was informed that the entire company of Captain Aranha had left their positions when first coming under fire, while half of the soldiers of the 'Marcilio Franco' and the 'Floriano Peixoto' Battalions had fled, so he gave the order to retreat across the Apiaí-Guaçu River. A Federal gun, guided by a group of defectors, was then moved to within just 30 metres of the command post and began to strafe the retreating Paulista troops. Many soldiers fled on foot along the railway to reach Itapetininga. The battle ended at midnight, with the rebels suffering more than 300 troops taken prisoner (453 according to government figures, with two 75mms gun, 800 rifles and four sub machine guns). The front was now completely open to an enemy advance.[18]

Finally, covered by the first intervention of the armoured train TB-1, the remaining Paulistas managed to consolidate their position to the north-east of Buri, in Vitorino Carmilo, still on the Sorobacana railway line to São Paulo.[19] The Federals were protected behind a lake formed by the damming of the Apiaí-Guaçu River in Santa Luzia.[20] Although several authors claim the loyalists enjoyed an overwhelming numerical superiority in this battle, the truth is that only the Varguistas' extreme vanguard was involved in the fighting, consisting of two battalions and a section of artillery, as the bulk of the force was delayed. The Federals were still surprised by the extent of the Paulista withdrawal in the previous confrontations, also having to detach troops to cover their flanks. Facing them, the Paulistas also had at least two battalions, one company and an artillery battery, so in all likelihood the sides were evenly matched in this clash, with about 1,050 Federals against some 850 rebels.[21]

The Battle for Ribeira (17-30 July)

While all this was happening in the middle section of the front line, both flanks of the government's vanguard were left hanging in the air, so Federal General Lima had to organise several new detachments and distract troops to cover them. Thus, in Faxina, Lima created the Detachment Lieutenant Colonel Boanerges, that was to march towards the south-east along the road to Ribeirão Branco, and then continue to the southern end of the front, attacking via Apiaí the rear of the rebel positions that were still defending Ribeira. Boanerges had about 1,550 soldiers (the II/13th RI and 13th BC of the 5th Division, II/8th RI from the 3rd Division and a platoon from the 2nd RC/Mixed Brigade).[22]

At the southern end of the front, or the Federal extreme right, the main road towards São Paulo started in Capela de Ribeira, on the border with Paraná, before passing through Ribeira. Ribeira was defended from the beginning of the war by a Paulista detachment of 100 soldiers divided into four battle groups under Lieutenant Silva Campos. On 17 July, these were reinforced by a cavalry squadron led by Captain Oliveira França. Against them, the Federal detachment of Captain Airton Playsant, consisting of about 100 soldiers of the 13th RI and Paraná FP, was being organised. On 18 July, Playsant reconnoitred the sector and on the 19th, having been progressively strengthened, he expelled the rebels from Pinhalzinho in Paraná, and then tried to outflank the Paulista right flank in Ribeira. During the following days, government forces managed to take the bridge across the Itararé River. However, the Paulistas, under Lieutenant Colonel Azarias Silva from 21 July, were also being reinforced and already had about 400 soldiers. Consequently, the attacks made on 23, 25 and 26 July were repulsed with heavy losses. The 400-strong 1st Battalion FP Paraná began to suffer many defections, including its deputy commander. Their morale was low and they had suffered at least 26 wounded. However, they were eventually reinforced to include almost 1,200 fighters, according to Paulista sources. Playsant was then able to infiltrate to near a ranch 6km behind the rebel front line, and attacked Ribeira from the rear, taking the city on the afternoon of 30 July. About 123 Paulistas escaped from the siege, and after a six-day cross-country march to the north-east, they crossed the Paraná Piaçaba ridges and reached Apiaí on the road to São Paulo city. The rest of the original defending force was either killed or imprisoned.[23]

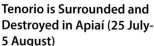

Paulista forces in the sector of Ribeira. (Higuchi)

Paulistas volunteers. As they wear just flat or cloth caps, only their white scarfs identify them as rebels. (Higuchi)

Tenorio is Surrounded and Destroyed in Apiaí (25 July-5 August)

While this struggle occurred in Ribeira, the Paulistas discovered that their right flank was being threatened by the Boanerges Detachment, which was marching south from Faxina, and whose 5th RCD had just taken Ribeirão Branco on 25 July. Some 400 Federal soldiers remained there without artillery. The next step for Boanerges was to move forward to Apiaía, to fully isolate Ribeirão from the rear. To avoid this, reservists from the town of Itapetininga's 'Tenorio' Battalion under Major Tenorio Brito were sent through Guapiara to Apiaí. The plan was to help Ribeira and recover Ribeirão Branco, attacking Boanerges on his left flank. However, when Tenorio arrived at Apaiaí on 31 July, Ribeira had already fallen. Nevertheless, Tenorio still sent part of his force to the right to attack Boanerges and the rest

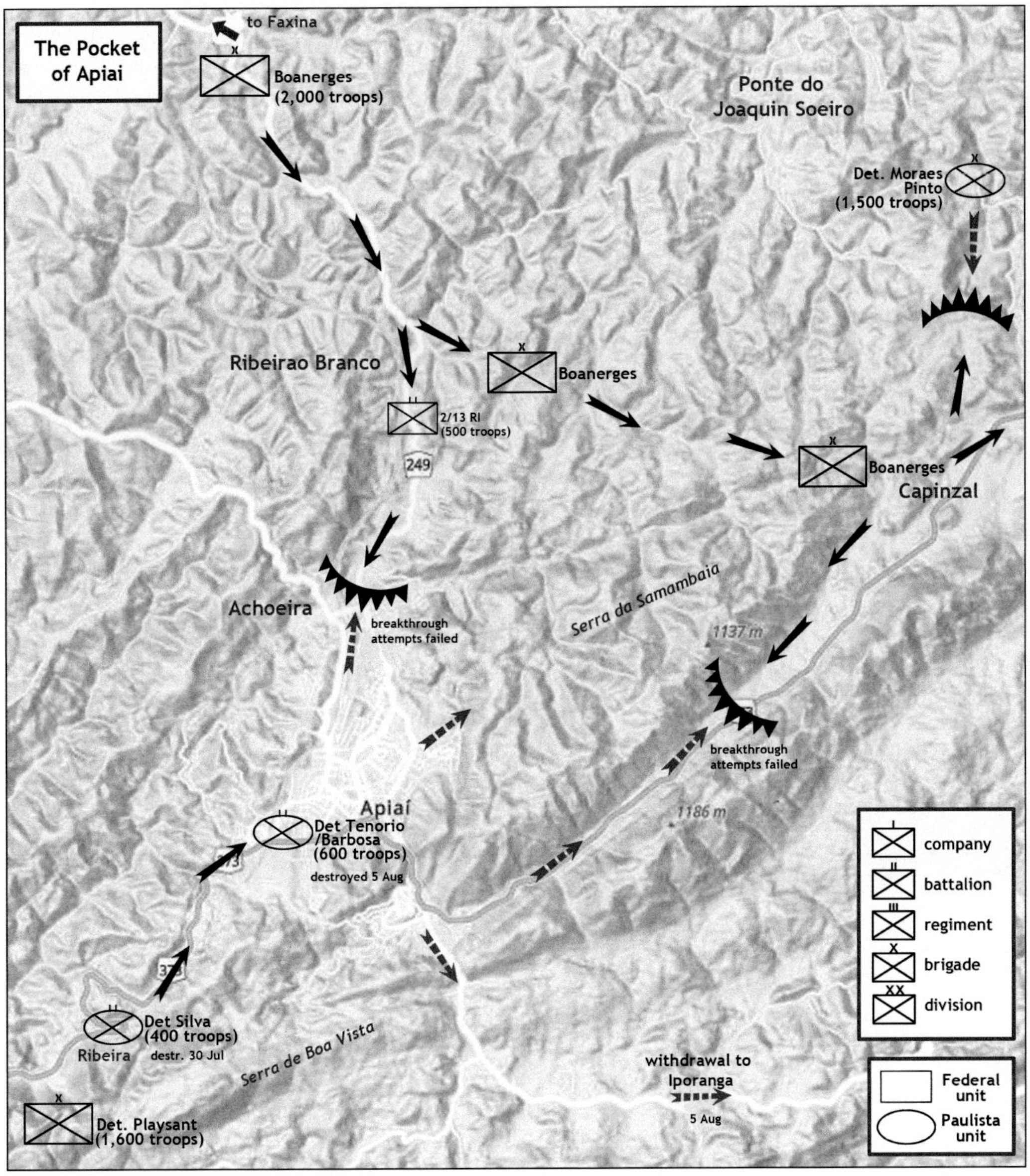

The Pocket of Apiaí. (Map by Tom Cooper)

to the south, but he received a counter-order from Colonel Taborda stating he should focus only on attacking Playsant in the south, so all the troops had to return to Apiaí. When Tenorio made contact with Playsant's Federal units, the Paulistas found that Boanerges had not been inactive. The Federal forces continued marching eastward, and after overcoming 150 Paulistas that were covering the rebel rear under Colonel Barbosa e Silva, had taken Capinzal and then turned to their right, to the south. Boanerges thus occupied Banhado Grande, behind Apiaí, surrounding the entire Tenorio Detachment.[24]

During the evening of 1 August and early the following morning, the 600 rebels under Tenorio attempted to break out and reopen the road north-east to Capinzal-Capão Bonito. To this end, Tenorio sent 130 recruits in six trucks to recover Fazendinha, but on the way they were ambushed by Boanerges, and suffering a direct artillery hit, the rebels fled after a 20-minute fire fight.[25] The isolated forces of Tenorio were now facing a ring comprising the Playsant

Table 3: The Extreme Southern Sector: Battles of Ribeira & Apiaí (17 July-5 August)				
Paulistas				
Colonel Basilio Taborda (since 26 July)				
Detachment	**Location**	**Composition**	**Strength**	**Notes**
Lieutenant Colonel Silva (since 20 July)	Extreme south: Ribeira		100 men. Reinforced to 180, then up to 400 men	Destroyed (30 July)
Major Tenorio/ Lieutenant Colonel Barbosa	South: Apiaí	Tenorio Battalion	Reinforced up to 600 men	Created 25 July. Destroyed 1-5 August
Colonel Moraes Pinto	South-centre: Guapiara	Marcilio Franco, 14 de Julho and 8th BCP Battalions, a company/7th BCP, three artillery pieces	1,300 men, three cannons	Retreated from the centre: Itararé, then Capão Bonito. Only one company sent to rescue Tenorio
Federals				
Playsant	Extreme south: vs Ribeira	13th RI, 1st FP Paraná Battalion	100, then 400, 1,200 and up to 1,600 men	
Boanerges	South-centre: Faxina to Ribeirão Branco	II/13th RI, 13th BC, II/8th RI Battalions, a platoon 2nd RC/Mixed Brigade, 3rd Squadron/5th RCD, 5th RAM	1,550, then 2,100 men	

Detachment (some 1,600 men) in the south, the 13th RI (5th Division) on the road from Ribeirão Branco to the north, and the rest of the Boanerges Detachment to the north-east, on the road from Capinzal (7th RI/3rd Division, 13th BC, 5th RAM, a squadron of the 5th RCD of 5th Division and several units of the Rio Grande do Sul Mixed Brigade). Outside the pocket, the rebel Taborda had a force in Guapiara, on the road to Capinzal, with which he could try to attack Boanerges from the north. These numbered some 1,300 soldiers (the Marcilio Franco, 14 de Julho and 8th BCP Battalions, a company of the 7th BCP and three artillery pieces). Surprisingly, Taborda only sent only one company of this force to reach the pocket on 1 August, probably because the Paulistas were also defending Capão Bonito from any potential Federal attack coming from Buri. This company was beaten off by Boanerges at Capinzal, just 14km from Guapiara and the south-east sector of the front was secured.[26]

Meanwhile, in Apiaí further south, the surrounded Tenorio Detachment was asked by Playsant and Boanerges to surrender. However, both Colonel Barbosa and Major Tenorio decided to try to escape across country to the south-east, toward Juquiá, via Iporanga and Xiririca, crossing the Paraná Piaçaba mountains and abandoning all their heavy materiel. At that moment, the 123 survivors fleeing from Ribeira arrived, and they joined the group in their retreat to the coast. The Federal cavalry pursued them to Iporanga, where they captured 50 fugitives. The rest of the force arrived at Xiririca on 5 August, completely demoralised and almost unarmed, reaching Santos 12 days later.[27] The Tenorio Detachment had been sent by Colonel Taborda into a trap that ended with its destruction.

Federal troops defending their lines with machine guns. Note the cloth caps and the large Gaúcho hat, which identifies them as Riograndense pro-government troops. (Higuchi)

The Paulistas Invade North-east Paraná (17-31 July)

As the reader will remember, we left the Army Detachment of the South with its spearhead in the central sector of the railroad to São Paulo city, taking Buri, while its General

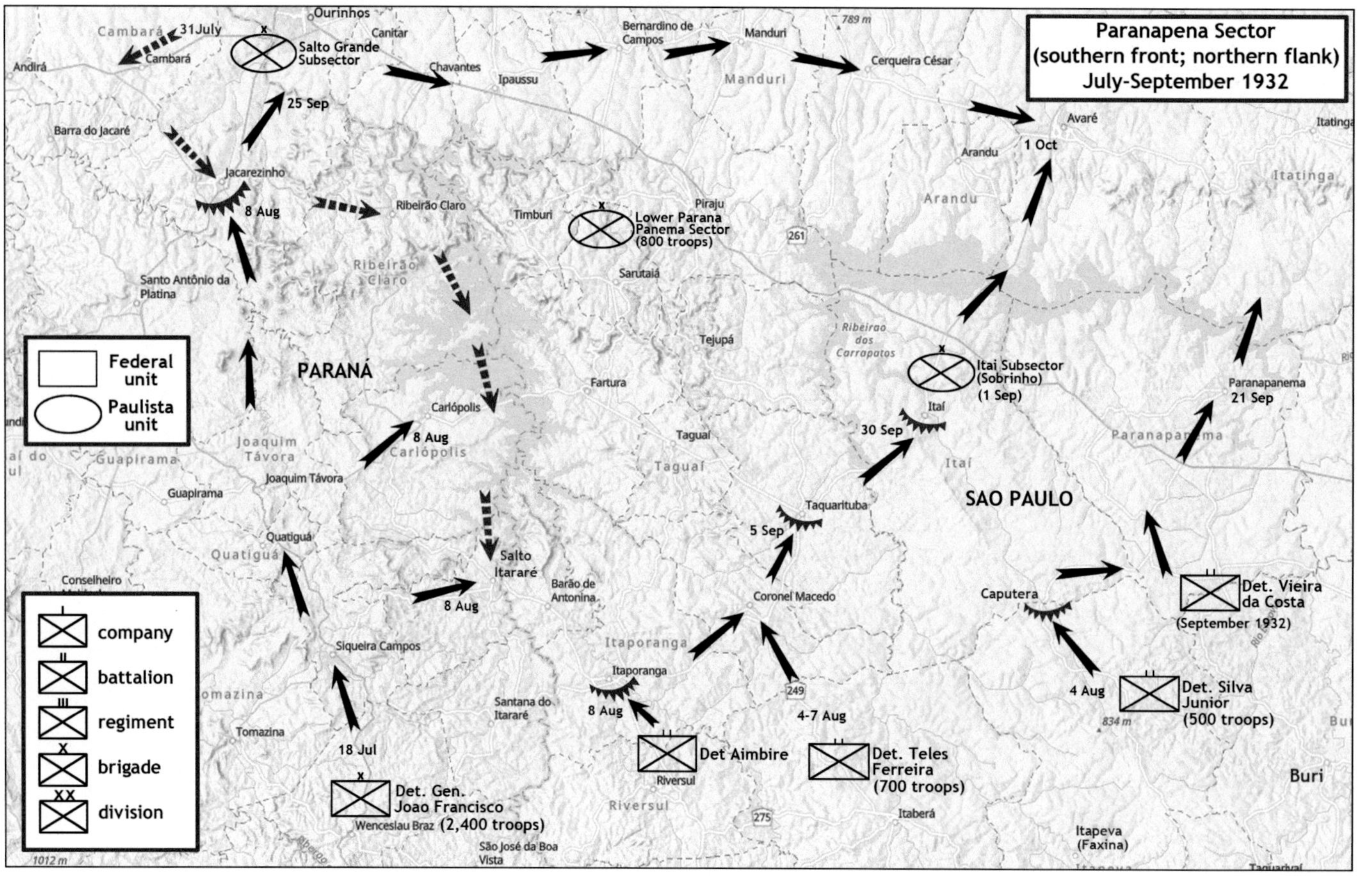

The northern flank of the Southern Front. (Map by Tom Cooper)

Valdomiro Lima cleared his right flank (south) by capturing Ribeiro and Apiaí. Now he had to do the same on his left or northern flank. This area, between the middle course of the Paranapanema River in the north and the railroad to São Paulo in the south, was defended by the Paulistas' 'Voluntarios de Avaré' under Captain do Vale e Silva, and the 9th BCP under Major Castro e Silva, about 800 soldiers in all. However, these were scattered in several groups of 100-200 men in small garrisons. They were deployed, during the first half of July, from south to north, at Itaberá, Itaporanga to the north-west, Fartura in the north, Chavantes further to the north-west (on the other side of the Paranapanema, on the railway to Presidente Wenceslão) and finally at Ourinhos and Palmital, in the same direction but further west, at the confluence with the railway line of North Paraná, which runs from north to south in this state in parallel with the border with São Paulo.[28]

In principle, the mission of this Constitutionalist deployment was purely defensive, to prevent the crossing of the middle course of the Paranapanema by the loyalists. Yet by 18 July, government patrols from the João Francisco Detachment, which was still being constituted, had taken several points on the Itararé River, the first Paranapanema tributary after crossing the state boundary. They now held Salto de Itararé, Carlópolis and a raft to cross the river, in the central area of the watercourse, a vital device since the Ourinhos bridge had been destroyed since 1930 so it was impossible to cross the Paranapanema there.

However, the defensive scope of the Paulista deployment changed when the Federals broke the front at Itararé and advanced to Buri. Commander Alfieri, then chief of the Paulista General Staff, gave instructions that some defensive elements were to be left in the sector to protect various villages, but to concentrate the other forces to attack the northern/left flank of Lima's Federal South Army. Consequently, a column departed from Avaré to Itaporanga, but when they were about to attack the government forces on 22 July they received instructions from the new Southern Sector commander, Colonel Taborda, to cancel the assault and withdraw to Pirajú, in the north-east, until he had analysed the situation in situ. With the fall of Buri, the operation was definitively cancelled. A Lower Paranapanema Sector was then created under Colonel Dias de Campos on 30 July, comprising two battalions (the 'Avaré' and 9th BCP), with the mission of protecting the Paranapanema crossing at Pirajú, Bom Sucesso, Itatinga and Avaré in the north of the sector.[29]

However, Dias de Campos was an active commander, so on 31 July[30] he invaded Paraná, contradicting his orders, rather than staying on the defensive. During his offensive he took Cambará, Jacarezinho and Rio Claro, all towns located south of Ourinhos, cutting the railroad from western Paraná and the northern part of Northern Paraná railroad, thus moving the front line far from the crossing points of the Paranapanema River. He marched further south and also took Salto de Itararé, in the middle course of the river, after a fight lasting half an hour. Once this sector was stabilised, Dias de Campos moved his command post east from Ourinhos to Bernardino de Campos, halfway on the railroad to Avaré.[31]

The Federals Conquer the Northern Flank (1 August-1 October)

After the Paulista offensive, the Federals' João Francisco Detachment began operations to reconquer the north-east of Paraná and cover Lima's left/northern flank. João Francisco's group comprised some 1,800 soldiers,[32] including volunteers, the Paraná FP, 2nd CR and 10th CA/Military Brigade.[33] In early August, Francisco cleared the entire North Paraná railroad from Venceslau Braz north towards Jacarezinho after fierce fighting against the troops of the Paulista Dias Campos Sector. João Francisco then recovered Cambará, turned east to take Ribeirão Claro and, further south, Salto de Itararé, suppressing enemy threats throughout the northern part of Paraná, taking the crossing points on the Itararé and clearing the entire border with São Paulo State.[34] From 8 August, João Francisco began attacks on Carlópolis, also on the Itararé River, and then across the river on Itaporanga and Vermelho.[35] In early August, Vermelho was occupied by the 3rd RC/Mixed Brigade.[36]

Shortly thereafter, the Federals sent the 14th BC (5th Division) north from Faxina to connect with João Francisco's right flank. These units occupied Itaberá, then on 7 August they were replaced by the new Detachmnet Teles Ferreir (8th BC, a battery of the 6th RAM of the 3rd Division and a platoon of the 9th RCI from the 2nd Cavalry Division). On 4 August, it was reported that a new Silva Junior Detachment was created when the 2nd BC (probably actually the 2nd RC/Military Brigade) went north-east to Catupera, also from Faxina. Apparently, in the fighting for Catupera the Federals had a superiority of three-to-one against Major Genesio Castro e Silva, whose rebels did not even have automatic weapons.

On 20 August, the offensive was halted when, upon hearing of the uprising in Rio Grande do Sul (see Chapter 2), the 3rd RC/Military Brigade in Fazenda Juca de Almeida, under Colonel Pelegrino, revolted. Fearing being cut off from the rear, the vanguard of Quim Cesar's column was forced to retreat. The mutiny was eventually halted when General Lima personally confronted the deserters and arrested their colonel. After this incident, and despite the significant lack of Paulista troops, Federal progress in this northern sector was

Federal soldiers in their barracks. (FGV CPDDC, Onete Diniz Junqueira collection, via Catalogo)

Table 4: Southern Front: Northern Sector (Lower Paranapanema), July-September				
Paulistas				
Lower Paranapanema Sector (30 July)				
Colonel Dias de Campos (30 July)				
'Avaré' Battalion		(deployed 9-15 July)		
9th BCP		(deployed 9-15 July)		
Total:		**800 men**		
Federals				
Detachments	**Location**	**Composition**	**Strength**	**Creation date**
João Francisco	North of the sector: Salto de Itararé-Ourinhos	Paraná FP, 2nd CR, 10th CA/Mixed Brigade, 3rd RC/Mixed Brigade	1,800, then 2,400 men (8 August)	Around 18 July
Teles Ferreira	Centre: Faxina-Itaberá	14th BC, replaced by 8th BC, a battery/6th RAM, a platoon/9th RCI	700 men	4-7 August
Silva Jr	Centre: Faxina-Catupera (north-east)	2nd BC or 2nd RC/Military Brigade	500 men	4 August
Aimbiré	Centre: Itararé road–Itaporanga			8 August
Vieira da Costa	Centre: Bon Sucesso to Paranapanema town			Around September

extremely slow, and the Teles Ferreira Detachment did not take Taguarí, further north, until 5 September, having joined with the Aimbiré Detachment. This latter unit had been created to his left, in the west and had taken Itaporanga coming from Itararé.[37] The fighting for Itaporanga (where 78 prisoners were taken on 8 August) and Taguarí had lasted several weeks,[38] due to the smart defence made by the troops of Dias de Campos.

This efficient Paulista defensive action was helped by reinforcements sent to the sector, mainly from the Minas Front: two companies from the 3rd and 7th BCP, followed by the 2nd and 4th/7th BCP Battalion under Major Hygino, departed from Eleutério on 28 August, just before the great Federal offensive in Minas (see Chapter 4). These units, arriving on 1 September, were sent to Itaí in the Paranapanema, also controlling the area around Itapeva, the Taquari River, the town of the same name, Caputera and

Table 5: Federal Southern Army Detachment (3 August)			
General Valdomiro Lima			
Location	**Detachment**	**Composition**	**Strength**
Northern Paraná railroad: Barbozaso – Jacarezinho	João Francisco	Volunteers, FP Paraná Battalions, 2nd CR, 10th CA/Mixed Brigade	1,800 men
Jaguariana (Paraná), facing Itararé	Reinforcements	9th BC, 14th BC, Pernambuco and Santa Catarina FP Battalions, 14th RCI, 5th GAM, 3rd GIAP	2,700 men
Itararé – São Paulo railroad	Line of communications troops	8th BC, a company/5th BE, a company/Railway Battalion	700 men
Vermelho	Line of communications troops	3rd RC/Mixed Brigade	500 men
Itaberá	Line of communications troops	14th BC	500 men
Caputério	Line of communications troops	2nd BC	500 men
Railway to Faxina	Line of communications troops	A company of a BC, a squadron/5th RCD, a section/5th BE, 9th RAM, a battery/5th RAM	850 men
Buri	Dorneles & Saião	1st Battalion and 2nd RC/Mixed Brigade, 8th RI, 5th GAM	2,700 men
Riberiâo Branco	Boanerges	13th RI, 7th IR, 13th BC, two artillery groups/5th RAM	3,900 men
Ribeira (São Paulo road)	Playsant	El. 13th RI, some battalions Paraná FP	1,200 men
Total:	**Author's estimation**	**15,350 soldiers**	**(7,800 men in São Paulo State)**
	Official records	**15,750 soldiers**	**(8,500 in São Paulo State)**

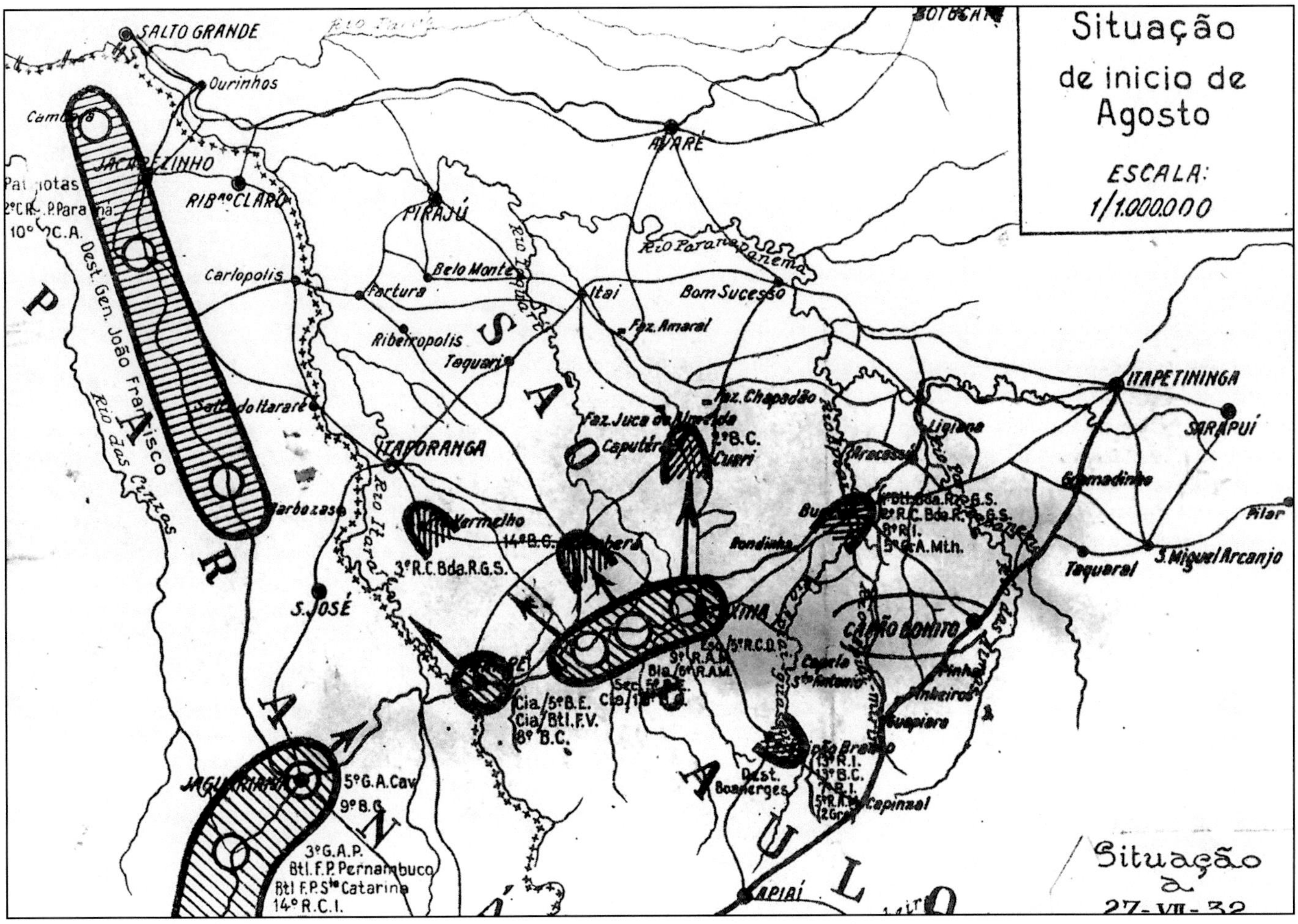

Jorge Mancini map of the deployment of Lima's Federal forces between 27 July and the beginning of August. On the left corner may be seen the deployment of the João Francisco Detachment, covering the lower Paranapanema and below – in a line running from Jaguarapava to Buri – the central front or main line of advance of the Southern Detachment. (Jorge Mancini, via Donato)

Pirajú, thus covering the whole north-west to south-east defensive line from the Paranapanema River to near Faxina. These units were later reinforced by another two companies of the 9th BCP that joined the volunteers of the 'Presidente Prudente' Battalion who were armed only with outdated Winchester rifles.[39] In total, there were now some 800-900 Paulistas in the area. The command of the Itaí Sub-Sector was now assumed by Lieutenant Colonel Carvalho Sobrinho, while the Salto Grande Sub-Sector in the north-west, near the frontier with Paraná, was under the Major Hygino, having successfully defended Eleutério for a month until finally being defeated on the Minas Front (Chapter 4).[40]

In the meantime, the Federals' João Francisco Detachment continued operations along the Paranapanema River against the Salto Grande Sub-Sector, on the extreme Federal left, occupying Leoflora and Presidente Muñoz stations with 2,400 soldiers on 8 August.[41] The Paulistas' two companies of the 7th BCP and 'Presidente Prudente' Battalions, some 400 men in all, had only two machine guns between them, with a mere five bullets per combatant, and had to rely on a large number of *matracas* (rattling machines that simulated the noise of a machine gun). They were forced to retire after realising that their old rifles had an effective range of just 40 metres. The Varguistas under João Franciso thus forced a crossing of the Paranapanema on 23 or 25 September, defeating the rebels under Major Hygino.[42] Also, on the far right (to the east), on 21 September, the Silva Junior Detachment took Fazenda Chapadão and Juca de Almeida, helped by a new Vieira da Costa Detachment created on their right. This new formation took Bon Sucesso, to the north-east, threatening the town of Paranapanema further east. At the same time, in the west, João Francisco reached the Sorocabana railway (that crossed São Paulo State from west to east), and took Salto Grande, defended by Major Hygino, thereby isolating the entire western part of São Paulo State from its capital. Meanwhile, the Teles Ferreira and Silva Junior Detachments, from Taquari and Fazenda Bernardes respectively, marched north-east to Itaí and then, after crossing the Paranapanema and defeating the troops of the Carvalho Sobrinho Sub-Sector, took Avaré on 1 October. They also cut the railroad that connected São Paulo with Mato Grosso, isolating the whole north-west of São Paulo and Mato Grosso State from the rebels' capital.[43]

Major Hygino's Paulistas fled from Salto Grande to Palmital on 30 September, and then to Assis. Finally, Lieutenant Colonel Carvalho Sobrinho, after trying to march to help Hygino with the 9th BCP, escaped from Itaí to Santa Cruz de Rio Pardo.[44] After these movements, the Paulista troops in Ourinhos, threatened by João Francisco (from Salto in the west) and by Silva Junior (from Avaré in the east), had to withdraw from Santa Cruz de Rio Pardo, Espírito Santo do Turvo and Cabralia, thereby leaving the front.[45] João Francisco's forces, marching east from the northern end of the front, now controlled Ourinhos, Ribeirópolis, Fartura, Pirajú, Manduri and Bernardino de Campos. When the war came to an end, a huge square formed by the border with Paraná in the west, the Paranapanema River in the north, Avaré in the east and the Itararé–São Paulo railroad in the south, was surrounded and isolated on the right flank of Lima's Southern Army.[46] However, the large number of troops employed in this Lower Paranapanema Sector, forgotten by most authors, meant that General Lima did not have enough soldiers for a new breakthrough in the central sector of the Southern Front until the end of September, which transformed into a painful campaign, his men advancing slowly almost inch-by-inch. On the other hand, the spectacular successes in this sector were instrumental in the final collapse of the regime in São Paulo, which saw that vast regions of the west and north-west, and Mato Grosso itself, were now isolated from the Constitutionalist capital.

The Federal Deployment in the Central (Main) Sector in August

Returning to the Central Sector of the Southern Front in early August, the Federal troops had advanced north-east to Buri. They then cleared their right or southern flank and began to deploy to clear their left or northern flank. At this time, the João Francisco Detachment was deployed on the left, still along the Northern Paraná railroad, from south to north between Barbozaso and Jacarezinho, with 1,800 soldiers (comprising volunteers, several FP Paraná Battalions, the 2nd CR and 10th CA/Mixed Brigade).[47] A 2,700-strong column made up of Lima's reinforcements was further south, in Jaguariana, Paraná, facing Itararé – with the 9th BC, 3rd GIAP (3rd Division), Pernambuco and Santa Catarina FP Battalions, the 14th RCI (3rd Cavalry Division), the 5th GAM and the 14th BC (5th Division). A number of forces were deployed further to the east, along the Itararé–São Paulo railroad, covering the line of communications for the Southern Army and beginning a march to the north to clear Lima's left flank. These included about 700 soldiers (a company of the 5th BE, a company of the Railway Battalion and the 8th BC) in Itararé, repairing bridges and railway tracks; some 500 loyalists (3rd RC/Mixed Brigade) isolated in the vanguard in Vermelho, further to the north; another 500 troops (14th BC) in Itaberá, further to the east; and a further 500 men (2nd BC) in Caputério, at the eastern end of the deployment. All these units were marching north to cross the Paranapanema River. Further back, some 850 soldiers – a squadron of the 5th RCD, a section of the 5th BE and the 9th RAM (all from the 5th Division), a battery of the 5th RAM (from the 3rd Division) and a company of BC – was deployed on the railway line to Faxina. The Dorneles and Saião Detachments, with about 2,700 men (1st Battalion and 2nd RC/Mixed Brigade, 8th RI from the 3rd Division and the 5th GAM), were in Buri. The Boanerges Detachment fielded 3,900 troopers – 13th RI, 13th BC and two artillery groups of the 5th RAM (all from the 5th Division), and the 7th IR (3rd Division) – was in Riberiâo Branco, south of Faxina. Finally, the Playsant Detachment had about 1,200 troops (with elements of the 13th RI and some battalions of the Paraná FP) in Ribeira, on the road to São Paulo.[48] In total, Lima's Southern Army had some 15,750 fighters. According to Lima, 8,500 of these had already penetrated Paulista territory.[49]

Federal troops panicking under attack by a Paulista aircraft. Note the absence of helmets and the machine gun carried by one of the troopers. (Museu da Imagem e do Som de São Paulo, via Donato)

The Federal Aviation Arrives (26-28 July)

As stated above, all the rebel combat aviation had been deployed since 16 July on the Southern Front, to compensate for the near absence of their own artillery there. This was made possible by the lack of any Federal combat aircraft on this front. The Federal General Lima sent numerous telegrams to Rio requesting the deployment of the government aircraft to the front, as he saw that his troops were frequently panicking when the Constitutionalist aviation appeared. The Federals eventually reacted on 26 July, when the Potez A-211, piloted by 1st Lieutenant Antônio Lemos Cunha, with 2nd Lieutenant Carlos Brunswick França as observer/gunner, took off from Dos Afonsos in Rio. The Potez crossed the entire State of São Paulo in a very risky action, as it could have been intercepted at any time by the bulk of the rebel aviation, but landed later that day at the recently taken Faxina airfield.[50]

On the same day, once refuelled, the Potez made a surprise attack on the Paulista headquarters at Itapetininga, and while returning also machinegunned a rebel supply convoy. On 27 July, the Potez made two further support missions, and on the 28th attacked the Itapetininga airfield itself, surprising on the ground an uncamouflaged Paulista Waco. However, the bombs dropped missed their target, causing little damage, and the Federal pilot did not dare descend to fire his machine

Table 6: Combat Aviation in the South (26 July-8 August)

Federal aircraft			
Type	**Plate number**	**Arrival date**	**Fate**
Potez	A-211	26 July	Bombed at Faxina (damaged on 27 July). Returned and damaged on 29 July, returning again on 4 August. Departed or damaged on 5 or 6 August.
Potez	A-117	5–8 August	Shot down on 8 August. Later repaired.
Paulista aircraft			
Constitutionalist 1st Fighter Group			
Major Lysias Rodrigues			
Type	Plate number		Notes
Potez	A-212		Bombed Federal Potez A-211 and downed A-117
Waco	C-2		Improvised armament
Waco	C-3		Synchronised weapons

A Paulista Waco with the pilots Xavier de Brito, Motta Lima and Pelegrini. Note that the aircraft is painted in red, like the famous Federal *vermelinhos* ('little reds'). (FGV/CPDOC/ Donation from João Baptista Periera de Almerida, via Donato)

Corvette Captain Djalma Petit, commander of the Federal Southern Mixed Aviation Detachment. He began his career flying Corsair fighters, providing escort for bombing missions. (Daróz)

guns because of intense anti-aircraft fire. While returning to base, the pilot also bombed several Paulista trucks. These flights warned the new rebel aviation commander, Major Lysias, of the presence of Federal aerial forces on the Southern Front, and he immediately ordered an attack to destroy the government aircraft. The rebel Potez A-212, piloted by 1st Lieutenant José Ângelo Gomes Ribeiro, with his observer-gunner 1st Lieutenant Arthur da Motta Lima Filho, took off from Itapetininga and caught the Potez A-211 on the ground in Faxina, damaging it slightly with machine gun fire. The Federal Potez was sent to Curitiba to be repaired. Two days later, the Potez A-211 was again decommissioned after breaking its landing gear following a mission, once more leaving the Federals without air support.[51] The Paulistas took advantage of the situation to bomb and strafe at low level enemy troops with the Potez A-212 on 30 July, and to make night reconnaissance missions with the aircraft flown by Silvio Hoetz.[52]

The First Aircraft Downing in the Americas

In late July, the São Paulo aviation continued its actions, leaving three Federals dead and five wounded in another attack. Desperate at his lack of aerial support, General Lima urgently asked for new aircraft to be sent. In the meantime, the busy Federal Potez A-211 was repaired again at Curitiba on 4 August, returning to Faxina airfield. This Potez then attacked Itapetininga airfield again, this time surprising three Paulista aircraft on the ground, but failing to hit any of them. Apparently, the next day, 5 August, the Potez A-211 was flown by Lemos Cunha on missions to attack Buri, Itapetininga, Aracassu, Vila Carmilo and Capão Bonito. Close to Buri, Cunha dropped bombs from 800 metres and struck a train convoy. No more is heard of this Potez on the Southern Front after this date. Perhaps it was sent once again to the Paraíba, or maybe it suffered further damage. Nevertheless, at the same time, a new Federal Potez, A-117, was sent to Faxina. In the meantime, the rebel aircraft were harassing Federal land forces on a daily basis.[53]

A close-up view of a Potez 25 TOE, with its engine apparently being maintained or repaired at Campo Dos Afonsos, Rio de Janeiro. (Daróz)

On the morning of 8 August, while the Paulistas were trying to recover Buri, the Federal Potez A-117 ran into the bulk of the rebel aviation. The Paulista

A picture of nearly all the available Paulistas pilots, in front of a pair of armed Wacos. Below, on the left, is fireman turned bomber-pilot João Negrão, and on the right, the lawyer Mario Machado Bittencourt, with his friend Jose Ângelo Gomes Ribeiro, standing behind and pointing at him. Bittencourt and Ribeiro would die together in action when trying to bomb a Federal cruiser (see Volume 1). (Daróz)

aircraft were Motta Lima's Waco C-3, Sebastião Machado's Waco C-2 and Lieutenant Mario Machado Bittencourt and Gomes Ribeiro's Potez A-212 (the Potez A-116 was having its engine worked on). The mission, led by Gomes Ribeiro, was to attack the Guapiara field, but they encountered the Federal Potez at Capão Bonito. The Federal aircraft turned to the south in a bid to escape, followed by Motta Lima's Waco and Ribeiro's Potez. Motta's Waco C-3 inched closer and closer to the Federal Potez, but he waited to open fire until he could be sure to hit the target, and the Federal aircraft shot at him first with its rear machine gun. Motta then fired into the fuselage of the enemy aircraft, and continued shooting until the Potez of Ribeiro, coming from above, joined in the pursuit, also opening fire on the Federal Potez. The Federal aircraft flew past its aerodrome at Itapeva, where the Paulista Potez and then the Waco, pulled back when they ran out of ammunition.[54]

That same afternoon, at 1500 hours, the Federal Potez A-117 flown by Captain Arquimedes Cordeiro and 2nd Lieutenant Oswaldo Carneiro Lima encountered the same three Paulista aircraft (this time with Lieutenant Ribeiro in the Waco C-2, Motta Lima Filho in the C-3, and the Potez A-212 piloted by Major Lysias Rodrigues, with Lieutenant Abílio Pereira Almeida as gunner) flying over the old Paulista lines at Buri that had just been taken by the Federals. The Federal Potez, flying towards the sun, apparently spotted the two Wacos but not the rebel Potez, and Cordeiro decided to make a dive from his higher altitude and slip through his enemies, hoping to gain enough speed to open fire and then escape before they could react. However, the Federal Potez then suddenly discovered Lysias' Paulista Potez. The rebel made a sharp turn, letting the light of the setting sun dazzle his enemy, while Pereira, in the observer seat (or Lysias with his nose guns; the sources are not clear), opened fired from below at the Federal aircraft, raking it from propeller to tail from barely 10 metres' distance. The aircraft almost crashed into each other, but Lysias turned his device at the last minute. With his radiator punctured and pouring gasoline and smoke, Cordeiro's Potez A-117 also turned and entered a near-vertical dive from 1,500 metres. The Paulista aircraft followed suit, but anti-aircraft fire

Land crew preparing a Vought O2U-Corsair for a mission. Note the absence of the engine protection in the nose. (Daróz)

Table 7: Federal Aviation in the South (10 August)		
Southern Mixed Aviation Detachment		
Lieutenant Commander Djalma Petit		
Type	**Plate**	**Arrival date**
1st Section		
Navy Corsair	1-0-4	12 August
Navy Corsair	1-0-6	12 August
2nd Section		
Navy DH-60 Moth		Around 10 August
Navy DH-60 Moth		Around 10 August
Navy DH-60 Moth		Around 10 August
3rd Section		
Potez	A-114	11 August
Potez	A-211 (probably)	26 July
Potez	A-115	11 August

forced Lysias to climb again to 500 metres, so the Federal was able to escape, making an emergency landing at the railway station at Rondinha. This was the first aircraft shot down in aerial combat in the Americas – indeed throughout the Western Hemisphere – some seven weeks before the first downing reported on 30 September in the Chaco War of 1932-35 between Bolivia and Paraguay, that is often wrongly claimed to hold that distinction. As we saw in Volume 1, the downed Potez aircraft was mentioned as having taken part in a mission soon after in the Paraíba Valley, so it is likely that despite being severely damaged, it was then evacuated, repaired and put back into service.[55] Nevertheless, although there were other aircraft destroyed on the ground by bombing or downed by anti-aircraft fire during the war, the Potez A-117 was to prove the only one shot down in aerial combat during the conflict.

The next day, taking advantage of the downing, the Paulistas continued to bombard the Federals. On 9 August, Major Lysias strafed a squadron of Federal cavalry on the Capão Bonito–Buri road, decimating its ranks and leaving the roadside ditches filled with dead horses, as later mentioned by a prisoner. On 11 August, the rebel aviation bombed Buri.[56]

Federal Air Supremacy in the South (10-12 August)

However, the Paulista aerial victory would have no long-term consequences, as on 4 August, the Federal Potez A-211 was back in action (although after 5 August it disappears from the records). This was followed on 11 August[57] by the Potez A-114, that departed from Resende to join the government aviation in Faxina. The next day, 12 August,[58] two Navy Vought Corsairs – numbers 1-0-4 and 1-0-6 under Lieutenant Commander Djalma Petit – also took off to join the Southern Group in Faxina. These were pure fighter aircraft, with a top speed of 269km/h, much faster than the 210-215km/h of the Paulistas' Waco and Potez aircraft, that were reconnaissance and bombing aircraft rather than interceptors. The presence of the Corsairs thus guaranteed the Federals air supremacy on the Southern Front from 12 August. It is not known whether the Paulistas were reacting to this move, or whether it was just by chance, but that same morning, all the Constitutionalist 1st Fighter Group flew back to Lorena to support the rebels in Paraíba and Minas. Federal dominion of the skies in the south was therefore now complete.[59]

On 10 August, General Lima organised the Federal Southern Mixed Aviation Detachment, an unprecedented unit in the world, mixing in one body both army and navy aircraft. The commander of the unit was Lieutenant Commander Djalma Petit, who was assigned to the 5th Infantry Division. He led a group comprising the 1st Section, with the two Navy Corsairs 1-0-4 and 1-0-6; the 2nd Section, with three observation DH-60 Moths, also from the Navy; and the 3rd Section, with two Potez aircraft from the Army, A-114 and A-211, which would soon be reinforced with a new Potez A-115 that arrived on 11 August, becoming operative several days later. In all, the detachment had eight aircraft, including five combat aircraft. Its first mission was a mass attack against the Itapetininga airfield on 12 August, but as we have seen, the rebel aircraft had already departed.[60] That same day, a Corsair and two Potez aircraft

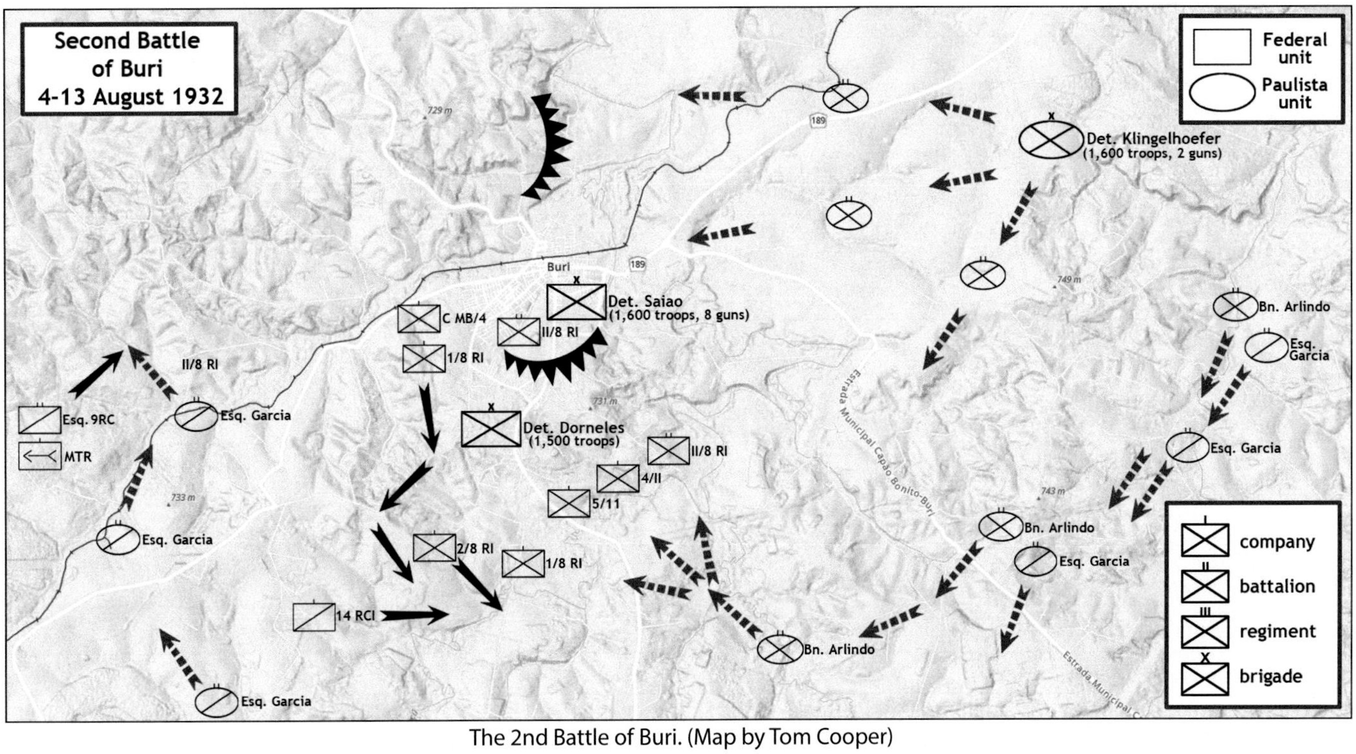

The 2nd Battle of Buri. (Map by Tom Cooper)

under Petit also bombed concentrations of rebel troops and train convoys.[61]

The Paulistas Strike Back at Buri (4-13 August)

After the conquest of Buri by the Federals, in the central sector of the front, the Paulista troops retreated to Vitorino Carmilo and then to Legiana, further north-east, protecting the railroad to São Paulo across the Paranapanema. On 4 August, the Paulista deployment on the heights of Vitorino Carmilo included the 7th BCR and a platoon from the Jardim Squadron on the right wing, and a second line made of a company of the 1st BRE, the 9th BCR in the centre and the 1st BRE and 6th BCR on the left wing. In the rear was the armoured train, half a company of the 7th BCR and a company of the 1st BRE on the railway in Aracaçú. Further to the south, or the left, was the García Feijó Squadron and the 'Arlindo' Battalion on the road to Capão Bonito, a company of the 14 de Julho Battalion in Fundão and the rest of the 14 de Julho in Capão itself.[62] The two-piece Mascarenhas artillery section was also in this sector. In all, there were thus some 2,400 Paulistas along a 12km front.

After a period of rest, Major Arlindo de Oliveira with the Arlindo Battalion conducted a local counterattack to the south-west, recrossed the river and recovered Vitorino Carmilo on 5 August. With the good news of the only Federal aircraft in the area being shot down on 8 August, the Paulistas planned a counteroffensive to regain Buri. For such a task, they gathered the 6th BCP, the 6th, 7th and 8th BCR, the 1st BCV and the Legião Negra ('Black Legion') Battalion,[63] these units being very divided or weakened, perhaps a mere 200 men per battalion.[64] Including the flanking units and artillery, they were no more than 1,750 men, who had to fight roughly the same number of Federals, or double that if their reserve units are added. At dawn on either 12 or 13 August,[65] the Paulista attack began, supported by the two artillery pieces from the Mascarenhas section.

Table 8: 2nd Battle of Buri (12-13 August)		
Paulistas		
Detachment Klingelhoefer		
Location	**Composition**	**Strength**
Extreme right flank: north	Jardim Cavalry Squadron	100 riders
Centre-right flank: north (Vitorino Carmilo)	7th BCR	200 soldiers
Main force (Centre)	6th BCP, 6th BCR, 8th BCR, 1st BCV, Legião Negra ('Black Legion') Battalion	1,000 soldiers
	Mascarenhas Artillery Section	50 soldiers, two cannons
Left flank: south (road to Capão Bonito)	Arlindo Battalion, García Feijó Cavalry Squadron	300 men
Total in Battle (including gunners etc) 1,750 soldiers, two cannons		
Rearguard		
Right: Vitorino Carmilo	Company/1st BRE	70 soldiers
Centre	9th BCR	200 soldiers
Right	Company/1st BRE	70 soldiers
Left wing	El. 1st BRE	70 soldiers
Railway in Aracaçú	Armoured Train, ½ company/7th BCR, company/1st BRE	200 soldiers
South: road to Capão Bonito & Fundão	14 de Julho Battalion	200 soldiers
Total Detachment 2,450 men, two cannons		
Federals		
Detachments Dorneles & Saião		
Reserve in Buri	1st Battalion and 2nd RC/Mixed Brigade, II/8th RI, 5th GAM (probably)	1,600 soldiers, eight cannons
Fazenda Quilombo (south-eastern Buri)	Battalions I & II/8th RI, 14th RCI	1,500 soldiers
South-west Buri	Squadron/9th RC	100 riders
Total in Battle 1,600 soldiers		
Total Federal Detachments 3,200 soldiers, eight cannons		

Troopers from the *Legião Negra* ('Black Legion') Battalion, preparing lunch for the unit. Note the many Gaúcho hats, that were not usually used by the Paulistas. (Museu da Imagem e do Som de São Paulo, via Catalogo)

Constitutionalist prisoners being escorted by Federal troops. (FGV, CPDDC, Yasuhiko Makemura, via Catalogo)

Constitutionalist prisoners on a train at Ponta Grossa, Paraná. (FGV, CPDDC, Jurendir Esteves Donation, via Catalogo)

However, with the Federal Aviation being increased in just four days up to eight aircraft, and the Paulista aerial forces leaving the front that same day, the Paulista infantry was left with no air cover. The Paulistas divided into two groups, marching on both sides of the railway line. The right was on the heights of Apiaí-Mirim, directly threatening Buri, putting it under fire but without assaulting or crossing the bends of the Apiaí-Gauçú River that protected them, trying to distract the Federals. Another diversionary attack was launched further north by the Jardim Cavalry Squadron. At the same time, the main attack was conducted on the left, with the Paulistas crossing the river to the south and surrounding the government positions on that flank, then appearing in the enemy's rear at Maria Mocinha. However, the force employed for this task was too weak, comprising only the Arlindo Battalion and the García Feijó Cavalry Squadron, a mere 250 soldiers.[66]

Furthermore, the Federals' Dorneles and Saião Detachments did not fall into the trap lain by the Paulistas, and after leaving a reasonable contingent defending Buri, transferred many units to contain the encirclement, blocking the Paulista attack south of the city at Fazenda Quilombo. These forces numbered some 1,500 Varguistas in all (the II/8th RI, the 4th/II, 5th/II, CMB/I Companies, the I/8th RI Battalion and 14th RCI, deployed diagonally from north-east to south-west). The Arlindo was able to hold these troops with its tiny rebel battalion, while the García Cavalry Squadron made a detour further west, almost reaching the railroad to cut off all the Federal troops. Nevertheless, a Federal squadron of the 9th RC was planted in the line of advance of Garcia and contained him, so the rebels were unable to reach their goal.[67] The Paulistas then dug in where they were and stayed in their positions, surrounding Buri to the east and south. Until now, the result of the fighting since the beginning of the war had been disastrous for the rebels, as by 10 August they had already lost as many as 1,000 prisoners on the Southern Front.[68]

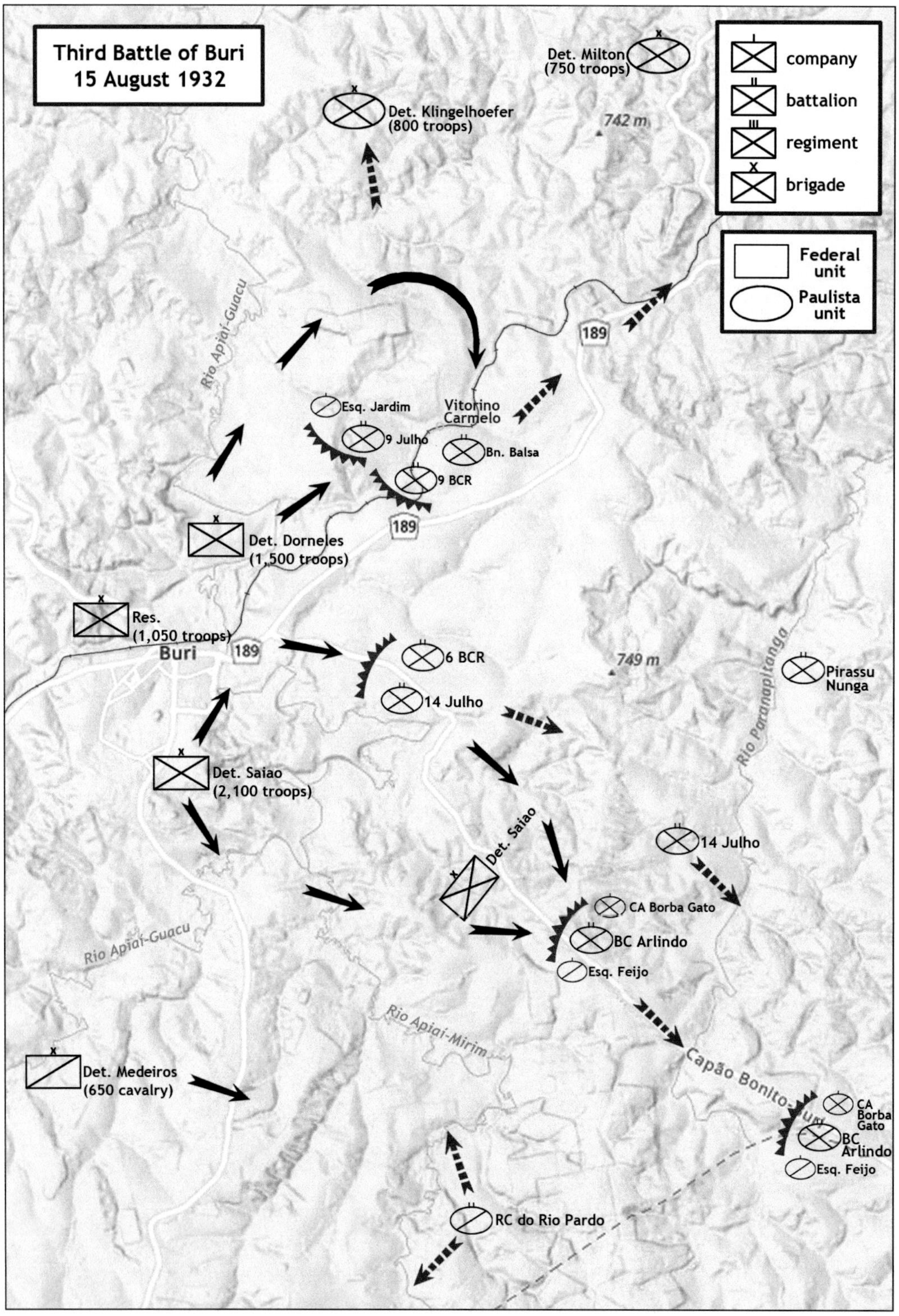

The 3rd Battle of Buri (15 August 1932). (Map by Tom Cooper)

The Third Battle of Buri (15-17 August)

The Paulistas risked being overrun in a counterattack, with their excessively extended wings in front of Buri, one behind the Apiaía-Guaçu and the other isolated across the river. A Federal attack was indeed ordered by Valdomiro Lima, with the aim of taking Vitorino Carmilo in the north and Capão Bonito in the south. The offensive was launched on 15 August, with devastating results. The Dorneles Detachment advanced towards Vitorino Carmilo, to the north-east but also to the south-east to clear the road to Capão Bonito, with some 1,500 soldiers (Pernambuco FP, 1st/Mixed Brigade and one battalion from the 8th RI). The Saião Detachment supported them by trying to take the Mata da Picada (Mata being a wooded area) with about 2,100 men (14th BC, one battalion from the 8th RI, Santa Catarina FP, 3rd Auxiliary Corps/Military Brigade and a company of the 13th RI). The right flank between Buri and Rondinha was covered by a force of about 700 soldiers (14th RCI and a battalion of the 8th RI). The left wing had about 150 men of a squadron and a machine gun section of the 14th RCI in the Bairro dos Costas. Colonel Medeiros was to cross the Apiaí-Guaçu south of the railway in the direction of Guari-Caputera with a force of some 650 men (17th Auxiliary Corps/Military Brigade and part of the 14th RCI). The 9th RCI, comprising about 500 riders, would attack the Usina region, towards Capão Bonito, linking with the Saião Detachment. Finally, as a reserve in Buri itself, were based some 1,500 troopers (2nd and 5th Battalions of the Military Brigade and a section of the 3rd GIAP).[69]

In all, there were about 6,650 Federal fighters involved,[70] although authors such as Donato claimed that only about 3,600 of them would attack the Paulistas, the others being in reserve or covering the flanks. Facing them were only 930-1,030 Paulistas of the Klingelhoefer Detachment, comprising a handful of very weak units: the 6th BCR (300 soldiers), the 2nd Battalion/14 de Julho Regiment (250 men), the 9th BCR (200 men), 1st BCR (100 men), 7th BCR (100 men), Jardim Cavalry Squadron (80 riders) and just one cannon.[71] The Federal numerical superiority for their attack was therefore more than three-to-one.

On 15 August, at 0650 hours, after an artillery barrage of 1,200 rounds fired by 32 cannons, the 8th RI, 13th BC and Santa Catarina FP Battalions moved against the Paulista trenches in the 6th BCR's sector, supported by Federal aviation forces. Three Federal airframes under Petit strafed and bombed troops and trains from 200 metres and dropped 18 bombs on a convoy of trucks, according to pilot Alves Cabral (Cabral claimed that such missions were made at least on 12, 15-17 and 21 August). Once the defending Paulista battalion had exhausted its ammunition, and without air support, it was finally

Table 9: The 3rd Battle of Buri (15 August)			
Federals			
Location	**Detachment**	**Units**	**Strength**
Left flank cover: Barrio das Costas		A squadron and machine gun section/14th RCI	150 riders
Left flank: north-centre (facing Vitorino Carmilo & Capão Bonito)	Dorneles	Pernambuco FP, 1st/Mixed Brigade, a battalion/8th RI	1,500 soldiers
Right flank (south, facing Mata da Picada-Capão Bonito)	Saião	14th BC, a battalion/8th RI, Santa Catarina FP, 3rd Auxiliary Corps/Military Brigade, a company/13th RI	2,100 soldiers
Right flank cover: Buri-Rondinha		14th RCI, a battalion/8th RI	700 soldiers
Apiaí-Guaçu, south of the railway to Guari-Caputera	Colonel Medeiros	17th Auxiliary Corps/Military Brigade, el. 14th RCI	650 riders
Facing Usina region–Capão Bonito		9th RCI	500 riders
Buri	Reserve	2nd and 5th Battalions/Military Brigade, a section/3rd GIAP	1,050 soldiers
Total: 6,650 soldiers			
(In the front line: 3,600 soldiers)			
Paulistas			
Detachment Klingelhoefer			
Unit	**Strength**		
Battalion 2nd/14 de Julho Regiment	250 soldiers		
9th BCR	200 soldiers		
6th BCR	300 soldiers		
1st BCR	100 soldiers		
7th BCR	100 soldiers		
Jardim Cavalry Squadron	80 riders		
Mascarenhas Artillery Section	1 cannon		
Total: 930–1,030 soldiers			
Reinforcements: 9 de Julho Battalion & Feijó Squadron 300-400 soldiers			

forced to retire by a bayonet charge of the Santa Catarina men, being replaced by other units of the rebel right flank at 2000 hours.[72]

The battle was hotly contested, and Donato – exageratedly – calls it the fiercest ever fought in the Republic of Brazil. On the Paulista side, Sergeant Ângelo Martin was left alone in his trench that was being stormed by the enemy, but by using his machine gun – and even the bayonet – managed to keep the Federals at bay until reinforcements arrived to save the position. Klingelhoefer rewarded Martin by awarding him a battlefield promotion to lieutenant.[73]

Nevertheless, such efforts proved in vain. During the combat, the rebel '9 July' Battalion arrived as reinforcement, but one of its companies then left their positions, forcing the withdrawal of the entire line.[74] At midnight, a general withdrawal of Paulista forces began, covered by the 14 de Julho Battalion, which withstood a massive Federal bombardment from 0600-1600 hours, and then a Federal assault over its trenches. The attack having separated one Paulista flank from the other, the right wing retreated north-east to Ligiana, protected by the Jardim Squadron. On the left, meanwhile, the Arlindo Battalion, Feijó Squadron and Hernani Company marched to Capão Bonito, to the south-east, halting at Fundão, where they were joined by a company of the 14 de Julho Battalion.[75]

During the battle on the left flank, the Dorneles Detachment had attacked in a north-easterly direction towards Vitorino Carmilo, and on 17 August took the heights north and north-east of the village after suffering 12 dead and 30 wounded. On the right flank, the Saião Detachment took the entrance to the path made into the jungle by the Paulistas, the Mata da Picada, where they could link up with the road leading to Capão Bonito in the south-east.[76]

The Deployment Against Capão Bonito

Once having cleared the São Paulo railway to the north-east, and the roads to the south around Buri, General Lima continued his projected offensive against Capão Bonito, to the south-east, which was threatening his right flank. To do this, Lima first reorganised his Southern Army, reversing the roles of the detachments: Saião would now fix the enemy, while Dorneles would continue the march through the Picada, along the path that was cut in the wilderness by the rebels, towards the road to Capão. The Saião Detachment would advance north-east on the railroad line to Aracaçú with about 2,950 soldiers and eight guns (14th BC, part of II and III/13th RI, Santa Catarina FP, Pernambuco FP and I/8th RI Battalions, a battery of the 9th RAM and a battery of the 6th RAM). The Dorneles Detachment would march off-road to the south-east, with about 3,300 fighters and 28 cannons (3rd and 17th Auxiliary Corps/Military Brigade, Pernambuco FP, Paraíba FP and one-third of the II/8th RI Battalions, the 14th RCI/3rd Cavalry Division, part of the 9th RAM and 3rd GIAP/3rd Division and the 5th GAMTH). Meanwhile, the new Lieutenant Colonel Ângelo de Melo's Detachment would cover the space between the other two detachments, but also directed towards Capão Bonito, to the southeast, threatening the right flank of the Paulistas in Fundão. This third detachment comprised about 750 Federals (one-third of the II/8th RI, the 5th Battalion and the 2nd Squadron/2nd RC, both from the Rio Grande do Sul Military

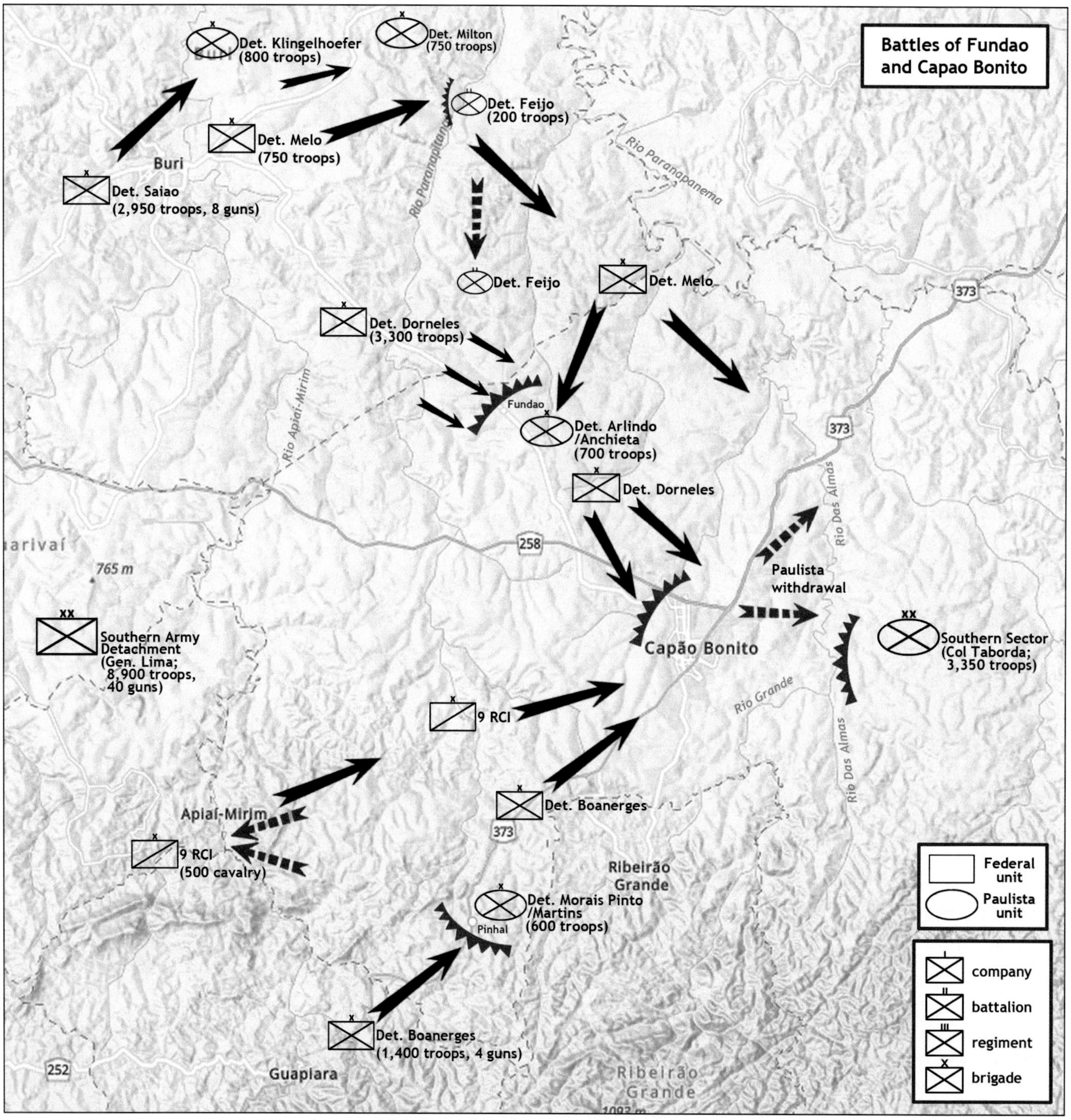

Battles of Fundão and Capão Bonito. (Map by Tom Cooper)

Brigade). Finally, the 9th RCI/2nd Cavalry Division would try to infiltrate from the Federal extreme right, to wrap around the Constitutionalist rear, at Serraria and Fazenda Santa Ines.[77] In total, these forces included about 7,500 Federals with 36 artillery pieces.

The Paulistas received reinforcements, so now had the Klingelhoefer Detachment in the north-east, defending the railway line and the Paranapanema and Ligiana river crossings with half of the units it had on 15 August. There was also a new detachment under Lieutenant Colonel Milton, comprising part of Klingelhoefer's old units, that made a brief counterattack from Aracaçú on 17 August with some 750 soldiers (from the 9th BCR, 10th BCR and '9 July' Battalions, the Jardim Squadron and a section of Mascarenhas artillery). The Captain García Feijó Detachment, with about 200 soldiers from the García Squadron and a company of the Borba Gato Battalion, would then cover the Paranapatinga River and link with the Fundão Detachment, based to the south. Finally, this latter group, which protected the village of Fundão, had some 300 soldiers (the Arlindo and a company of the 14 de Julho Battalions).[78] In total, the Paulistas could count on some 2,050 combatants, thus again being outnumbered by at least three-to-one.

The Sporadic Return of the Paulista Aviation (15 August-19 September)

Although the Federal air dominance was absolute, there is some diffuse information about small and sporadic rebel aviation interventions on the Southern Front. Apparently, the aircraft returned to Itapetininga briefly on 15 August, from Lorena, making a temporary stop in Campo de Marte.[79] Then, on 20 August, some Paulista aircraft are mentioned again in the Paraíba, so this foray must have been brief.[80]

Table 10: The Offensive against Capão Bonito (20 August)			
Federals			
Southern Army Detachment			
General Valdomiro Lima			
Location	**Detachment**	**Composition**	**Strength**
Left (north): the railway to Aracaçú	Saião	14th BC, el. II and III/13th RI, Santa Catarina FP, Pernambuco FP, I/8th RI Battalions, a battery/9th RAM, a battery/6th RAM	2,950 soldiers, eight cannons
Centre, facing Fundão	Ângelo de Melo	⅓ II/8th RI, 5th Battalion and 2nd Squadron/2nd RC/ Military Brigade.	750 soldiers
Right (to the south-east)(through the Picada)	Dorneles	3rd and 17th Auxiliary Corps/Military Brigade, Pernambuco FP, Paraíba FP, ⅓ II/8th RI Battalions, 14th RCI, el. 9th RAM and 3rd GIAP, 5th GAMTH	3,300 soldiers, 28 cannons
Extreme right (facing Serraria & Fazenda Santa Ines)		9th RCI	500 riders
Total at the Beginning: 7,500 soldiers, 36 cannons			
Marching to envelop from the south: Capinzal–Pinhal	Boanerges	El. II//13th RI, 13th BC, ⅓ II/8th RI Battalions, platoon/2nd RC of Rio Grande, el. 5th RCD, battery/5th RAM	1,400 soldiers, four cannons
Total Troops Involved			**8,900 men, 40 cannons**
Paulistas			
Southern Sector			
Colonel Basilio Taborda			
Location	**Detachment**	**Composition**	**Strength**
Right flank (north): Paranapanema and Ligiana crossings	Klingelhoefer	Battalion II/14 de Julho Regiment, 6th BCR, 1st BCR, 7th BCR	800 soldiers
Right-Centre: Aracaçú	Milton	9th BCR, 10th BCR, 9 de Julho Battalions, Jardim Squadron, section of Mascarenhas artillery	750 soldiers
Centre: Paranapatinga River	Feijó	García Feijó Squadron, a company/Borba Gato Battalion	200 soldiers
Left: Fundão	Arlindo/Anchieta	Arlindo Battalion, a company/14 de Julho Battalion	300 soldiers
Total at the Beginning			2,050 soldiers
Protecting long south flank (Capinzal–Pinhal)	Morais Pinto/Martins	8th BCP, 3rd BCV, Marcilio Franco Battalion	600 soldiers
Reinforcements Fundão (23 August)	Anchieta	Company/Legião Negra, Company 14 de Julho Battalion, Rio Pardo Cavalry Regiment	400 soldiers
Reinforcements Ribeirão Branco River (around 1 September)		Fernão Dias Battalion, cavalry squadron	300 soldiers
Total Troops Involved			**3,350 soldiers**

On the Federal side, the Djalma Petit Southern Detachment was strengthened with the arrival of new equipment. On 20 August, a new Corsair left for Faxina, but was destroyed when it crashed in the heights of Jacarezinho.[81] On 24 August, a new Federal Potez 25 was appointed to the Southern Detachment, although its number plate is unknown.[82]

There is also some mention of a possible second Paulista raid to the south. At an indeterminate time – but in any case after the defection of the Nid-72 K-423, which occurred on 20 or 21 August,[83] and probably even after 23 August, when the Federal bombing of Guaratinguetá destroyed the Paulista Potez A-116 and forced all the rebel aviation to retreat to the Campo de Marte[84] – the Nid-72 K-423 piloted by Adherbal and the Wacos C-2, C-3 and C-5 flown by Motta Lima, Bittencourt and Camargo bombed the government command centre at Buri, although apparently the Nid had to make an emergency landing, perhaps having been hit by anti-aircraft artillery fire.[85] These aircraft were quickly called back to Resende, in the Paraíba Valley, and from there to Mogi Mirim, in the Minas sector, around 26 August. Thereafter, probably just the three Waco CSOs (C-2, C-3 and C-5) returned to Itapetininga on 27 August[86]. From there, they apparently bombed government positions and covered the rebel withdrawal from Fundão on 28 August. On this date, an aircraft flown by Silvio Hoeltz, along with two other aircraft, attacked the Buri area from an altitude of 200 metres,[87] before returning to Campinas on the Minas Front.[88]

With these sporadic Constitutionalists interventions, the loyalists decided to further strengthen their Southern Detachment. On either 30 August or 1 September, they sent two of the five brand new Wacos recently received from the United States, with the license plates C-9 and C-10,[89] probably equipping a new 4th Section. The

A line of post-war (see plates) Navy Vought O2U-A Corsairs, like the ones that were destined for the Southern Front. (SDM, via Sergio Luis dos Santos)

An anti-aircraft position, perhaps Federal, due to the absence of white scarfs worn by the soldiers and the canvas headgear. (Coleção Paulo Florançano, Taubaté, via Donato)

Federal doctors and nurses in the Blood Hospital at Itararé. (Coleção Dorothy Moretti, photo taken by Claro Gustavo Jansson, via Donato)

Southern Mixed Aviation Detachment now had 10 or 11 aircraft, including seven or eight combat aircraft – two Corsairs, three or four Potezs (A-211, A-114, A-115 and perhaps another one) and two Wacos (C-9 and C-10) – and three reconnaissance DH-60 Moths.

Throughout September, the Paulista aviation again appeared in the southern theatre on ill-defined dates. On 10 September, they are cited as bombing a hospital in Capão Bonito.[90] Lysias Rodrigues cites in his memoirs another useless mission, "throwing pieces of paper [leaflets]" over Capão Bonito on 16 September, with the Nosso Potez A-212, being surprised by three Federal aircraft (two Wacos and a Potez). He was only able to escape due to defensive fire from his gunner, Mario, who was promoted to lieutenant for this action. Despite being lower than the Federals, Lysias attacked the closer Waco, but his nose machine gun jammed, so he ordered his gunner to fire at the Waco. Mario did this so effectively that the Federal aircraft was seen to dive suddenly, trailing smoke behind. The Paulistas thought that the Federal Waco had been downed, but it actually made it back to base. In the meantime, the other Federal aircraft reacted. The Federal Potez kept its distance, but the other Waco fell upon the Paulista Potez and began a dogfight. As the light Waco was more manoeuvrable than the heavy Potez (0.19 to 0.14 thrust-to-weight ratio), it had all the advantages. Furthermore, the Waco had 1,200 rounds of ammunition against the 300 of the Potez. Hence, Mario had to fire only in short sweeps, saving his ammunition, but the Paulista aircraft was eventually left without any bullets to fire. Nevertheless, with all seeming to be lost, Lysias turned his Potez against the Federal Waco, making as if to fire on three occasions, and the Waco finally desisted and broke off the engagement.[91] After surviving this mission, the Paulista aviation abandoned the region for the Viracopos airfield, in Campinas on the Minas Front on 19 September, as they were being threatened by the Federal advance towards Itapetininga.[92] Nevertheless, they soon had to return, as on 22 September they were again mentioned as bombing Capão Bonito's hospital.[93]

These Paulista aviation interventions resulted in the sending of further aircraft to reinforce the Federals. Four Wacos from the third batch were sent to the south, although two of them, the C-13 and C-17, were destroyed on the ground in transit at Mogi Mirim on

Table 11: Aviation in the South (September)			
Southern Mixed Aviation Detachment			
Lieutenant Commander Djalma Petit			
	Plate Number	**Arriving date**	**Type**
1st Section			
Navy Corsair	1-0-4	12 August	Fighter
Navy Corsair	1-0-6	12 August	Fighter
Navy Corsair	1-0-2 or 1-0-3	September	Fighter
2nd Section			
Navy DH-60 Moth		Around 10 August	Recce
Navy DH-60 Moth		Around 10 August	Recce
Navy DH-60 Moth		Around 10 August	Recce
3rd Section			
Potez	A-114	11 August	Bomber
Potez	A-211 (?)	26 July	Bomber
Potez	A-115	11 August	Bomber
Potez	Unknown	24 August	Bomber
4th Section			
Waco	C-9	1 September	Fighter-Bomber
Waco	C-10	1 September	Fighter-Bomber
5th Section			
Waco	Unknown	Around 22 September	Fighter-Bomber
Waco	Unknown	Around 22 September	Fighter-Bomber
Paulistas			
Units sent back and forth to the theatre at the end of August/beginning of September, returning then to Minas/Paraíba			
Nid-72	K-423	Since 24 August	Fighter
Waco	C-2	Since 24 August	Bomber
Waco	C-3	Since 24 August	Fighter-Bomber
Waco	C-5	Since 24 August	Bomber

21 September.[94] The other two survivors may have formed a 5th Section in the Southern Mixed Detachment. Finally, this group was reinforced once again, with what is believed to be a Corsair on an unspecified date during September,[95] so the government ended up with some 13 or 14 aircraft in the theatre, 10 or 11 of them being combat aircraft (three Corsairs, three or four Potezs, four Wacos and three DH-60 Moths). Even if the rebels sent all their aviation forces to the south, they would now be outnumbered by two-to-one. According to reports by the pilot Alves Cabral, the Federals made

Paulista armoured train TB-1 in Soracabana, heading to the Southern Front. (A Gazeta, São Paulo)

A soldier of the Legião Negra, with his complete combat uniform. (Subtil)

Paulista armoured truck FS-6 or -7, perhaps like the one that defended Capão Bonito and Fundão. This is a Fordson 1922 Model, two of which were built for the Paulista FP, FS-6 and FS-7. (A Gazeta, via Catalogo)

several bombing and strafing missions on trains and troops on 5, 9 and 21 September, without meeting any opposition.[96]

The Battle for Fundão (18 August-1 September)

Returning to the land front, after the battles for Buri in the central sector, but before the Federal offensive, the Paulistas made a quick counterattack with the Fundão Detachment under Major Arlindo and recovered the Balsa region. Arlindo then advanced to Chácara do Alemão, where he entrenched on 18 August. After this brief interlude, on 20 August the government forces finally launched their attack against the rebels, who had been deployed in a cordon a little to the east running north–south, behind the Apiaí-Mirim and Paranapitanga rivers, concentrating on the crossing points. The Federal Melo Detachment moved south of the railway line and turned to the south-east, crossing the Paranapitanga over the Manteiga bridge and ejecting the Paulista Pirassununga Battalion that was defending it with just 100 soldiers on 30 August.[97]. To its right, the Dorneles Detachment followed the Capão Bonito road and crossed the river further south, clashing directly with the Paulista Fundão Detachment, now commanded by Colonel Torres Anchieta. Anchieta entrenched his forces and held the government assault from 18-22 August. The Federals then attacked using 75mm and 105mm artillery on 23 and 24 August, shelling the defenders with around a thousand rounds plus air support, while all the rebels could respond with was a pitiful three artillery shots.

In Fundão, a company of the Legião Negra Battalion and the 14 de Julho were left as a reserve, while the Rio Pardo Cavalry Regiment covered the left flank along the Apiaí-Mirim River. However, the 9th RCI/2nd Cavalry Division surrounded the Paulistas' positions and crossed the Apiaí-Mirim River after beating back the Rio Pardo Regiment (which fled to Serraria, north-west of Capão). The Federal cavalry then crossed the Paranapitanga River at two points, flanking the north of the Fundão Detachment with its 14 de Julho Battalion, while in the south at Capela Santo Antonio and São Roque, the new Lieutenant Colonel Martins Detachment was expelled on 26 August, Capão Bonito thus being threatened from the south-west. Seeing its left flank was outflanked, the Anchieta Detachment retreated to Fundão under pressure from the Federal forces under Dorneles.[98]

Armoured train number 2 or 3 and three rebel aircraft (the C-2, C-3 and C-5 Wacos) covered the Paulista withdrawal on 30 August.[99] The rebel aviation, however, soon disappeared from the skies once more. At the same time, the Federals of the Melo Detachment passed around Martins' right flank, reaching Fazenda Santa Ines, north of Capão, on 2 September. There, they were held by the Rio Pardo Cavalry Regiment, which had reached the area after their escape from the Apiaí-Mirim River, but the route to the east for Anchieta's Fundão Detachment was cut. Anchieta thus had to follow their withdrawal directly to the south-east, to Capão Bonito, being about to be surrounded again by the Federals in the north (Melo Detachment), north-west (Dorneles Detachment) and south-west (9th RCI).[100]

On 31 August, a Paulista armoured truck cleared the government positions on the road, but nevertheless, Dorneles took Fundão that same day. Its fall affected the whole Paulista deployment at the southern end of the front. In early August, the Federal Boanerges Detachment had succeeded in destroying Tenorio's rebels at Apiaí. Later, Boanerges' forces were held up by the rebel Morais Pinto Detachment in Capinzal (which finally fell on 11 August),[101] and then in Pinhal, south of Capão Bonito. With the Federal advance in the north, the space available for the Paulistas in Pinhal was drastically reduced, so they were forced to abandon this sector. Meanwhile, Lieutenant Colonel Alvaro Martins assumed command of the detachment (which now comprised the 8th BCP, 3rd BCV and Marcilio Franco Battalion, about 600 soldiers in all), but being harassed frontally by the Boanerges Detachment, and with his right flank threatened by the 9th RCI (which broke through the Franco Battalion at Capela San Antonio, on the Apiaí-Mirim River), he had to accelerate its withdrawal towards Capão Bonito to the north-east. Boanerges at this time had a strong formation of some 1,400 fighters and four cannons (part of the II/13th RI, the 13th BC and one-third of the II/8th RI Battalions, one platoon of the 2nd RC of the Rio Grande Brigade, elements of the 5th RCD and one battery of the 5th RAM).[102]

Paulista armoured car FS-2, built by the engineer Francisco de Sales (hence the 'S' in its identification). (Tom Cooper)

Federal troops in Capão Bonito, having conquered the town. (Coleção Dorothy Moretti, photo taken by Claro Gustavo Jansson, via Donato)

To cover the withdrawal of Martins and Anchieta, a small Paulista detachment was formed further east by the Fernão Dias Battalion and a cavalry squadron, a mere 300-400 soldiers, who were following the Ribeirão Branco River. In their withdrawal on 1 September, the rebels of Anchieta's and Martins' Detachments, instead of stopping at Capão Bonito, continued, turning east and crossing the Das Almas River to set up a new defensive line.[103] Between the third Battle of Buri and the taking of Capão Bonito, the Federals had spent 15 days of hard fighting to advance some 52km, in contrast to the initial offensive in which they advanced 104km to Buri, also in 15 days. Operations were now gradually transforming into a war of position, thanks to the arrival of reinforcements, the narrowing of the front and the efforts of the rebel Colonel Taborda. Taborda had started awkwardly with his untimely attempts to launch a counterattack but was now becoming a master in positional warfare.

Deployment on the Paranapanema and Das Almas Rivers (7 September)

After these battles, the Paulista front line retreated behind the wide Paranapanema River, except at the southern end of the front, where they deployed behind its tributary, the Das Almas River, a little further to the west. At the other end of the line, in the north, to prevent the rebels bringing reinforcements from the central sector (where the Battle of Fundão-Capão Bonito was fought), the Federal

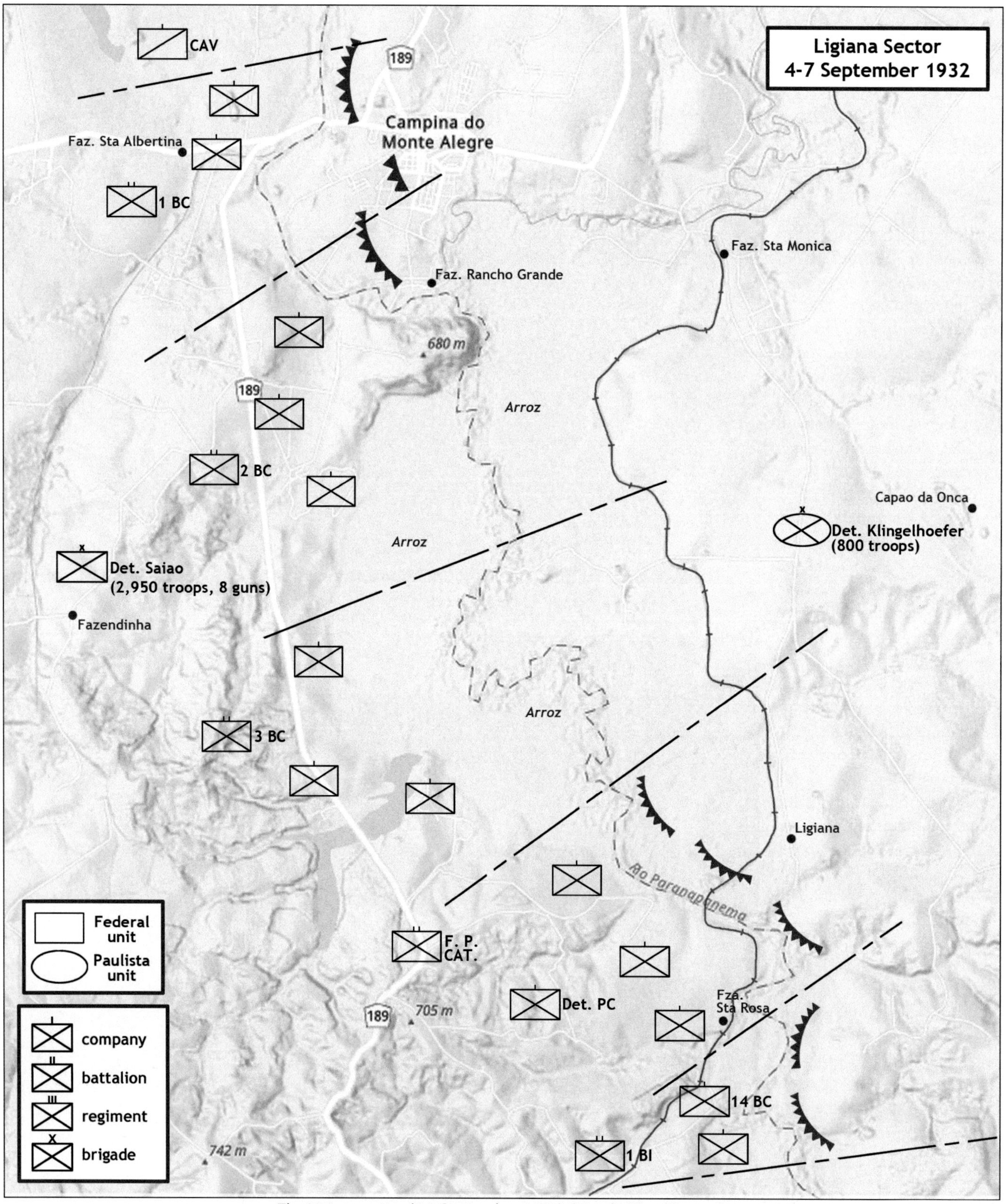

The Ligiana sector (4-7 September 1932). (Map by Tom Cooper)

Saião Detachment advanced slowly on 25 August, pushing back the forces of Klingelhoefer at Aracaçú. On 5 September, the step-by-step Federal progress continued. They deployed, from north to south, a squadron of the 12th RCI, the 1st, 2nd and 3rd BC, probably from the Pernambuco FP,[104] the Santa Catarina FP Battalion and the 1st/ Military Brigade Battalion, with about 2,500 fighters in the front line, supported by another 600 soldiers from the 8th Auxiliary Corps/ Military Brigade and a battery of the 6th RAM. With these troops Saião expelled the rebels from Aracaçú, reaching the Paranapanema River on 7 September. The Paulistas were now behind the river, protecting Ligiana, following the railroad to São Paulo.[105] There, the front was stabilised until shortly before the end of the war, being defended, again from north to south, by some 1,100 soldiers on the front line (a squadron of the 2nd RCD, the 9th BCR, II/'9 July' Battalion, 7th BCR, 10th BCR and 6th BCR),[106] plus an additional 300 soldiers in reserve (1st Reserve Battalion of Engineers, a two-piece artillery section, one piece of 150mm heavy artillery mounted on a train and the Armoured Train Number 1).[107]

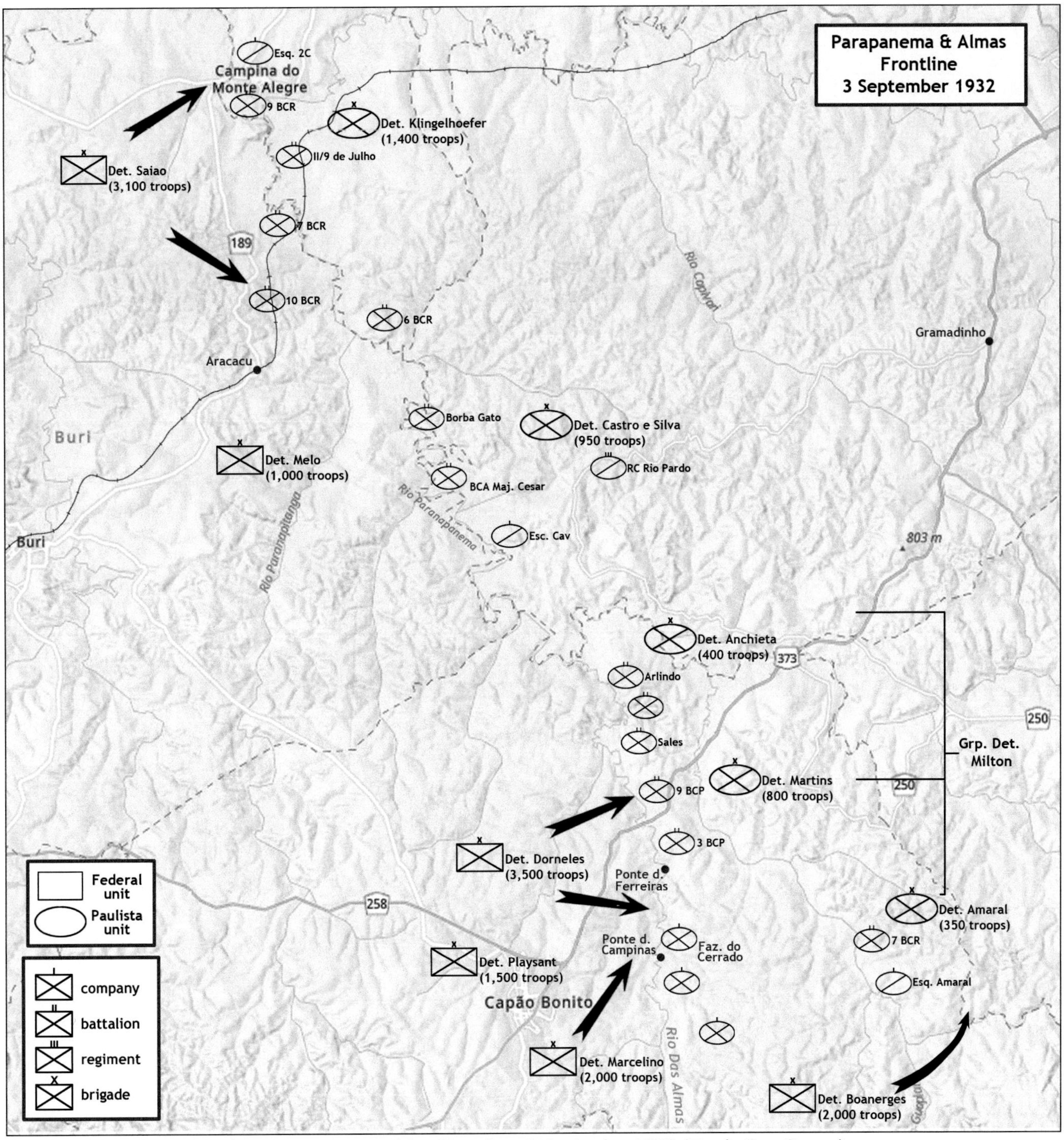

The Paranapanema and Das Almas front (3 September 1932). (Map by Tom Cooper)

Further to the south were units that would carry the weight of the struggle to cross, or impede the crossing of, these river barriers. From north to south, there was the Federal Melo Detachment – that once it crossed the Paranapitanga River, pushed the Paulistas against the Paranapanema – consisting of about 1,000 troops (2nd RC and 5th/Military Brigade), against the rebel Detachment Castro e Silva, based in Faxenda Bom Retiro, with some 550 Constitutionalists (Borba Gato and Major Cesar Battalions, a cavalry squadron and a section of artillery). Further south was the Rio Pardo Regiment, comprising about 400 additional Paulistas.

Then there was the Federal Dorneles Detachment, poised to cross the Das Almas River. To do so they would first have to take the bridge at Brizolas. This unit was composed of about 3,500 soldiers (7th RI, I/8th RI Battalion, 3rd Auxiliary Corps/Military Brigade, a Paraíba FP Battalion and the 5th RAM). Opposing them was a group of detachments under Lieutenant Colonel Milton, who would defend the entire das Almas. The 400-strong rebel Anchieta Detachment was almost cornered between the curve of the Paranapanema at its rear and right flank, but protected by the mouth of its tributary, the das Almas (the Arlindo and Alipio Ferraz Battalions), while further south was the Martins Detachment, holding the Brizolas and Ferreiras bridges, adding another 800 soldiers (the Fernão Sales, Marcilio Franco, 8th BCP and 3rd BCV Battalions).

Finally, at the southern end of the front, the Federals had about 1,500 men in the Playsant Detachment, formed from several Paraná FP Battalions, who were attacking the Damião Ferreira bridge over the Das Almas River. The 2,000-strong Boanerges Detachment (the II/8th RI, 13th BC and II/13th RI Battalions, and the 17th Corps/ Military Brigade) and the Colonel Marcelino Detachment (the 14th BC, 1st Santa Catarina FP, 2nd Paraíba FP and 8th/Military

Table 12: Paranapanema–das Almas Front (7 September)			
Federals			
Southern Army Detachment			
General Valdomiro Lima			
Location	**Detachment**	**Composition**	**Strength**
North/left flank, facing Aracaçú	Saião	1st, 2nd and 3rd BC (perhaps part of Pernambuco FP), Santa Catarina FP, 1st/Military Brigade, 8th Auxiliary Corps/Military Brigade Battalions, a squadron/12th RCI, a battery/6th RAM	3,100 soldiers, four cannons
Centre: Paranapitanga River	Melo	2nd RC, 5th/Military Brigade Battalion.	1,000 soldiers
Right flank: Das Almas River (Brizolas bridge)	Dorneles	7th RI, I/8th RI, 3rd Auxiliary Corps/Military Brigade, Paraíba FP Battalions, 5th RAM	3,500 soldiers, 24 cannons
Extreme right flank: Das Almas River (Damião Ferreira bridge)	Playsant	Paraná FP Battalions	1,500 men
Reserve: Capão Bonito	Boanerges	II/8th RI, 13th BC, II/13th RI, 17th Corps/Military Brigade Battalions	2,000 soldiers
Reserve: Capão Bonito	Marcelino	14th BC, 1st Santa Catarina FP, 2nd Paraíba FP, 8th/Miltary Brigade Battalions	2,000 soldiers
Total Federals: 13,100 soldiers, 28 cannons			
Paulistas			
Southern Sector			
Colonel Basilio Taborda			
Location	**Detachment**	**Composition**	**Strength**
North/right flank: Aracaçú	Klingelhoefer	9th BCR, II/ Regiment 9 de Julho, 7th BCR, 10th BCR, 6th BCR, 1st BRE, a squadron/2nd RCD, Mascarenhas Artillery Section	1,400 soldiers, two cannons, armoured train with 1 x 150mm gun
Centre: Faxenda Bom Retiro	Castro e Silva	Rio Pardo Regiment, Borba Gato, Major Cesar Battalions, Cavalry Squadron, Artillery Section	950 soldiers, two cannons
Left flank: Das Almas River	Anchieta/Milton Group of Detachments	Arlindo, Alipio Ferraz Battalions	400 soldiers
Das Almas River (Brizolas & Ferreiras bridges)	Martins/Milton Group of Detachments	Fernão Sales, Marcilio Franco, 8th BCP, 3rd BCV Battalions	800 soldiers
Extreme left flank (south): Das Almas (Dos Ferreiras bridge)	Amaral/Milton Group of Detachments	São Miguel Platoon, a company/7th BCP, Amaral Squadron, Quintâes Battery	350 soldiers, three cannons,
General Reserve: Itapetininga	Taborda	14 de Julho Regiment, 2 companies/ Legião Negra	400 soldiers
Total Paulistas: 4,300 soldiers, eight cannons			

Brigade Battalions, in all another 2,000 Federal troops) would stay as a reserve at Capão Bonito. They were to support Playsant's assault across the Das Almas River. In front of them, the Paulistas had the Major Amaral Detachment at dos Ferreiras bridge, just 250 soldiers in total (the provisional São Miguel Platoon, a company of the 7th BCP and the Amaral Squadron, which was still part of the Milton Group of Detachments). The artillery of the Milton Group comprised the Quintâes Battery, a mere three cannons with some 100 soldiers. Colonel Taborda had another 400 soldiers (from the 14 de Julho Regiment and two companies of the Legião Negra Battalion) as a general reserve for all the Southern Sector in Itapetininga.[108] Thus, in total, throughout the Paranapenama–Das Almas line, 13,100 Federals under General Valdomiro Lima were to attack 4,300 Paulistas under Colonel Taborda. The above calculations of the numbers of troops are consistent with the fact that according to the payrolls, the loyalists had in the Southern Army in late August some 12,900 soldiers, while the rebels, according Taborda, had 3,975 soldiers in late September (and their number always ranged between 3,000 and 5,000 fighters).[109]

Forcing Crossing the Das Almas River (9-23 September)

On 9 September, the government's Playsant Detachment began the attack on the Das Almas River at the southern end of the Federal line (its right), attacking the weak Amaral Detachment across the river and forcing a bridgehead. Only the arrival of the 14 de Julho Battalion, coming from the Paulista reserve, managed to stabilise the line. To restore its general reserve, Taborda moved back the 10th BCR and added the new Taunay Battalion, just arrived from

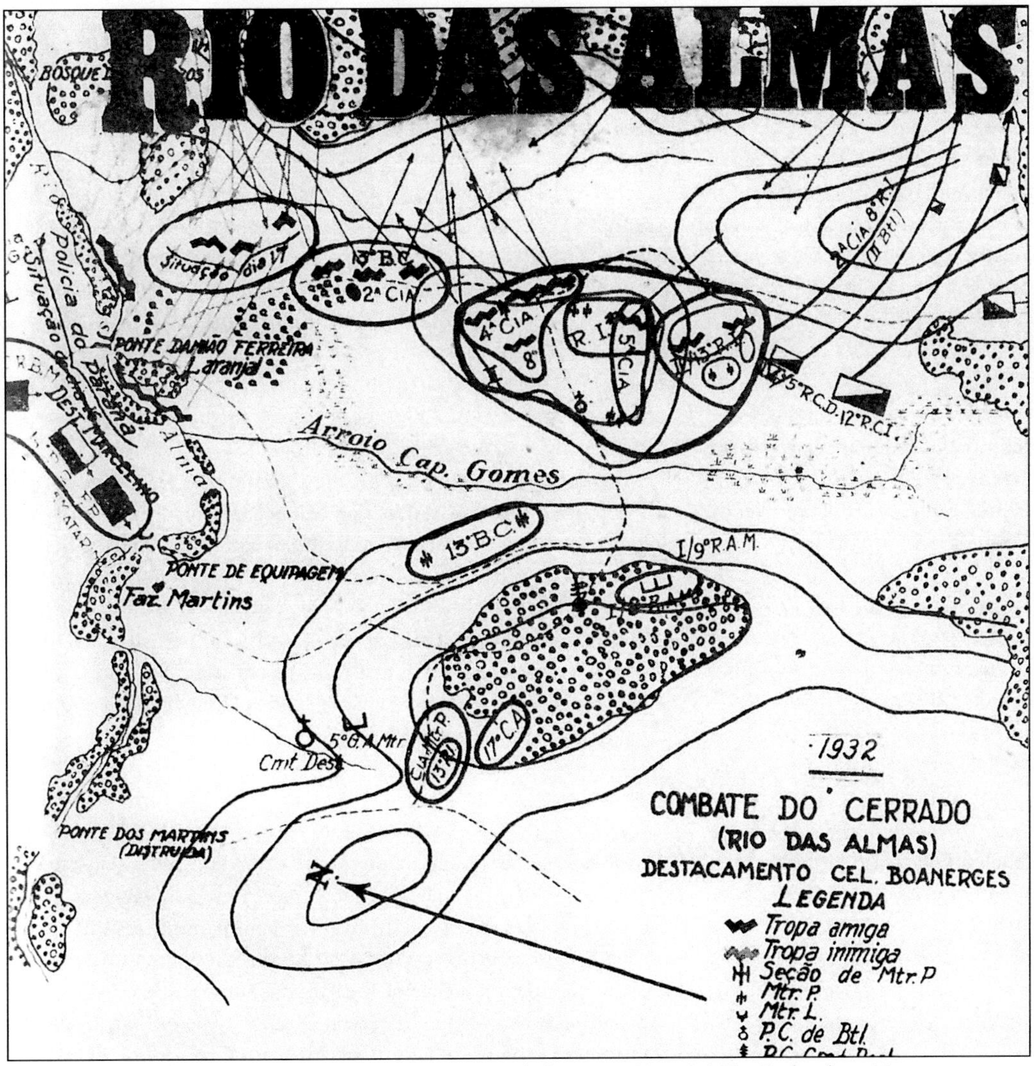

A sketch of the Rio Das Almas crossing made by Jorge Mancini. The Federal positions can be seen, with the Marcelino Detachment on the left, while in the centre, in two lines, is the Boanerges Detachment. (Jorge Mancini, via Donato)

continued to expand their bridgehead across the river. There, at the Damião Ferreira bridge,[112] Captain Gomes do Santos led a bayonet charge by a Paraná Provisional Battalion to take the bridge, knowing that once occupied they could outflank the rebel trenches, but his assault was beaten back by heavy machine gun fire. In a second assault on the bridge, Captain do Santos was shot in the head and had to be evacuated to hospital. When rebel artillery fire began falling near the hospital, the brave wounded officer told the surgeon to move away to safety and then to care for the other badly injured soldiers rather than himself. This heroic act would cost him his life.[113]

In the meantime, heavy fighting continued for the bridge. Playsant, unable to take it, focussed instead on securing a bridgehead. The location of this bridgehead is not specified in the sources, but thanks to a map made by Mancini we know that it would have been between the Damião Ferreira and dos Martins bridges (the latter one being destroyed).[114] Playsant used a raft and a ferry to cross the river here. When his vanguard was on the other side, they were vigorously attacked by the rebel Martins and Amaral Detachments, so Playsant had to call for aid from Boanerges. Meanwhile, Marcelino came from the Federals' reserve on 18 September, reinforcing the front line. Marcelino crossed the river with the 14th BC and took Fazenda Cerrado, in the Amaral Sector. On the 20th, the beachhead across the river managed to break through the defences of the 14 de Julho Battalion, which retired north to Capela dos Ferreiros, which formed Martin's left flank,[115] leaving behind 35 men to defend the trenches. These brave soldiers fought on until they were all dead or overcome and captured.[116] With that action ended the fighting in the Cerrado region. The rest of the Amaral Detachment had already retreated to the east, following the Paranapanema River, on 19 September.[117]

However, Martins and Anchieta, further to the north, were still behind the Das Almas River. They were faced by the troops of Dorneles, still on the west bank of the river, who were halted at the Brizolas bridge by Martins' rebels. The Federals, having already crossed the river further south, turned to their left, to the north, to take Martins in the flank and force him to evacuate Brizolas, attacking Santa Cruz dos Ferreiras. To do this, Marcelino's 8th Reserve/Military Brigade Battalion replaced Playsant's badly depleted Paranenses and the 14th BC, who were sent to the rear, forming new reserves along with the 13th BC, 12th RCI and 17th Auxiliary Corps/Military Brigade. The Marcelino Detachment

Mato Grosso. Anticipating that the Federals were about to launch further attacks, Taborda decided to go ahead with a series of minor sectional offensives along the front on 15 September, to disrupt the Federal assault before it was carried out. The main effort was made in the Fazenda Santa Ines area, threatening the Capão Bonito. Here, Taborda launched an ad-hoc group set up under Lieutenant Colonel Otelo-Franco with the reserves (some 500 Paulistas of the 10th BCR, the Taunay Battalion and the Rio Pardo Regiment) that took advantage of a gap in the Federal detachments to occupy an area, surprising the 9th RCI and the Dorneles Detachment. However, government cavalry forces counter-attacked and the rebels were forced to retreat, covered by the Rio Pardo Regiment.[110] A little further to the north, Melo's Federals had forced the Cesar Battalion under Castro e Silva to abandon Capão do Papagaio, Fazenda Rodrigues Alves and Capão do Lageado. On 13 September, Castro's rebels launched a further counterattack with a contingent under Captain Ribeiro Junior, which was fought off by the Federals, the young Paulista captain being killed during the fighting.[111]

General Lima then ordered the Federal attack on 16 September. The Saião and Melo Detachments fixed the Paulistas of Klingelhoefer and Castro e Silva in the north so that they could not send reinforcements to the south, where the main point of the loyalist effort was to be launched. The Melo Detachment pushed Castro e Silva back against the Paranapenama River. Further south, near the Das Almas River, the Playsant Detachment, supported by Boanerges, comprised about 1,600 soldiers and four pieces of artillery (II/8th RI, 8th Reserve/Military Brigade and 14th BC Battalions, with a battery of the 5th GAMTH). On its right was the Boanerges Detachment with some 1,700 fighters and eight heavy guns (II/13th RI, 17th Auxiliary Corps/Military Brigade, a machine gun company of the 13th RI and Santa Catarina FP Battalions, the 4th Squadron/5th RCD and the I GAM/9th RAM), which was to advance to the next river, the Paranapanema, then take the dos Souzas bridge, cross it and continue along the road north-east to São Miguel Arcanjo, thereby cutting off the withdrawal of the Paulista forces under Martins still located at the Ferreiras bridge and Santa Cruz. On 21 September, the rebel resistance in Ferreiras gave way, and in order not to be enveloped between the two rivers, both the Anchieta and Martins Detachments retreated behind the Paranapanema River, leaving their das Almas positions. To cover their retreat, the Brizolas bridge was destroyed. Dorneles was finally able to cross the river on the 23rd, when the fighting ended, using a pontoon bridge.[118]

Crossing the Last Barrier: The Paranapanema River (25 September-1 October)

At the same time, Boanerges, on the extreme Federal right, continued his advance to the north-east to reach the Paranapanema River. There, he found that the Paulistas protected the Ana Romana pass, so he left his 17th Auxiliary Corps/Military Brigade there to distract the rebels, while the main force, comprising the II/13th RI and 13th BC, crossed the Paranapanema further south at the Passo das Formigas, defended by only one rebel company, on 23 September. After breaking through the front, Boanerges launched through the gap the 3rd and 4th Squadrons/5th RCD, whose riders galloped to try to take São Miguel Arcanjo, but were stopped halfway there by the Paulistas in Taquaral, with some reinforcements from the 14 de Julho Battalion. At the end of September, Boanerges took Taquaral Abaixo. A little further north, the Federal Marcelino Detachment also crossed the das Souzas bridge and continued north-eastward on 26 September, defeating the Paulistas at Passo do Jango and dos Tenentes, in the Ponte Bueno region. Even further north, the Melo Detachment also broke the barrier of the river after expelling the Castro e Silva Detachment, threatening Campina and Angatuba, along with the rear positions of the northernmost Paulista detachment.[119]

There, with all the rebel lines collapsing, the last battle of the Southern Front happened when Federal troops of Colonel Jurandir Mamade (from Detachment Melo) forced the passage of the river on 1 October in the region of Salto after an artillery barrage of 70 rounds at 0840 hours, while the Paulistas, knowing that an armistice was being negotiated, remained silent. The Federals then attacked and opened fire but were beaten off by a counterattack from the Paulista civilian volunteers. At 1430 hours, after a further artillery barrage, the government troops managed to cross the river and the rebels fled to Angatuba. That same day, in the Campininha Sector, in Perigo, the Tenorio do Brito Battalion had two of their trenches taken by the loyalist forces; in the third trench, the volunteer Lieutenant Martin continued fighting despite being alone, and had to be dragged 800 metres to safety by another volunteer, Salvador Assumpção, while the officer continued shouting orders to his non-existent troops.[120] Meanwhile, further north, the loyalist forces under Saião also forced a passage across the Paranapanema against Klingelhoefer, and took Ligiana and Campina Monte Alegre.[121]

Despite the stiff resistance in the Rio das Almas brilliantly executed by Taborda, all the Paulista front collapsed and the Federal forces advanced all across the line. At this time, Lima's Southern Army had some 18,000 soldiers opposing the 3,975 Paulistas of Taborda.[122] Taborda's surviving forces were now only thinking about saving their lives. While all this was happening in the central sector, on the Federal left (the northern flank), the government troops also crossed the lower reaches of the Paranapanema River and cut the railroads that connected the capital with the west and north-west of the state and the friendly territory of Mato Grosso. On 3 October, the Marcelino Detachment was still advancing when the news came of the surrender of São Paulo, stopping all operations.

2
THE FAILED CONSTITUTIONALIST REBELLIONS

As we have seen, although the rebellion against Getúlio Vargas to re-enact the constitution in Brazil succeeded in São Paulo and southern Mato Grosso, there were other attempts in Rio Grande do Sul, along the Amazon River and in the states of Bahia, Paraná and Minas Gerais, all of which failed. While the events in Minas proved a threat rather than a real danger, there was fighting in all the other states. The most serious was the uprising started in Rio Grande do Sul, followed by that around the Amazon. Nevertheless, none of these had the slightest chance to flourish and endanger the rule of the government.

The Minas Gerais Revolts (8 August-22 September)

In the Minas region there were several movements to try to support the rebel Paulistas. We have already seen in Volume 1 how General Horta Barbosa tried to subvert the 4th Division but was arrested and replaced by Colonel Pinheiro. However, there were other attempts, though less serious. The principal one involved Artur Bernardes, the Mineiro Republican Party leader, former president of the State of Minas Gerais (1918-1922) and former President of Brazil (1922-1926) during the Mineiro turn in the so-called 'coffee with milk' regime. Bernardes was a vociferous enemy of the Vargas regime and the tenentismo (Lieutenants Movement) and participated in the conspiracy by the Paulista Colonel Figueiredo to raise São Paulo in revolt to become the leader of the resistance to the Mineiro loyalist government.

Artur Bernardes, retired at his residence in Viçosa, was being closely observed by the Mineira police, but as yet he had not done anything illegal, so they were unsure whether or not to arrest him. However, Barbosa had gathered 500 of his followers, known as the 'jagunços', and most of them were armed, so any operation against Bernardes would not be an easy one for the police. Emboldened, Bernardes issued a manifesto on 8 August in which he stated: "São Paulo took up arms and stood for Brazil, why we do not accompany them?" That was too much for the government, and Federal Delegate Moura Filho marched to Viçosa with a Mineiro FP Battalion. Nevertheless, Bernardes met Filho and convinced him that the presence of Barbosa's armed men was only to protect him; if the government did not arrest or attack him, they would not revolt. However, this excuse for their existence proved hollow shortly afterwards, when it was discovered that Bernardes was receiving weapons via the Leopoldina railway. Documents unearthed in Rio de Janeiro on 6 September also incriminated him.

The Federal reaction was swift. The Hacienda Ipanema, owned by a nephew of Bernardes, was taken by assault after a 20-minute barrage on 7 September. At the same time, the government ordered the arrest of Bernardes. However, he had already fled from Viçosa, and his supporters at last began their rebellion after a

Gustavo Capanema, Minister of Justice for Minas Gerais, on a hospital train. He had to deal with the Barbosa rebellion. (Unknown author, FGV, CPDDC, Donation by Guilhermo Figueiredo, via Catalogo)

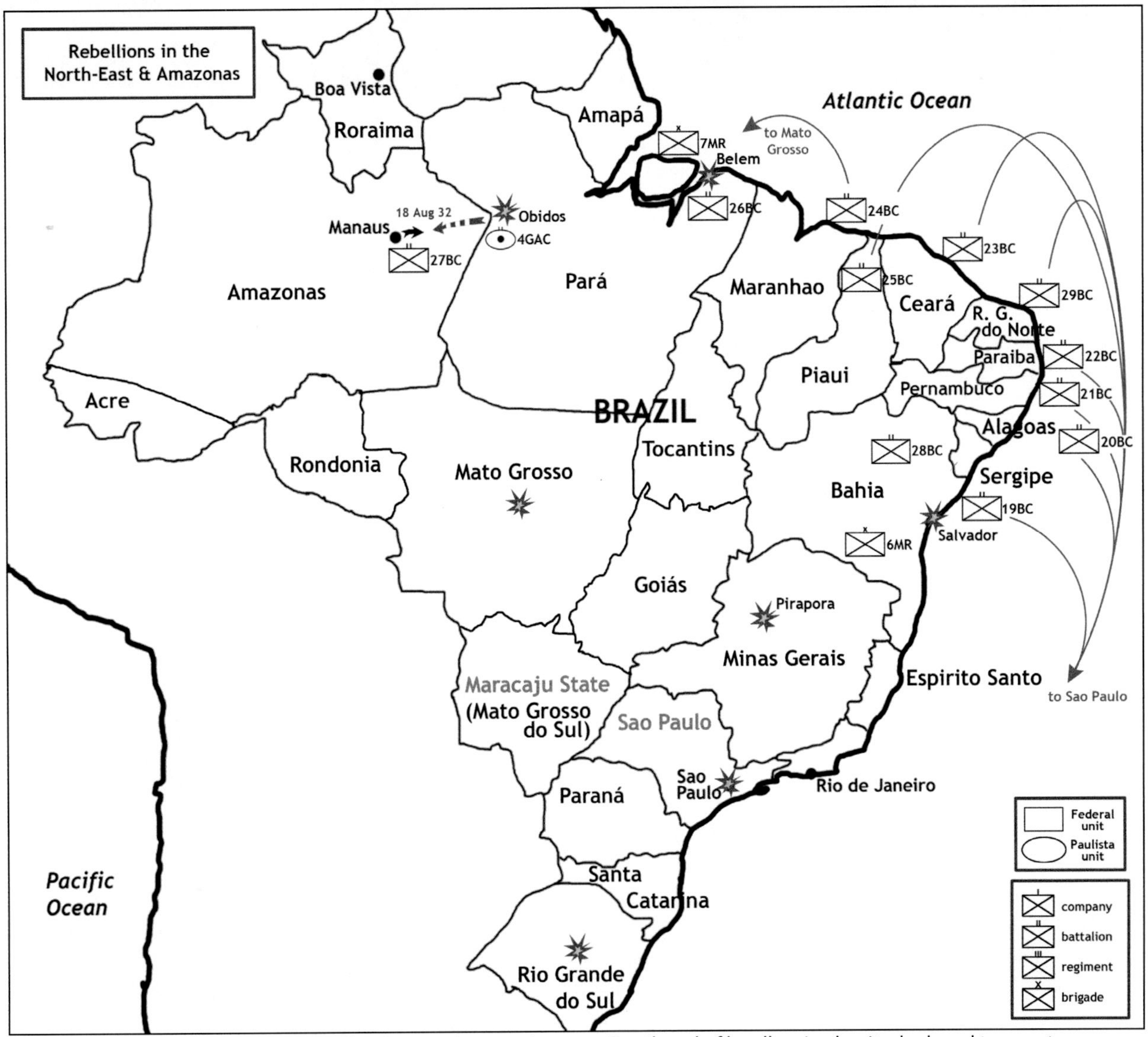

A map of Paulista-related rebellions in northern and eastern Brazil, and of locally raised units deployed to counter the Paulista rebellions in the Federal States of Mato Grosso and Sao Paulo. (Map by Tom Cooper)

A Federal soldier with a boy, also in uniform and armed, probably his son. Due to the owner of the picture being Gustavo Capanema, it was probably taken in Minas Gerais. (FGV, CPDDC, Gustavo Capanema archives, via Catalogo)

tense wait of nearly two months. In Pirapora, the rebels briefly seized the town, but they surrendered after being blockaded for three days in Lassange. Other armed insurgent groups operated in the Mata area. On 11 September, up to 800 rebels under Freitas Bastos were driven out of Iraponga. Bernardes, meanwhile, evaded the police for two weeks until he was located alone at a farm near Viçosa on 22 September, and arrested, signalling the end of the revolt. In the end, the numerous but poorly armed rebels had stood no chance of success.[1]

The Rebellion in the Amazon and the North-east (17 July-24 August)

One of the first attempted uprisings occurred in Belém, the capital of the state of Pará and a port located to the east of the Amazon delta. There, on 17 July, a naval captain along with several soldiers tried to overthrow the State Governor, Joaquim Magalhaes Barata and seize the river battleship *Floriano*. This was a very old battleship, dating from 1899, that since 1931 had been acting just as a hydrographic survey vessel and that would be decommissioned shortly thereafter in 1934. However, with two Armstrong 240mm guns, four 120mm guns, four 57mm guns and two torpedo tubes, the *Floriano* could still be a dangerous opponent which might have been able to lift the blockade that was being implemented in Santos harbour. The ship also had a 350mm armoured belt, so it was only vulnerable to projectiles fired from guns with a calibre larger than 300mm (which only existed in other battleships or coastal artillery batteries) or from close-range attacks carried out by torpedo or aerial bombing. Its weakness was its speed; just 14 knots at the time of its launch, but now even that would be much less because of its age. It also had poor navigation instruments, so was only able to perform coastal navigation in calm weather.[2] However, governor Barata quickly brought the situation under control, imprisoning the rebels or forcing them to flee.[3]

In the meantime, attempts at rebellion continued. Again, in Belém, on the night of 2 August, law and medical students, along with some graduates, marched to the headquarters of the tiro-de-guerra (arsenal), where they seized 12 rifles and occupied the firefighter and police barracks, taking advantage of the town's garrison, the 26th BC, having been sent to the south to take part in the Paulista War. Governor Barata summoned firefighters, police and armed volunteers and managed to corner the students at the Police Headquarters. Most of them surrendered, but gymnastics student Paulo Cícero Teixeira barricaded himself with a Hotchkiss machine gun and held off the government troops all night until a sharpshooter killed him from a neighbouring roof. The last pockets of resistance were silenced by a detachment from the Navy Arsenal.[4]

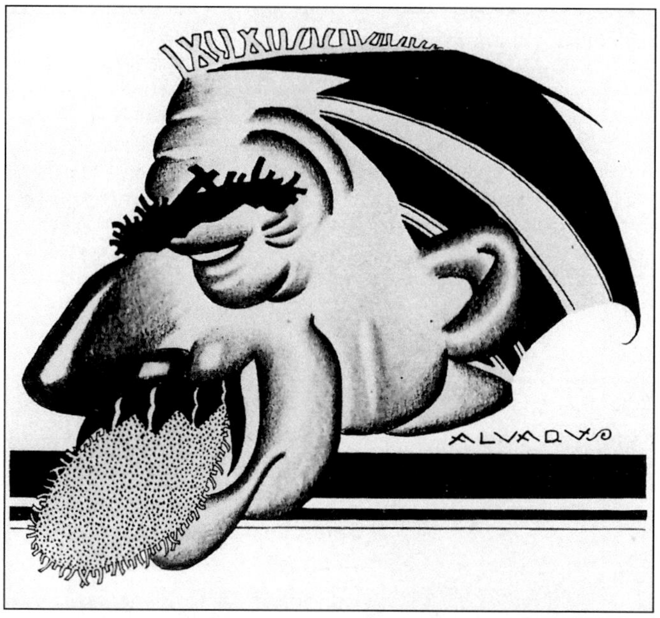

Cartoon of Borges de Medeiros, President of Rio Grande do Sul for 25 years. Despite being supported by Vargas in a previous local civil war in 1923, he turned against Vargas in 1932, and in 1934 he was a candidate for the presidency. Drawn by Alvarus. (Diários Associados, via Donato)

Borges de Medeiros. (Diários Associados, via Donato)

Recruitment poster published by the MMDC Militia, with the legend, 'They are waiting for you. Enlist to complete the battalion!' Notable is the Brazilian flag near that of the Paulistas, a testimony that the Paulista rebellion was not about establishing an independent nation. (Courtesy Eric Apolinário)

This small poster by an anonymous artist was used to glue onto the doors of houses from which a volunteer joined the Paulista Army. It included the inscription, 'A soldier of law departed from this house'. It demonstrated the fact the purpose of the war was not independence but the defence of legal order: democracy. (history.uol.com.br)

Anonymous poster of the P.R.P. political party, including inscription, 'Paulista, defend your country, vote for P.R.P.' Inspired by the famous Italian poster from the times of the First World War, it was published after the war, probably for the elections of 1933-34. (Courtesy Eric Apolinário)

Perhaps the most impressive Paulista poster was published by the MMDC Militia as a call for recruitment. Inspired by the well-known 'Uncle Sam needs You' poster from the USA in the First World War, it was the most graphic document of the 1932 War. The legend in Brazilian Portugues read, 'You have a duty of fulfil. Check with your conscience!' (Donato)

This Paulista FS 2 armoured truck, as most rebel vehicles, was designed by professor and engineer Francisco de Sales Vicente de Acevedo, hence its designation, starting with FS (Francisco de Sales), followed by a number (from 1 to 8). All designs made use of the chassis of various Ford, Chevrolet, and Mc Coornick Deering cars or trucks, protected with 11-12mm steel plates. The FS 2 was capable of reaching 30-45km/h and was painted in a French camouflage pattern using the sky blue colour rather than grey. This example, based on a Ford truck, was armed with a Hotchkiss 7mm machine gun in a turret, and used in all sectors for reconnaissance. (Artwork by David Bocquelet)

Similar to the FS 2, this was the Paulista FS 4 'Piolinho'. Having steel plates of 4-6mm thickness, it was less-well armoured, and had its wheels entirely unprotected. The turret included a Hotchkiss 7mm machine gun and – like the FS 2 – it could carry up to four troops. While the original chassis remains unclear, this illustration is based on that of a Ford truck. Ultimately, a total of five armoured trucks of this kind were manufactured, designated FS 1 to FS 5. (Artwork by David Bocquelet)

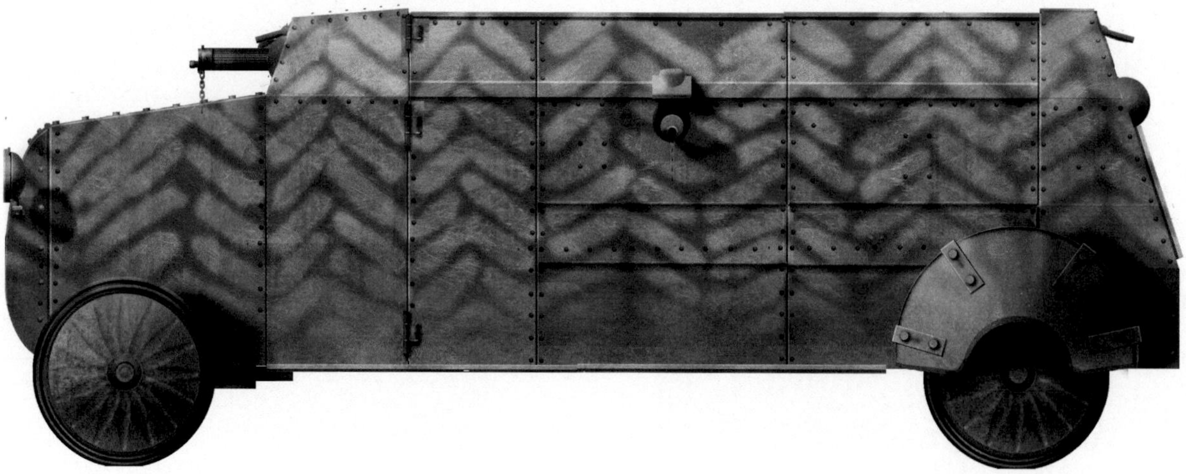

This Paulista FS 8 armoured personnel carrier could transport up to eight troops and was equipped with three Hotchkiss 7mm machine guns. As far as is known, this example was operated in the Paraíba Valley Front (covered in Volume 1) and formed a part of the 2nd BE. Its sole entry point was a door at the rear of the superstructure, armoured with 4-6mm steel plate. The wheels were protected with a round steel plate. (Artwork by David Bocquelet)

The FS 6 and FS 7 were made from Fordson Model F 1922 farm tractors. Each was armoured with thicker steel plate (11-12mm) and armed with up to three Hotchkiss machine guns. Their wheels were made entirely of iron, and they had a ventilation tower atop of the superstructure. Each had a crew of five, and their sole entrance was at the back. With their maximum speed of only 11km/h, neither was ever deployed on the frontlines: instead, they were kept back in Sào Paulo, and used for security tasks or parades. (Artwork by David Bocquelet)

This armoured vehicle with a flamethrower was designed by Reinaldo Ramos de Saldanha da Gama for the Paulista FP in 1931, before the war, to equip an Armoured Section for the police. It was based on a Caterpillar tractor Model 22, and it had two Hotchkiss 7mm machine guns installed in the front, two to the rear, and a turret equipped with a flamethrower that had a range of 100m. The crew consisted of six. It was operated in the Paraíba Valley, protecting – and saving – the 2nd Division during its massive withdrawal from Cruzeiro to Guaratinguetá (described in Volume 1). (Artwork by David Bocquelet)

As of 1932, this Renault FT-17 light tank was one of only three surviving examples out of 12 acquired by Brazil in 1921. One of these was equipped with a cast Berlier turret and a 37mm Puteaux cannon, shown here, while the two others had an octagonal turret made by Renault, equipped with one Hotchkiss 7mm machine gun. They formed a section of the Federal forces, deployed in the Sierra de Mantiqueira area (covered in the Volume 1). (Artwork by David Bocquelet)

French Engineer and resident of Sào Paulo. Clement de Baujeanau, designed the rebel armoured trains. This TB-1 (*Trem Blindado* or Armoured Train Number 1) was manufactured in cooperation between the Polytechnic School (USP), the Institute of Technological Investigations (IPT) and the Sorocabana Railway Company, under supervision by engineer Augusto Ferreira Velloso. TB-1 had a protected wagon to transport soldiers, with firing ports for automatic weapons and rifles, and was equipped with strong spotlights to blind and confuse the enemy soldiers at night. TB-1 fought in the Battle for Buri on the Southern Front, nearly retaking the village on 26 July 1932. Locomotive Number 216 was used to create the TB-2, and the wagon was used to create the TB-3: instead of an armoured wagon, the TB-2 and TB-3 were equipped with an unarmoured one, positioned in front of the locomotive, and the other behind it. The front wagon carried one 75mm Krupp or Schneider gun, and both wagons carried 7mm Hotchkiss machine guns. The total complement was 18, including three engineers and 15 weapon-handlers. (Artwork by David Bocquelet)

The success of the TB-1, TB-2 and TB-3 encouraged the USP and IPT to contract the Central Brazil ECFB and the Mogiana Railways companies to design two similar armoured trains. The resulting TB-4 and TB-5 were deployed on the Paraíba and the Minas fronts, respectively. The locomotives number 730 and 732 were slightly smaller than the ones used in TB-1, -2 and -3, and the wagons were smaller, but each was equipped with two turrets mounting machine guns. Crewed by 18, each of these trains received a new camouflage pattern: the top was painted in sky blue, to better hide the train in the mountains, while the rest was camouflaged in two shades of green. The TB-5 fought valiantly in Eluterio in August 1932, while the TB-4 was eventually sent to Mococa, on the Minas Front. (Artwork by David Bocquelet)

Christened the *Phantasma da Morte* (Phantom of Death), the TB-6 was the most powerful of the Paulista trains. Its armour consisted of two layers of steel plates, with wood in between, and it was equipped with three armoured wagons, the front of which (shown to the left) had one 75mm Schneider or Krupp gun, multiple Hotchkiss machine guns – fired through four quadratic windows – and several automatic rifles fired through port holes higher up. A Schwarzlose machine gun was installed in a turret for air defence purposes atop the superstructure of the third wagon (shown to the right). The locomotive (see next illustration) was bigger than the ones used on the narrow-track TB-1/3 and protected by armour covering the engine and funnel. Sometimes, a smaller, lighter and unarmoured car was attached in front as protection against mines, and to carry repair materials, while another was to the rear, carrying gasoline necessary to power the generators used for spotlights. The crew consisted of four engineers, and 11-13 gunners. The TB-6 had a colourful operational history, including a 'blue-on-blue' incident in which its crew gunned down 20 friendly troops. In the Morro Verde area, and during the retreat from Vila Queimada it was stripped of its primary weapons and used to transport troops. Re-equipped by Captain Saldanha, it was subsequently deployed to bombard Cachoeira, defend Lorena and cover the Paulista withdrawal to Guaratinguetá, where it received flamethrowers and grenade launchers – and survived multiple hits by 75mm shells and air strikes. (Artwork by David Bocquelet)

The final noteworthy train deployed by the Paulistas included a Baldwin 1927 4-6-2 wide-track locomotive of the Central Brazil ECFB. This was used to pull a specially modified flatcar, carrying a 150mm Canet coastal gun taken from Fort Itaipú. This car was followed by another, carrying shells, and a third wagon that served the crew. Not being intended to serve as an assault weapon, this train was entirely unprotected. It provided heavy artillery support in the Paraiva Valley where it would approach the combat zone by night, conduct its fire mission, and then be replaced by the *Phantasma do Morte* by day. (Arwtork by David Bocquelet)

As identified by his white scarf, this irregular Matogrossense was a rebel cowboy. He wore typical local clothes, included *bambachas* (baggy pants), and *tirador* (leather apron) to protect his legs. The *guaiaca* – a boar-leather belt – held a holster for his Smith & Wesson 1917 revolver. He is shown holding a Winchester Model 1892, the most-widely used civilian weapon in Brazil of the time. (Artwork by Anderson Subtil)

This cavalry Captain of the Federal forces served in the Ayrton Plaisant Detachment of the Paraná State forces. Note the Hungarian bows on shoulders, the field hat, riding trousers and boots – all part of the standard Brazilian uniform – and his red scarf, typical of Geutlist troops. The leather belt and suspenders hold a.38 Smith & Wesson Model 1906 Military & Police revolver. (Artwork by Anderson Subtil)

This Federal trooper is shown wearing the outdated green wool overcoat over his khaki campaign uniform from 1908, a field cap from 1920 instead of the new 'cloth helmet', and *borgeguins* (short boots). His leather gaiters and the belt were also dated to the times of the First World War. His firearm is the 7x57mm Brazilian Model 1908 rifle – the local version of the German-designed Mauser 1898. (Artwork by Anderson Subtil)

Two Vougth O2-UA Corsairs of the Federal air force were equipped with floats for operations along the coastal sector (covered in Volume 1). Notable on this example is the blue band, denoting it as the aircraft flown by the section leader, and the darker frontal half visible on several photographs: this might have been the same sky blue as on several Mexican operated Azcárates of the time. Powered by a 337Kw engine, and weighing 2,161kg when fully loaded, the Corsair had a maximum speed of 260km/h, and a manoeuvre ratio of 0.21. It could reach the ceiling of 5,670m, and a range of 1,094km. Its armament consisted of two 7.62mm machine guns (one firing fore, the other to the aft), and up to two 226.5kg bombs. (Artwork by Luca Canossa)

This Potez 25TOE was operated by the Paulistas, and – probably from September 1932 – had its entire upper wing painted in white, with black bands on the top side, to keep it consistent with markings on other aircraft operated by the movement. Its maximum speed was 215km/h, manoeuvre ratio 0.14 (the engine had an output of 357Kw, and the aircraft weighed 2,558kg when fully loaded), could reach a ceiling of 5,500m, and it had a range of 600km. Armament consisted of one or two 7.7mm Vickers machine guns firing forward, two 7.7mm Darne machine guns served by the gunner, and up to two 240kg bombs. (Artwork by Luca Canossa)

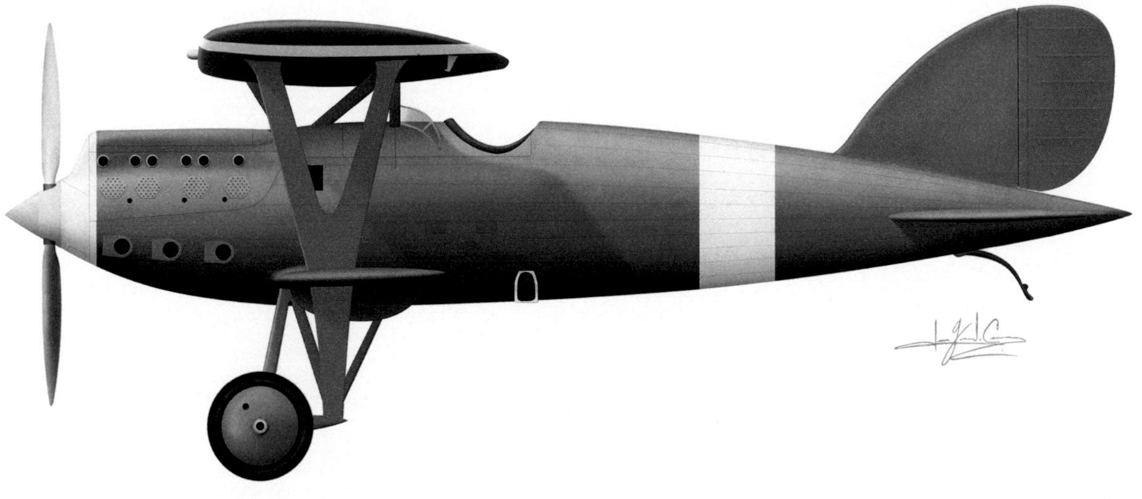

This Nieuport Nid-72 fighter (original serial was K-423) was flown by a defector to the Paulistas on 20 August 1932. Originally painted in olive green overall, it received white stripes on the nose, the rear fuselage, and around the upper wing. The Ni-72 could reach speeds of up to 260km/h and had a manoeuvre ratio of 0.3 (with an engine output of 447Kw, and weighing 1,471kg fully loaded). Its principal advantage was its high maximum ceiling of 8,200m; however, at 400km, it was quite short ranged. Armament consisted of two 7.7mm Vickers machine guns firing forward. (Artwork by Luca Canossa)

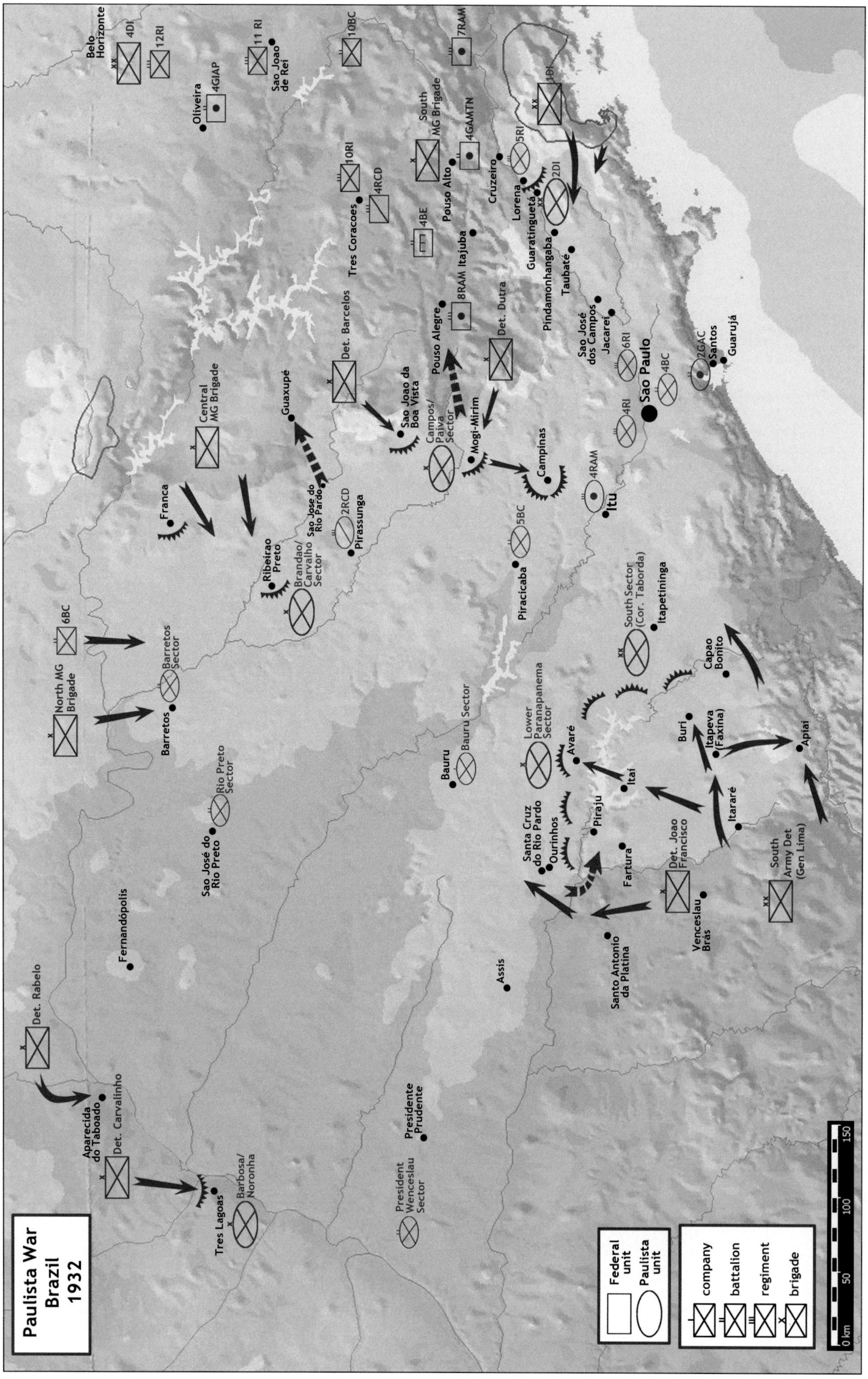

Map drawn by Tom Cooper.

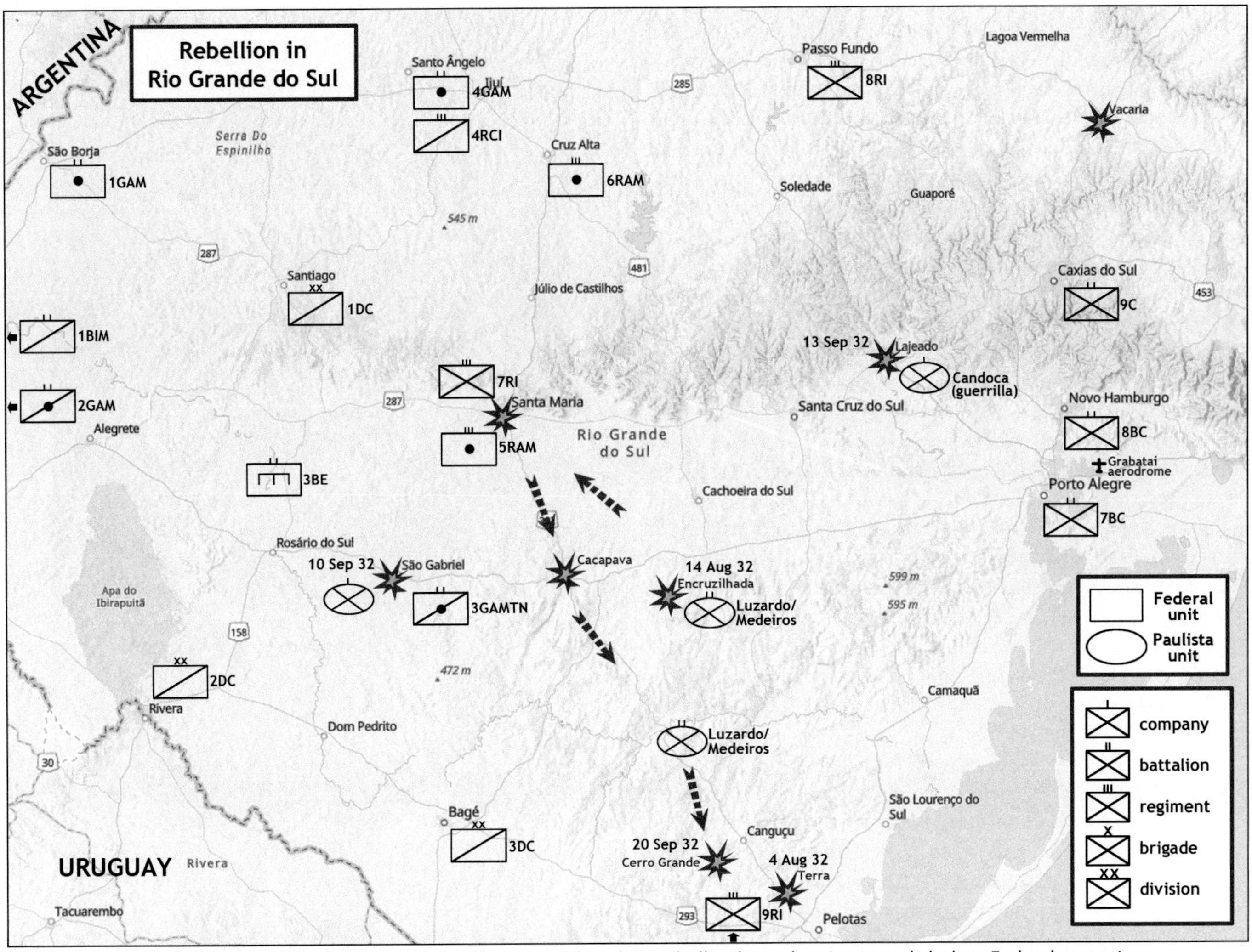

A map of the central Rio Grande do Sul, with scenes of Paulista rebellionhs and major armed clashes. Federal operations were made by local RGS Military Brigade units, as nearly all 3rd DI (7, 8, 9 RI; 5, 6 RAM; 3BE), 3rd DC (except 3 RCI) and one RCI each from 1st and 2nd DC (1st and 5th RCI) departed to Sao Paulo. (Map by Tom Cooper)

However, the danger was not over for Vargas, as another outbreak emerged on 18 August when the gunners of Fort Obidos, from the 4th GAC, located at the narrowest and fastest-flowing part (only 1.7km wide) of the Amazon River rose up for the return of the constitution. This rebellion was a serious one for the government, as the position held by the rebels was ideal to block the course of the Amazon, which was the only line of communication between the northern and interior states of Brazil and the rest of the country. It should be borne in mind that the Amazon is a huge impenetrable forest except for riverine communication. The fort's gunners tried to expand their territorial base and marched west against Manaus, capital of the adjacent State of Amazonas. However, unable to transport their howitzers, they carried only some machine guns and rifles, loading them onto two small river steamers. The government, aware of the gunners' expedition, sent against them two large Lóide Company steamers from Manaus, loaded with an infantry battalion (perhaps the 27th BC, that made up the garrison in the capital) under Commander Alberto Bastos Lemos. In a clash lasting 40 minutes at Itacoatira, the loyalist steamer *Baependi* rammed the rebels, sinking their boats and then strafing the survivors. Fifty-four rebels were killed, with virtually no survivors.[5]

The last rebellion in north-eastern Brazil took place on 22 August, with a student uprising in Salvador de Bahia. That day, a Lóide Company boat was due to set sail to transport troops from the State Police to fight the Paulistas. To prevent this happening, the students planned to rise up at 1700 hours, taking control of the police stations, fire stations and finally the Government Palace, and to depose the governor, Juraci Magalhaes. However, a group of students from another state precipitated the revolt at 1200 hours (according to Donato, enticed by money from Juraci). The rebels seized 50 rifles from the arsenal of the School of Medicine and barricaded themselves in the building. Water and light to the building were cut, and police surrounded the rebels, deploying machine guns. As the students refused to abandon their positions, the authorities opened fired on the university until 2000 hours. The students, after suffering dozens of wounded, surrendered; they numbered 427 boys and 312 girls, aged between 16 and 20. The uprising thus failed, but was immortalised at the reopening of the School of Medicine when Professor Prado Valadares greeted the students with verses from the Brazilian poet Castro Alves: "Those Leanders from the new Hellespont, they slipped, they ended on the floor of History, foundered, they ended in the Glorious sea."[6]

The Rebellion in Rio Grande do Sul (20 July-20 August)

In this extreme southern state bordering Argentina, Uruguay and Paraguay, a series of individuals of great importance in the history of the Rio Grandense became involved in the fighting: firstly, the Federal State Governor, Flores da Cunha, who held doubts over his support for his friend President Vargas as he sympathised with the rebel movement. As we saw in Volume 1, his friendship with Vargas and sense of order prevailed in the end, and he acted against the rebellion. Flores had fought for the government in the civil war in the southern state of 1923, and then had rebelled and supported Vargas in the Revolution of 1930. Both Flores and Vargas had defended Borges de Medeiros' state government in 1923, but now Borges would rebel against them in this Constitutionalist civil war. What is even more paradoxical, Borges Medeiros' rival in the 1923 civil war, Batista Luzardo, now joined Borges against Vargas. Batista Luzardo was a hero for many Riograndenses. He had revolted in 1923 to depose Borges de Medeiros, who had ruled Gaúcho State for 24 years and had committed electoral fraud to ensure his re-election. Although Batista Luzardo lost this war, he ensured a peace agreement that forced Borges de Medeiros to leave power, so it was rather surprising to see him now as his ally.[7] In 1932, Batista Luzardo would rise again to ensure the triumph of legality.

On 20 July, Batista Luzardo rose up in Vacaria to honour his commitment with the São Paulo rebels. There, he rallied a few hundred anti-Varguista Gaúchos waiting for the reaction in the rest of the state of Rio Grande do Sul. However, a general revolt did not occur, and State Governor Flores da Cunha was able to bring in Federal troops to surround the city. Realising he had failed, Batista Luzardo surrendered without a fight and was sent to Porto Alegre, where he was placed under house arrest in the Cidade Hotel.[8] Meanwhile, the commander of the 3rd Region, General Francisco Andrade Neves, began sending some of his troops to reinforce the Southern Army that was invading São Paulo: the 9th BC, the 8th RI and components of the Military Brigade.[9]

However, Batista Luzardo escaped from the hotel dressed as a priest on 5 August. After several days roaming around Porto Alegre, he managed to contact his old enemy, the leader of the Republican Party and former governor of the state, ex-president Borges de Medeiro, at the harbour. Both were taken to a sugar mill on 14 August, hidden in a gasoline tank, from where they set sail in a small motorboat to Arroyo dos Ratos, then riding a horse (or in a Ford Model A, depending on the source) to Encruzilhada. Once there, they gathered their followers, some 200 men, and launched a revolt. The initial plan was to go to Santa Maria, in the centre of the state, and to recruit the local cavalry regiment to their cause. However,

A cavalry trooper from the Rio Grandense Mixed Military Brigade. Note his sabre and the typical large Gaúcho hat. (Cody Images via Jowett)

A Federal Army de Havilland DH-60T Moth, plate number 2-0-3. Only two of every three of these were armed, whether with bombs or machine guns. This aircraft was mainly used for reconnaissance missions and artillery correction, apparently being vital in the detection and destruction of the rebel column in Rio Grande do Sul. (SDM, via Sergio Luis dos Santos)

there was no cavalry unit in this city, according to the organisation of the 3rd Military Region, so perhaps the Federals had temporarily placed a cavalry unit there, or the reference could be to the 7th RI and 5th RAM, a total of about 2,000-2,500 soldiers from the 3rd Infantry Division. If the plan had succeeded, it would have been a serious setback for Vargas, who would have been forced to halt his offensive with the Southern Army and send back the rest of the 3rd and 5th Divisions to destroy the rebels.[10] Meanwhile, further attempts at insurrection occurred in other parts of the state. On 4 August, a party of rebels under Colonel Marcial Terra overcame a small government force in Pelotas that was trying to prevent them from attending a meeting with Borges de Medeiro and Batista Luzardo at Santa Maria.[11]

Meanwhile, elements of the Military Brigade of Rio Grande do Sul who were supporters of Borges de Medeiro tried to persuade several units that were fighting in the Southern Army to revolt. Some units from the João Francisco Detachment, on the extreme left or northern wing of the Southern Army (see Chapter 1), were tempted to join them. The army's vanguard under Colonel Quim Cesar had to retreat temporarily to avoid the risk of being cut off by the uprising. One of the regiments of the detachment, the 3rd RC from the Military Brigade, tried to rebel, and their commander, Colonel Peligrino, had a personal confrontation with General Valdomiro Lima, commander of the Southern Army, on 20 August. Only the vigorous reaction of the general ended the attempted rebellion.[12]

The Battle of Cerro Grande (20 August-20 September)

Also on 20 August, the governor of Rio Grande do Sul, Flores da Cunha, managed to uncover a plot that was being organised for a rebellion in Santa Maria, arresting those involved and sending troops to the region. The rebel forces of Borges de Medeiros and Batista Luzardo, realising that the possibility of a revolt had failed, fled, being harassed by columns sent in pursuit by the new commander of the 3rd Region, General Franco Ferreira.[13] On 22 August, Batista Luzardo's column was intercepted in São João by government troops, leading to the death of three of their number; all the brothers da Rosa.[14] Other attempted risings at Soledade, Vacaria and Nononai failed, while a plan to launch a revolt by Lindolfo Collor and Marcial Terra in Tupanciretá and Santiago was a fiasco.[15]

On 10 September, in São Gabriel, near Santa Maria in the centre of the state, 80 guerrillas who were trying to join Batista Luzardo were attacked by 140 loyalists under Captain Abelardo Rubim, who was wounded, while his unit also suffered three dead and five taken prisoner. Six rebels were killed in the clash. Three days later, on the Fão River near Lajeado, guerrillas under Candido Carneiro Junior 'Candoca', who were also trying to join Batista Luzardo and Borges de Medeiro, were intercepted by a squadron of the Presidential State Regiment (the future 4th RC/Military Brigade) under Colonel Helio Moro Mariante. After both sides suffered 12 casualties, the rebels were forced to disperse across country, ending their activity in the area. Meanwhile, also on 13 September, in Reizinho Macedo near Caçapava, the main column comprising 210 rebels under Borges de Medeiros and Batista Luzardo, formed by contingents from the villages of João Vargas, Martim Cavalcanti and Fábio Garcia, surprised 120 government troops from the Detachment Figueira/Efetiva Brigade, dispersing them and taking all their payroll.[16]

This now 204-strong rebel column of Luzardo and Medeiros was eventually located and surrounded on 20 September at Cerro Alegre, near Piratini, by 670 Federal soldiers. The Varguistas included 400 riders from São Gabriel Auxiliary Corps under Colonel Adel Bento Pereira, 150 men of the 15th Don Pedrito Corps under Major Leopoldino Dutra and 120 men of the 1st Battalion/Military Brigade under Captain Figueira. The Constitutionalists, blockaded in a cabin, caused more than 62 casualties to the government forces, suffering only nine in return during a fierce battle lasting several hours. Batista Luzardo managed to escape the siege with a group of his followers, taking refuge in Uruguay and then Argentina. Borges de Medeiros stood with his men, making *mate* (a traditional South American caffeine-rich drink) for them during the combat. When they had only three bullets per combatant left, they refused to surrender until they were out of ammunition.[17] It is thought that the six Federal reconnaissance DH-60 Moth aircraft that were operating in the area from the first week of September had much to do with the location and destruction of this rebel column. It was probably these aircraft that detected the guerrillas from the air. These had been sent to Gravatati, Rio Grande do Sul, from the coastal forces at Ilhabela (see Volume 1).[18] Whatever the case, with this action the rebellion in Rio Grande do Sul ended.

Epilogue in Paraná

Despite being quoted by no other author but Ramos, there were some minor uprisings supporting the Paulistas in the north-east of Paraná, on the coast, near the border with São Paulo State. To overcome these rebellions, General Valdomiro Lima, commander of the Southern Army, created a detachment under 1st Lieutenant Federico Trota in early September, about 500 soldiers in total (a company of the Paraná Fire Brigade and the 15th BC, and the 25th Auxiliary Corps/Military Brigade). These troops took Guaraqueçaba, Porto Morato, Porto Faria Bonvier, Posto Evaldo, Santa Maria, Boa Vista and Rio Mina. Then, in São Paulo, they also occupied Itapitangüí, and on 4 October the island of Cananeia.[19]

According to other sources, this Littoral Detachment was directed by fire brigade commander Van Erven and had the same components with the addition of another auxiliary corps from the Military Brigade and a reserve squadron of the Paraná FP,[20] with some 900 soldiers in total. This was most likely the composition of the detachment at the end of the operations.

3
THE FRONT OF MATO GROSSO

The southern part of the state of Mato Grosso, which corresponds approximately with the modern state of Mato Grosso do Sul, was the only major region that was aligned almost entirely with the Paulistas. They even continued fighting after the surrender of São Paulo. Indeed, during the war the rebels from Mato Grosso proclaimed their own state, calling it Maracajú, splitting from the distant Cuiabá, capital of the old state, and designating Campo Grande as their new capital, located in the centre of the region.

Table 13: Mato Grosso Fronts			
Paulistas			
Location	**Detachment**	**Composition**	**Strength**
North: Campo Grande to Coxim	Cavalcanti	D Company Cavalcanti (El. Araçatuba and Antonio João Battalions), 18th BC (inc. 180 men of Visconde de Taunay Battalion)	300-400 men, two cannons
East: Porto XV de Novembro	Correia/Pereira Martins	Saravi Battalion	200-300 men
North-east: Cassilandia, then Três Lagoas	Morbeck/ Dutra/ Barbosa Martins/ Noronha	El. 18th BC, El. 6th BE, Mato Grosso Police, cavalry volunteers, Antonio João Battalion, Gustavo Rodrigues Column, Gato Preto Battalion	400 men, two cannons, then 1,000 men
West: facing Ladário	Gomes Coelho (18 August)	(18 August) El. 6th BE, 18th BC, a squadron/10th RCI	400-500 soldiers
South-east: facing Bellavista, then Porto Murtinho	Bronze Column (Silvestre)	El. 10th RCI, Escalón de Dourados, Ponta Porã volunteers, Kiki Martins, Nogueira, Barcelos, Lima, Garcia, Muzzi, Novais, H. Lima, Correia, Fagundes, Sancery volunteers, a company/6th BE, a company/18th BC, AC Company (perhaps field artillery), Guaicuru Indians under Lieutenant Moreira.	1,000 soldiers, two cannons
South: Ponta Porã facing Foz de Iguaçú	Kiki Barbosa/ Mattos	11th RCI, Marques, Ribeiro, Cabrera, Barbosa e Dantas, Gaúcho volunteers, Kiki Barbosa cavalry, a company/6th BCP	400-500 soldiers
Federals			
Detachment Rabelo			
Col. Manuel Rabelo (since August, overall commander of the region, independent from 4th Division & East Army Detachment).			
Location	Detachment	Composition	Strength
North: Cuiabá to Coxim	Unknown	Unknown	400 men
North-east: Goiás facing Paranaíba–Taboado–Tres Lagoas	Carvalinho	Mato Grosso, Minas Gerais and Goiás FP units; reinforced 20 August by Carvalinho, Atanagildo Franco, 21st BC Battalions	500 men (1,000 men, 20 August)
West: Ladário, Corumbá and Porto Esperança, then to Porto Murtinho	Neri de Fonseca	17th BC, Naval Fusiliers Company, Ladário Riverine Flotilla (Pernambuco, Parnaíba river monitors, gunboat Oiapoque, tug Voluntario)	600 men, then 800, with heavy artillery from monitors
South-west: Belavista, then retreating to Porto Murtinho	Garcia/Jacques	Silvino Jacques volunteers, el. 10th RCI	100-200 men
South: Foz de Iguaçú, facing Campanario & Ponta Porã	Foz de Iguaçú	Naval Fusiliers Company, other units	200-300 men

Maracajú is a remote, beautiful and wild area of about 365,000km^2, approximately the size of Germany, or half as large again as the UK. The area is flooded in the west by the marshes of the Pantanal and the Gran Chaco and is crossed by two major mountain ranges roughly on a north–south axis, those of Bocodenha in the west and Maracajú towards the centre. The rest of the region is made of savannas, with few lines of communication other than the railway (which crossed the state from east to west), the Paraguay River on the western border with Paraguay and Bolivia, and the Paraná River in the east, on the border with São Paulo State. The end of the conflict brought Maracajú state back into Mato Grosso state, but in 1979, due to their desire for greater self-government and ideologically armed by the historical precedent of the 1932 revolt, the local people finally obtained their own state of Mato Grosso do Sul.

In principle, Mato Grosso was the headquarters of the Mixed Brigade, whose commander, General Bertoldo Klinger, was to revolt and redeploy it entirely to São Paulo to lead the Constitutionalist Revolution. However, Klinger, tired of delays, sent an incendiary letter to the Defence Minister which forced Klinger's dismissal and brought forward the revolt from 14 to 9 July. Thus, Klinger left for São Paulo alone, rather than be accompanied by some 5,000 soldiers of the 1st Military Circumscription. Even the Fleet aircraft under Silvio Hoeltz that departed from São Paulo to take the general to Campo Grande on 10 July never arrived due to an engine failure in Baurú, so Klinger had to make the trip by train (see Volume 1).

At the beginning, the only units that revolted were the 18th BC and the Mixed Artillery Regiment, comprising about 1,000-1,500 soldiers and 16 pieces of artillery, all based in Campo Grande. The 16th BC in Cuiabá, in the north of the state, remained loyal to the government, as did the 17th BC, deployed in Corumbá in the west of the state, on the Paraguay River, controlling the border with Bolivia. The Federals appointed Colonel Oscar Paiva as the new commander of the Military Region. The 10th RCI in Bela Vista, on the Apa River, a tributary of the Paraguay which forms the border between the countries (in south-western Mato Grosso), and the 11th RCI in Ponta Porã (further to the south-east and on the same border), remained neutral, awaiting the outcome of subsequent actions.[1]

Once the revolt erupted in Campo Grande, the mayor of the town, Dr Vespasiano Barbosa Martins, proclaimed the secession of the southern part of the state on 10 July. After the departure of Klinger, Colonel Horta Barbosa took command of the local rebel forces. Seeing the situation in Mato Grosso, São Paulo ordered that a battalion formed in Araçatuba (in the north-east of the state), that had marched to Baurú, should go back and move by train to Campo Grande. These forces were integrated with the soldiers of the 18th BC, commanded by Colonel Joaquim Tardié de Aquino Correia. After carrying out a short but effective period of training, they put down a revolt from the Mixed Artillery Regiment. This artillery unit was then commanded by Major Salaberri.[2] Due to the lack of artillery for the Paulistas, the regiment was split into several sections and batteries of two or four pieces that were sent mainly to the Paulistas' Southern Front, but also to other sectors. They formed the major artillery deployment of the rebels, who had only one artillery regiment, the 4th RAM, compared to the eight Federal artillery regiments. Consequently, the rebels had almost no cannons left in Mato Grosso.

The Struggle for the North: Coxim (14 July-29 August)

With only Campo Grande under control, in the centre of southern Mato Grosso, it was essential for the rebels to expand their bases to increase their resources, help the Paulistas and stop the expected Federal counterattack. The position of Campo Grande was very important strategically because it controlled the only railroad that crossed the state from east to west, linking with São Paulo State, until reaching the Paraguay River in the west (on the frontier with Bolivia), where the Federals controlled Corumbá and the Ladário and Porto Esperança naval/military bases. Although the sources say nothing about it, at Aquidauana, between Campo Grande to the east and Porto Esperança to the west, was the 6th BE, which also went over to the rebel side.[3]

With the east–west axis controlled due to the railway, it was then necessary to dominate the north–south axis of the state. Consequently, a small column moved overland from Campo Grande to reach Coxim, occupying it without a fight on 14 July, cutting off communications with Cuiabá to the north and destroying the bridge over the Piquiri River.[4] This became the northern boundary of the state, which would only be threatened in early August when a weak Federal column was formed from Cuiabá to attempt to take it. Informed of this, the rebels sent two artillery pieces and a company under 1st Lieutenant Dechaus Cavalcanti to Coxim, including elements of the São Paulo Araçatuba Battalion.[5] According to other sources, they sent the Antonio João Battalion, formed by youths from Rochedo under Captain João Pessoa Cavalcanti.[6] Donato, who gives more details about the forthcoming clash, mentions the 18th BC under Major João Pessoa Cavalcanti and 180 men of the Visconde de Taunay Battalion. It is likely that those units were incorporated into the 18th BC, as happened with the Araçatuba men, so that all the authors were right. On 29 August, the rebels clashed with the Federal column, which fled after receiving 16 artillery shots, leaving behind 37 rifles and 173 uniforms. No other actions were registered in this sector during the war, although the Federals camped nearby.[7]

The Western or Paraná River Front

The Western or Três Lagoas Front was very important to the rebels, as the railway between São Paulo and Campo Grande passes through this town, over the bridge of the broad Paraná River. Indeed, all shipments of reinforcements and supplies from one state to the other were made through this area. Two Paulista sectors protected these communications on the São Paulo State side of the river (which was also navigable), that curved in a north-east to south-west direction. The first was the President Wenceslau Sector, located in the south under Captain Shakespeare Ferraz, defending against any attack that might be made on the river from the neighbouring state of Paraná. To protect the other bank of the river, the Matogrossenses sent the Saravi Battalion under Alves Correia and Etalívio Pereira Martins, defending Porto XV de Novembro.

The second sector was the Baurú Sector, further north, under Major Castro e Silva. This was formed to protect the river and railway from attacks by troops from neighbouring Minas Gerais. All the Paulista reinforcements sent to Campo Grande had to cross this sector, such as the previously mentioned Araçatuba Battalion.

From left to right, General Pedro Aurelio Góis Monteiro, in white summer parade uniform, perhaps from the Air Arm; his rival Manuel Rabelo, who led operations in Mato Grosso do Sul; Miguel Costa, the hero of the Lieutenants Revolt in 1924-27; and João Alberto, designated governor of São Paulo in 1930-31. The appointment of Alberto was one of the causes of the Paulista rebellion, despite him adopting popular measures such as establishing a 40-hour working week and increasing salaries by 5 percent. (Diários Associados, via Donato)

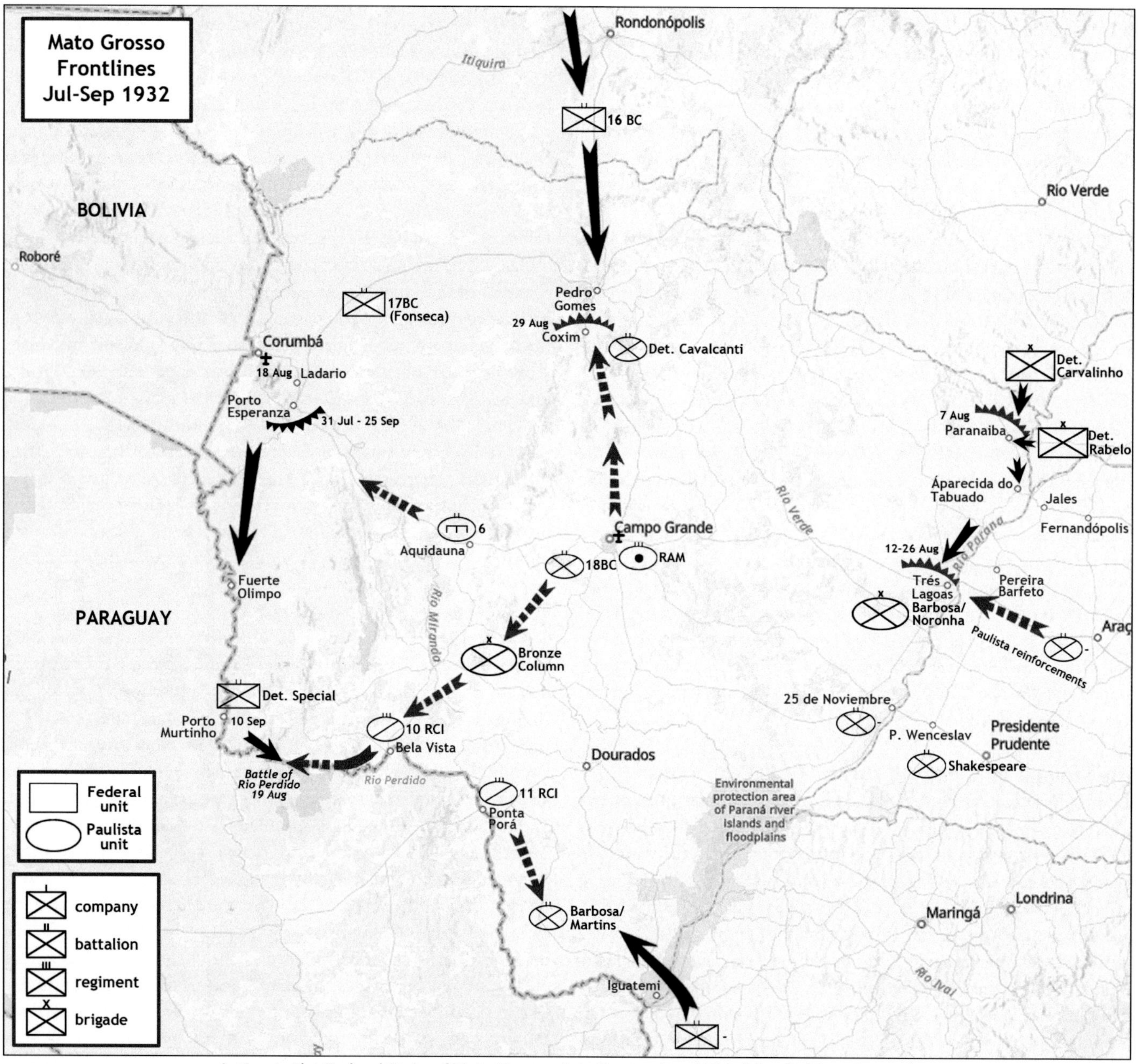

Action in the Federal State of Mato Grosso, July-September 1932. (Map by Tom Cooper)

Later, 339 soldiers under Captain Teófilo Rodrigues Lemos were sent by rail to Campo Grande on 29 July, followed by 90 soldiers from the 4th BCP. These two contingents created the new 6th BCP. This unit, divided into three companies, was dispersed to cover several fronts, with the 3rd Company sent to Três Lagoas, the 1st to Campo Grande and the 2nd to the south, to Ponta Porã. Captain Alves Pacheco repeatedly had to cross half of Mato Grosso for the payment and supply of these fragmented sections of the unit. Later, and likewise, they were also sent forces from Rio Preto to defend Porto Taboado. This route was also used by the Matogrossenses to send some reinforcements to the Paulistas, as part of the Mixed Artillery Group, sent to the Southern Front, or the Visconde de Taunay Battalion and elements of the 11th RCI.[8]

The Federal detachment under Colonel Manuel Rabelo was created in the Mineiro Triangle or wedge, in the north-east, to attack the Matogrossense Três Lagoas Front and to cut the Campo Grande–São Paulo railroad. Rabelo intended to attack Ribeirão Preto (in São Paulo), but soon focussed on attacking Mato Grosso instead, assailing Santana de Parnaíba and Porto Tabuado. His unit was formed from Mato Grosso, Minas Gerais and Goiás FP units, these latter under Carvalinho.[9] Góis Monteiro actually wanted these troops to marched against the northern Paulista sectors, while Rabelo insisted on his Matogrossense offensive, appealing directly to Vargas and going over the heads of his superiors, General Monteiro in the Eastern Detachment Army and the 4th Division commander, Colonel Pinheiro. The continuous petitions for more troops from Minas Gerais created new frictions in August, and when Rabelo finally disobeyed direct orders from Góis Monteiro, he separated his detachment from the Eastern Army. Even on 12 September, Rabelo's refusal to cede one of his Mineiro battalions was almost enough to cause the resignation of Góis Monteiro.[10]

The Federal Invasion in the West: from Paranáiba to Tabuado (28 July-12 August)

Whatever the cause, the Rabelo offensive in Mato Grosso did not start on the right foot. Paranáiba, in the north-east corner of the state, at the confluence of São Paulo, Minas Gerais and Goiás states, declared for the rebel government of Campo Grande on 11 July. The Carvalinho Column from Goiás, with some Mineira police, was sent to subdue the area, but they were defeated in an encounter with local

A volunteer from the rebel Gato Preto Battalion. Note the typical large Gaúcho hat and the chiripa, or male skirt, despite this trooper being a Matogrossense and not from Rio Grande. In Mato Grosso do Sul, there were a huge number of Rio Grande do Sul migrants who shared cultural aspects with Uruguayan, Argentinian and Brazilian Gaúchos. (Cody Images, via Jowett)

Matogrossense forces under Morbeck in Paranáiba on 28 July.[11] Nevertheless, seeing the danger they were in, the rebels sent the Gato Preto Battalion – some 400 soldiers under Henrique Barbosa Martins – to this sector, specifically to the Cassilandia area in the mountains of Morangas.[12] They arrived some time between 7 and 12 August to reinforce the units already there (elements of the 18th BC and 6th BE, 50 men from the Mato Grosso Police, 150 cavalry volunteers, the Antonio João Battalion and the Gustavo Rodrigues Column, some 400 men in all, armed with four heavy machine guns and two cannons), commanded by Major Francisco José Dutra.[13] The rebels in the area thus numbered some 800 soldiers.

In the meantime, after recovering and being reinforced, the Federals finally managed to advance and take Porto Alencastro on 6 August, where the strategic bridge over the Paraná River between Mato Grosso and Minas is located. Then, turning to the west, they entered Paranáiba on 7 August, almost without resistance. The rebel Gato Preto Battalion retreated to new positions 72km south, following the Quitéria River. Federal forces then took Aparecida do Tabuado, where they destroyed a Paulista contingent coming from Rio Preto with a machine gun section under Lieutenant Commander Sespadini. These Paulistas retreated to Lussanvira, being reinforced by 50 soldiers from the 9th BCP, now being led by Major Goès Nogueira.[14]

From the Battles of Quitéria to the Sucuriú River (12-26 August)

The government's vanguard of Captain Odilo Denny with the Goiás FP then advanced to the Quitéria River, where on 12 August they clashed again with Barbosa's troops. About 500 Federals under Carvalinho were up against some 400 rebels. The rebels hit the Federal forces with their artillery, following up with a rain of hand grenades. When the fire slackened, Commander Carvalinho on the Federal right attacked the enemy left flank, while another Federal force, perhaps under Denny, fixed the rebels in front. However, Carvalinho failed to envelop the enemy and attack them from the rear, being forced back by the rebels, who scattered his unit. On the frontal sector, the fighting continued until 1400 hours. Then, with the Matogrossenses behind the Quitéria River, the Federal 3rd Platoon, thinking for unknown reasons that it was being enveloped, withdrew, being followed by the 1st Platoon. To make matters worse, Colonel Salomão de Faria got into his car and fled to Santana de Paranáiba, followed by Major Benedito Quirino. Seeing this and panicking, all the government soldiers ran for their transports. Captain Denny reacted by placing a truck crossing the road to prevent any further retreats and was able to organise a more orderly withdrawal after having spent all his ammunition, covering his rear with two sections of heavy machine guns. The government troops retreated to the Santana River, 9km from the city of that name. Despite being totally disorganised, they had only suffered two casualties.[15]

On 22 August, the Federals, duly reinforced by Colonel Rabelo, tried again. This time their forces comprised the Carvalinho, Atanagildo Franco (only 50 soldiers) and 21st BC Battalions, plus some artillery. In all, there were perhaps some 1,000 soldiers against the 400 rebels from Barbosa Martins' Gato Preto Battalion. The Federals, rather than frontally attack, made a detour to a ford at Quitéria, the Franco Battalion crossing it with the water up to their waists at 0500 hours. An hour later, the Federal artillery began to bomb the Matogrossense positions, which duly answered with their own artillery. The shooting started a fire in the bush, which prevented the Federals from launching their infantry assault, having to fall back towards the shore. The next morning, the rebels continued their artillery fire against the 21st BC and Captain Carroberto's troops, exploding the projectiles in the air and setting fire to the treetops. The Federal forces remained there quietly for three days, hoping not to be attacked through the gaps in the line made by some deserters from the Franco Battalion.

Eventually, more than a square kilometre of the front – from the road to the river – became a sea of ashes, devoid of all vegetation. Throughout 23 and 24 August, rain extinguished the fires, but also prevented any movement. On 25 August, the Federals planned to launch again, at dawn the next day, the manoeuvre to cross the ford which had been prevented by the fires, but on the 26th there was only silence along the front. The Gato Preto rebels, leaving 120 soldiers under Major Dutra to cover them, retreated to the right bank of the Sucuriú in Puerto Galiano, further south, where they barricaded themselves along a 40km line to prevent any new crossing being made by the Federals. Behind them was Tres Lagoas (Calcula in these days), with the vital railway linking the two Constitutionalist estates. The sector was then reinforced, so that eventually there were some 1,000 rebels under the newly appointed Major Ramiro de Noronha. However, the front around the Sucuriú would remain stagnant for the rest of the war. Only on 5 October did the Federals under Lieutenant Colonel Flávio do Nascimento enter the village of Calcula with the 21st BC, the Goiás FP and some volunteer units.[16]

Portrait of the young bandit and pro-government leader Silvino Jacques. (Arumba)

The North-western Pantanal Sector: Porto Esperança and Ladário (18-19 August)

As São Paulo was being blockaded, the rebels could not export their sugar and coffee production, their main source of income, so the Paulistas would be doomed to surrender unless the blockade could be broken somewhere. One way to do so was to secure the west of Mato Grosso, along the Paraguay River, whose northern section made the border with Bolivia. There were the cities of Corumbá – with its adjacent Ladário naval base – on the west bank of the river, and to the south-east, Porto Esperança on the eastern shore. At the base of Ladário there was a small contingent of Naval Fusiliers, perhaps a company, and the 17th BC, a total of about 600 soldiers who remained loyal to the government. In addition, there was the Mato Grosso Riverine Flotilla, blocking the passage of any merchandise along or across the river. To defend these facilities, the Neri da Fonseca Detachment was created.[17]

Initially, throughout Mato Grosso there were no aircraft operations, with the exception of occasional civil transport and liaison missions. For example, the Federals used a civilian Junkers F-14, which in the past had flown the Corumbá–Campo Grande route, for reconnaissance missions. This aircraft detected an advancing rebel column along the railway towards Porto Esperança. When the Junkers made a pass over the train, it came under anti-aircraft fire, returning to Corumbá with more than 20 bullet holes in its chassis. With this information, the Mato Grosso Riverine Flotilla set sail from Ladário at full steam, heading for Porto Esperança to support the Federals based there. Part of the units that were present in Corumbá/Ladário were probably also landed there. Due to these moves, the Matogrossense attack that began on 31 July and lasted until the end of August ended with the defeat of the rebels.[18]

However, aware of the importance of this front, the rebels continued their pressure, and after probably leaving a force blockading Porto Esperança (perhaps part of the 10th RCI that was present later, on 3 September, along with other troops),[19] on 18 August a Matogrossense column under Major Luis Silvestre Gomes Coelho arrived at Corumbá/Ladário, to the north on the Paraguay River. This column was made up from elements of the 6th BE under Lieutenants Moreira and Tourinho, the 18th BC under Lieutenants Simão and Laroque, a squadron of the 10th RCI (that passed over to the rebels after the fall of Bela Vista, see below) under Captain Alcides Alves da Silva and several volunteers. There, Fonseca's government troops were pushed to the perimeter of the naval base, where they were cornered, but thanks to their artillery and naval gunfire support from the river monitor *Pernambuco*, they held on throughout the remainder of the war.[20] Moreover, from this base, the positions of Porto Murtinho and Puerto Esperança were reinforced, making a vital contribution to the Varguista cause, especially the monitor. As we shall see, these places were never taken, or if they were, it was too late, at the end of war, to be of any value to the rebels.

These Riograndense volunteers fought in the 1930s revolt, but their appearance would be very similar to the Gaúcho government volunteers that were part of Silvino Jacques' group, with their sinister bandit appearance. (Subtil)

The Struggle in the South: Bela Vista and Ponta Porã (19 July-10 September)

The control of the southern sector by the rebels was complicated because there were a lot of Gaúchos there, sympathisers with the government of Vargas. Bela Vista, near the border with Paraguay, in the south-west of the state, as we have stated, was garrisoned by the 10th RCI, which at this time was still neutral, but which eventually rebelled against Vargas. The prefect of Bela Vista, Mario Garcia, along with local forces under Saladino Nunes and Silvino Jacques' Gaúchos, stormed the headquarters of the rebel regiment at night. Saladino, on horseback, tried

Guaraní Indians of the Indian Battalion, used by both sides as auxiliaries for transportation and logistics duties, as in the 'Bronze Column' under Lieutenant Moreira. (Coleção Paulo Florençano, Taubaté, via Donato)

to drag away an enemy machine gun with a lasso, but the rebels gunned him down, cutting Saladino's body into two parts at the waist. The barracks eventually fell, but the survivors of the 10th RCI still fled to join the rebel forces.[21]

The rebels returned shortly after with the so-called 'Bronze Column' under Major Silvestre, who arrived at Bela Vista on 19 July, retaking the headquarters of the 10th RCI. Silvino Jacques and Mario Garcia, who now commanded the Federal part of this regiment, were forced to leave the village. Some loyal soldiers of the 10th RCI fled to Paraguay, but others defected to the rebels. The origin of the 'Bronze Column' is unclear in the sources, but it was possibly formed with troops from Três Lagoas, in the north-east, and Campo Grande, then being reinforced by local elements from Ponta Porã (perhaps after 20 July, as we shall see) and Dourados (with the so-called Escalón de Dourados), in the south-east of the country. These troops would recreate the 10th RCI that joined the 'Bronze Column'.[22]

The fall of Bela Vista meant that one day later, on 20 July, Ponta Porã, home of the hitherto neutral 11th RCI, also passed to the rebels under Dr Raphael Bandeira.[23] This unit would move to watch the southern end of the state against the Federal detachment that was forming in Foz de Iguaçú, on the border between Paraguay, Brazil and Argentina, probably from the existing company-size garrison based there, perhaps from the Naval Fusiliers. The mission of this new Federal detachment would be to move to the north-west, against Campanario and Ponta Porã. Small groups of Gaúcho fighters who entered the state under Major Americano Marques, Captain Telmo Ribeiro, Lieutenant João de Paula Cabrera and Osvaldo Barbos e Dantas, and a Paulista company of the 6th BCP under 1st Lieutenant João Rodrigues, joined the rebels. Soon these troops were reinforced and replaced in the abandoned railway area of the Matte Larangeira Company by Kiki Barbosa's civil cavalry, who assumed control of the sector. At the same time, the 11th RCI under Colonel Jaguaribe Mattos, pressed the loyal Gaúchos on the right bank of the Iguatemi River, near the state of Paraná and Paraguay. From there, they wanted to move back to join the 'Bronze Column' for a second attack on Porto Murtinho, that, as we will see, had failed. However, permission was denied as it was felt by Campo Grande to be more important to retain the left bank of the Iguatemi.[24] The contemporary authors are very vague about this event and do not give dates, but this must have been after 10 September, the date of the attack on Porto Murtinho. In this position, they were surprised at the end of the war.

The 'Bronze Column' Marches to the Paraguay River (20 July-19 August)

In retrospect, as already stated, with the São Paulo coast blockaded by the Federal fleet, the only possibility of receiving supplies and imports of war materiel from abroad was via the Paraguay River, which drew the border roughly between Brazil, Paraguay and Bolivia. Consequently, control of the river was vital for the Paulistas. However, it was along the Paraguay River where the strongest concentrations of Federal troops in the area were based, especially in Corumbá, to the north, with the barracks besieged at Ladário and Porto Esperança, and further south, in Porto Murtinho. It was along these points that the Neri Fonseca Detachment was formed, with the mission to defend them against any rebel attack,[25] as it did at Ladário. It was against the southerly village of Porto Murtinho that the 'Bronze Column' under Major Silvestre began its march after taking Bela Vista on 20 July.

The 'Bronze Column' was progressively reinforced by small civilian contingents under the civil Altivo 'Kiki' Barbosa Martins[26] (who was appointed civil commander of the column, and likely contributed with his Detachment Kiki Martins), Avelino Nogueira and Laudelino Barcelos (perhaps with their Detachments Nogueira and Barcelos), Ulisses de Lima, Guinarte Garcia, Nestor Muzzi, Vasco Novais, Hermenegildo Lima, Valdomiro Correia, Ataliba Fagundes and Colonel Sancery. As regular troops, they had a company of the 6th BE and the 18th BC, and an AC Company (perhaps field artillery) from Campo Grande. They also had several Guaicuru Indians under Lieutenant Moreira, who were in charge of the construction of telephone lines and bridges and had a heavy machine gun to defend themselves and 400 horses for transportation. Indeed, in Mato Grosso, due to the lack of viable roads, most movement was still made on horseback. Furthermore, the rebels had a section of two Schneider 75mm guns.[27]

In front of them, slowing the rebel march with constant guerrilla actions, were the former governor of Bela Vista, Mario Garcia, and the troops of Captain Silvino Jacques, only some 100 fighters, who were retreating westward after the fall of Bella Vista. It is difficult to follow the actions fought by Jacques against the 'Bronze Column' in its march towards Porto Murtinho due to the lack of chronological data, but it can be summarised as the blowing up of bridges at the Piripucus River (which is still destroyed today, consisting of just a

A Paulista Falcon that had just arrived at Campanario from Chile at the beginning of September, before receiving the Paulista aviation colours. (Jose Leal Collection, via Higuchi)

The Avro 504-N with plate number 445 and the marks of the Brazilian Navy. These were deployed in Mato Grosso, but rarely intervened as the Paulista Falcons were also there. Note below the upper wing the extra fuel tanks (which were often confused with machine guns). (SDM via Sergio Luis dos Santos)

few stone pillars and a wooden board) that was the scene of a minor loyalist victory. During its march, the 'Bronze Column' was again ambushed near the Teré River, which flowed into the Paraguay River on their right or northern flank. The rebels were camped there when they were attacked by the Varguistas. A truck carrying the column's two guns then arrived at the scene, and Captain Teófilo cut the moorings of one of them, which fell pointing directly toward the enemy. The gun was quickly fired, scattering Silvino Jacques' loyalist forces.[28]

The Arrival of the Falcon Paulista Aircraft (1-19 September)

While the 'Bronze Column' was continuing its march against Porto Murtinho, the most important and almost unique acquisition of war assets received by São Paulo from abroad (due to the effectiveness of the physical and diplomatic blockade) was made. These were 10[29] reconnaissance-bomber Curtiss D-12 Falcon aircraft that were acquired by the Paulistas. The data available is rather contradictory, but we may summarise it. The rebels contacted the American agent C.W. Webster in Buenos Aires, Argentina, making him believe that the purchase of the aircraft was for Paraguay, to avoid any international intervention from Rio. Webster received US$292,500 for the acquisition, an amount much inflated to pay multiple commissions and to obtain rights of travel through the various countries involved. Accordingly, in late August, the aircraft began departing from the Curtiss factory in Santiago de Chile in several batches of three aircraft each. However, one crashed on the Chilean border[30] and another, although officially also destroyed in Concepción, Paraguay, was in fact paid for by São Paulo for Paraguay to allow these devices to refuel on Paraguayan soil on 25 August.[31] Finally, on 1 September the first Falcon arrived from Encarnación, Paraguay. Klinger ordered it to be sent immediately to São Paulo to be used there, so Gomes Ribeiro took off that same evening with it.[32] This was probably the *Taguató* that was soon after badly damaged when its weapons were being synchronised to the propeller, as it is no longer heard of.[33]

The rest of the Falcons then began to arrive at Campanario and were retained on the Mato Grosso Front for a while.[34] The exact dates are unclear, but it is known that on 3 September, one of these Falcons landed in Capitán Bado, Paraguay, and was held by the local authorities. The Ponta Porã commander, Major Telemaco Rodrigues, sent Major Lysias Rodrigues himself, commander of the 1st Constitutionalist Fighter Group, which was in the area to organise the reception of these aircraft. Lysias arrived armed to the teeth to obtain the release of the aircraft, which he got in exchange for ammunition and two machine guns on 6 September.[35]

Another Falcon was already present at this time, as on 3 September, Orton Hoover, who had brought one of these aircraft, piloted its first combat mission, attacking the Mato Grosso Flotilla.

This small Federal armada was made up of the river monitors *Parnaíba* and *Pernambuco*, the gunboat *Oiapoque* and the tug *Voluntario*. The attack was carried out at Porto Esperança on the Paraguay River, near Brazil's border with Bolivia. Hoover bombed the *Pernambuco*, and did so again two days later, on 5 September, causing some damage to the vessel. The monitor retired to Ladário, not having any anti-aircraft defence, which permitted the rebels in the area to receive part of the 10th RCI, increasing their pressure on the government naval base.[36]

Then on 6 September, the Paulista Falcons *Kyri-Kyri* and *Kavuré-Y* departed for São Paulo, probably partially armed, escorted by the Nid-72 K-423 nicknamed *Negrinho* ('Little Black').[37] The Paulista Falcons were some of the fastest and best-armed aircraft in the conflict. Therefore, the arrival of eight of these at one time could have turned the balance of the air war in their favour, or at least given them parity. Unfortunately for the Paulistas, however, these aircraft only arrived piecemeal. Later, the other four Falcons arrived, but only shortly before the Paulista surrender, on 28 September, just in time to be given to the Federal government. Of all the Falcons, only four – those that received names (*Taguató*, *Kyri-Kyri*, *Kaburé-Y* and *José Mario*) – saw any action, but never at the same time (despite most sources claiming that only two served in the war). When the conflict came to an end, Brazil was able to equip up to seven aircraft of this type (one had been downed by anti-aircraft fire on the Coast Front, as related in Volume 1), with the license plate numbers 3-111 to 3-117.[38]

To compensate for the presence of the Falcons in Mato Grosso, on 7 September, the Federals sent two Navy Avro 504Ns, which were based at Ladário, just 60km away from Porto Esperança. Yet these reconnaissance and liaison aircraft dating from the First World War could do little against the Falcons. They had departed on 15 August to strengthen Neri da Fonseca Detachment, but because the runways available near Ladário were held by the Paulistas, these aircraft were sent along the route of the da Prata and Paraguay Rivers, so they arrived much later.[39] To protect them against air strikes, the gunboat *Oiapoque* received some 47mm and 57mm guns that had a high angle of elevation, making them suitable as anti-aircraft guns.[40]

The Assault of Porto Murtinho (19 August-10 September)

Re-joining the epic march of the 'Bronze Column', it continued advancing with more prudence to the west, and on 19 August its units were crossing the bridge over the Perdido River, near the Porto Murtinho defensive perimeter.[41] This time Silvino Jacques' guerrilla loyalists were surprised as they camped in Recreio, leaving their horses to forage at nightfall, so Major Silvestre's rebels were able to ensnare the Federals. Jacques reacted by taking 38 soldiers chosen from the 2nd Squadron, and after making a 5km cross-country detour by night, they stormed the rebel camp at dawn. Armed with automatic weapons, the loyalist guerrillas attacked the rebel trucks, with devastating results: one ammunition truck exploded in a huge fireball, throwing shrapnel over 200 metres, and then a gasoline truck also burst into flames. Within five minutes, Jacques retreated, having destroyed much of the rebels' ammunition, which was going to be critical for the imminent assault on Porto Murtinho.[42] Thereafter, the march of the 'Bronze Column' was still difficult, as Major Silvestre's men had to fight all the way through Ipajim, Perdido, Mandioca Assada, Muquém and São Roque. A minor clash of Mandioca Assada against a light Federal force on 7 September was of great importance since the rebels captured two artillery pieces.[43]

Finally, on 10 September, the column launched the assault on Porto Murtinho. Continually adding soldiers to their ranks, the rebel force now had more than 1,000 men,[44] compared to the 800 Federals of the Neri da Fonseca Detachment.[45]. As Neri could foresee the attack due to the slow progress of the rebels, the Federals had also been reinforced since early September with all the 17th BC from Corumbá, the Naval Fusiliers from Ladário, some units of the Military Brigade of Rio Grande do Sul, and the Simâo Coelho and Mario Garcia civil Gaúchos (survivors of the Bela Vista clashes). Furthermore, they had the Mato Grosso Flotilla, which came from Ladário, with the monitor *Pernambuco* equipped with 90mm (some say 120mm) guns,[46] which would be of great use in the coming fight.

Gaúcho bandit Silvino Jacques, who fought for the Federals in Mato Grosso. His surprise attack with 38 men ended up preserving Porto Murtinho and all of Mato Grosso for the Vargas cause. (Arruda)

The clash began at 1300 hours and lasted until about 2200 or 2300 hours, during which time the rebels fired on the Federal trenches located just outside the base. The rebel vanguard, formed by cavalry followed by infantry and artillery, moving from the road and forming the right flank of the column, was the first to hit the Federals. It was composed of the platoons of Captain Costa Lima and Colonels Waldomiro Correa and Teófilo Azambuja, supported by 14 heavy and 33 light machine guns. The shells of the *Pernambuco*, docked in the harbour, and the rest of the Federal fire struck the rebel vanguard. Subsequently, the rebel artillery located the monitor, bombarding it and forcing it to withdraw upstream, but the ship found an even better position from which to attack the Constitutionalists' lines. At the same time, a Federal aircraft, perhaps one of the Avro 504s, located the rebel deployment and helped direct the loyalists' artillery fire, forcing them to move 600 metres closer to the Federal trenches. Meanwhile, the hoarse song of a government Maxim gun situated on the railway line, which could fire 500 shots per minute, was heard. The fighting continued overnight, but eventually the Federal fire stopped: their resistance has collapsed. The rebels sent forward several men to discover what was happening, and they found that many of the defenders were embarking on a ship and barges sailing up the Paraguay River. Others crossed Margarita Island, to the west, and took refuge over the border in Paraguay. However, the rebels had exhausted their ammunition. Although they had victory within reach, the risk of a counterattack from the *Pernambuco*, that could bombard the city from a bend in the river and land fresh troops, and the inability to defend themselves due to lack of bullets, forced Silvestre to order a withdrawal and retreat to Santa Cruz and São Roque. Subsequently, he urgently asked for ammunition from Sào Paulo for a second attempt.

Neri da Fonseca himself recognised the panic in his Federal ranks: he had to appear at the front with a machine gun in hand, threatening his soldiers and forcing them to return to their defensive lines. According to him, "with a little more tenacity [by the rebels] the village would have fallen". The 'Bronze Column' realised it had to try to neutralise the *Pernambuco*, but as the rebels did not receive any further ammunition, they stayed quietly in Santa Cruz until the end of the war.[47]

A Wasted Effort: Taking Porto Esperança (25 September-1 October)

Paradoxically, the attack on Porto Murtinho was, along with that made by Cuhna on the coast (see Volume 1), the most successful offensive which the rebels made during the war, and which was most likely to result in not only a tactical or operational success, but also a strategic one. In the end, it only failed due to the lack of ammunition. Here we can also see one of the rare cases in history in which an insignificant action, such as that of Silvino Jacques' 38 men on the Perdido River destroying most of the Matogrossenses ammunition, had immense consequences on the later battle and even on the course of war.

With the 'Bronze Column' resting and waiting for more ammunition, the rebels split off a portion of their forces and sent them to the north-west of the state, upstream on the Paraguay River against Porto Esperança, between Ladário/Corumbá in the north and Murtinho in the south, hoping to neutralise the monitor *Pernambuco* in the case of it being there. Porto Esperança had been harassed by the rebels earlier that month: on 24 September, it was bombed by a Paulista aircraft, forcing the monitor to fall back as it had no anti-aircraft defences.[48] The aircraft involved probably the new Falcon *José Mario*, since the other two available aircraft were attacking the Federal fleet in Santos that same day. The name of this aircraft was a tribute to the rebel pilots killed in an attack to Santos, Jose Gomes Ribeiro and Mario Machado Bittencourt (see Volume 1).

With the monitor away from the front in Porto Murtinho, the rebels launched their offensive against Porto Esperança on 25 September. As the war was almost over, with the initiation of first contacts between the Paulistas and the government to sign a peace treaty, the Federal resistance was not very intense. The *Pernambuco* appeared in the village again and tried to disembark its Naval Fusiliers, but without much conviction.[49] Thus, the Matogrossenses rebels finally took the village and secured a point on the Paraguay River, opening the door to the importing of war materiel and exporting of coffee, but this victory proved futile as the conflict ended a few days later.

In support of this offensive, in late September or early October, three rebel Falcons – the *Kyri-Kyri*, maybe the *José Mario* and perhaps the *Taguató*, if it was by then repaired – departed from Campo Grande and attacked the Ladário Arsenal, dropping four bombs and strafing the tug *Voluntario*, causing some damage. The Federal Avros did not take off, but the gunboat *Oiapoque* finally saw off the enemy aircraft with its anti-aircraft artillery.[50] This was probably the last attack by the rebels during the war and the final intervention of the Paulista Falcons, but it all proved in vain.

4
THE MINAS GERAIS OR MINEIRO FRONT

Returning to events at Minas Gerais in July, after several days of confusion, the government had to dismiss General Firmino Borba for being a supporter of the Paulistas (see Volume 1). With the appointment of Colonel Pinheiro to command the 4th Federal Division, located in Minas Gerais, the loyalists were able to organise the unit against the rebels.[1] However, the division's troops proved insufficient and were still poorly organised. For example, on 16 July, they still numbered only 4,340 soldiers, fewer than half the official staff of a standard division.[2] The Federals had barely 250-300 troops per battalion at this time, and all of them were dispersed in their barracks, back in the rear. This position of weakness was exploited by the Paulistas, who started an offensive to bring the war to Minas, and they almost succeeded.

However, the Paulistas also had their own problems, being unable to send the necessary forces against Minas Gerais. First of all, the commander in charge of the Minas Front also had to protect more than 1,500km of border in the north, north-west and north-east of Paulista state, covering communications with the allied state of Mato Grosso do Sul, while in the south-west facing the northern Paraná state border. To protect this huge area, seven different commands were created, from south-west to north-east, starting with the President Wenceslau Sector near the Paraná

Paulista soldiers defending the line in Silveiras, in the Paraíba Valley (see Volume 1), wearing a civilian hat, an Adrian 1915 helmet with the typical Brazilian dome instead of the French crest, and a straw hat. (Abril, Nosso Século, Paulo Florençano Collection, via Catalogo)

The Federal commander of the Eastern Front, Góis Monteiro, in the centre, with Colonel Barcelos, commander of a detachment in Minas, the sixth from the left. Note the Adrian 1915 type helmets on both commanders. (FGV/CPDOC/ Coleção Cristovão Barcelos, Donato)

River, under Captain Ferraz Shakespeare, the Baurú Sector under Major Castro e Silva (who would later command the Taborda Southern Sector, and would cover, as we saw in Chapter 1, the lower Paranapanema or the right/northern flank of Taborda) for communications with Mato Grosso, taking advantage of the only railroad that connected their capital, Campo Grande, to São Paulo; then the Rio Preto Sector under Colonel Eduardo Lejeune and the Barretos Sector commanded by Captain Antenor Musa (later Commander Joviniano Brandâo) against the Minas salient, also named the 'Mineiro Triangle'. Further to the east, there was the Ribeirão Preto Sector in the northern part of the eastern border with Minas, under the aforementioned Commander Brandâo, the Mogi Mirim Sector, commanded by Colonel Dias Campos, protecting the railways that linked Mogi Mirim in the north, north-west and east with Campinas, and finally, in the south-east, supporting and liaising with the Paraíba Valley Front, the Bragança Paulista Sector under Captain Labieno Gomes.

To defend this immense front with its seven sectors, the rebels had only two battalions and a cavalry squadron under Captain Amaral, with about 1,000 soldiers of the 3rd and 7th BCP. Of these units, the 7th BCP was assigned to the main front east of Minas, together with the Riberão Preto Squadron (although in the second half of July this unit was withdrawn to the Southern Front), thus leaving only the 3rd BCP to cover the entire northern border, west and south-west of São Paulo. Later, after recruiting several volunteer battalions, these borders were protected by some 4,000 soldiers, their number occasionally reaching 7,000, which gave between 500 and 1,000 soldiers in each of the sectors, with perhaps 1,000-3,000 in the vital Mogi Mirim Sector.[3]

Opposing them, the Federals were configuring two detachments consisting mainly of regular troops, to be joined by two brigades made up of the Minas Gerais FP (a third brigade, the 'South', was watching the Paraíba Valley, and therefore was out of this theatre, as narrated in Volume 1). These two detachments, both under the command of Colonel Pinheiro, acting commander of the 4th Division, protected the flanks of the Mineiro Front, the two state brigades being placed in the centre. The group on the left flank was the detachment of Colonel Cristovão Barcelos, covering the entire south-central part of Minas' eastern border with São Paulo, from Guaxupé in the north to Ouro Fino in the south, then turning east following the railroad to Pouso Alegre, and thence parallel to the Paraíba Valley.[4] Colonel Barcelos was sent from Rio on 15 July to take control of the large Minas sector. However, Barcelos also wanted to control all the Minas state troops, a move which was opposed by the division commander, Colonel Pinheiro, and the front leader, General Góis Monteiro.[5] Several efforts had to be made to adjust the deployment of the overextended Barcelos Detachment: elements of this command (the 4th RCD, the 10th RI from Tres Coraçoes and the 11th RI from São João de Rei) were deployed in another theatre of war, the Paraíba Front, as related in Volume 1, protecting the Tunel de Mantiqueira until around 18 July, when they would be relieved by the Minas 'South Brigade'.[6] All these regular troops of the 4th Division would then reinforce the Barcelos Front, joining with the 12th RI, already further west near Pouso Alegre.[7] In the vanguard of this detachment, the General Esteve Sector was being formed, perhaps under Major Pedro, based in Jacutinga and protecting the route that led from Mogi Mirim in São Paulo, to Ouro Fino in Minas Gerias. This was most likely a sub-unit of Barcelos' group.[8]

The Minas 'Central Brigade' was located further to the north, comprising local troops of the state, with their headquarters in Poços de Caldas under Colonel Amaral (who reported in turn to Colonel Barcelos). This brigade would soon defend the Guaxupé area against the rebel forces in Ribeirão Preto to the north and São João de Boavista to their front. Further north-west, in the Mineiro Triangle around Frutal, was the 'North Brigade' under Colonel Fonseca,[9] also composed of Minas FP troops, threatening the Uberaba rebel forces. Góis Monteiro ordered a battalion of Minas FP to march against Ribeirão Preto via Itaperí.[10] These two Minas Brigades each fielded some 3,000 men.[11] Also in this area of Uberaba was the 6th BC, perhaps coming from Ipameri in Goiás, part of what was now the Paulista 2nd Infantry Division but that had remained loyal to the government. This unit, with the 4th Minas FP Battalion, was threatening the rebel positions at Igarapava and Jaguará, in the Ribeirão Preto Sector, at the northern end of the railway leading to Campinas and São Paulo.[12] The 'North Brigade' was protected by the Rio Grande River, a vast tributary of the Paraná, but on the flip side, this river also had to be crossed for them to start any offensive.

Finally, in the extreme west of the Mineiro salient or triangle was the detachment of Colonel Manuel Rabelo, threatening Ribeirão Preto, but which would soon be diverted further to the west against Mato Grosso, via Santana de Parnaíba and Porto Tabuado. To do this, although his left flank would be protected by the Rio Grande, Rabelo had to cross the incredibly wide and mighty Paraná, the

Table 14: Forces Covering the Minas Gerais & Mato Grosso Frontiers (July)				
Paulistas				
Location	**Sector**	**Commander**	**Units**	**Strength**
West: Paraná River	President Wenceslau Sector	Capt. Ferraz Shakespeare	El. 3rd BCP	150 men
North-west: Railway to Campo Grande, Mato Grosso	Baurú Sector	Major Castro e Silva	El. 3rd BCP	150 men
North: facing Minas salient	Rio Preto Sector	Colonel Eduardo Lejeune	El. 3rd BCP	150 men
North: facing Minas salient	Barretos Sector	Captain Antenor Musa/ Commander Joviniano Brandâo	El. 7th BCP	150 men
North-eastern or left flank: facing Minas Gerais	Ribeirão Preto Sector	Commander Joviniano Brandâo	1st BPCM, Ribeirão Preto Squadron, el. 7th BCP	500 men
East or centre (main sector, railway to Campinas)	Mogi Mirim Sector	Colonel Dias Campos	El. 7th BCP, Piratininga Group (Plinio Prado, 14 de Julho, Paes Leme Battalions), 23 de Maio Battalion	1,150 men
South-east (connecting with Paraíba Valley)	Bragança Paulista	Colonel Labieno Gomes	El. 7th BCP, Cícero Battalion	450 men
Total: 2,700 soldiers				
Federals				
4th Division/East Army Detachment				
Colonel Pinheiro				
Location	**Detachment**	**Commander**	**Units**	**Strength**
North-east: Mineiro Triangle, facing Mato Grosso	Rabelo (later independent)	Colonel Manuel Rabelo	6th BC, 4th FPM	800 men
North: Frutal facing Uberaba	Northern Brigade	Colonel Fonseca	about five FPM Battalions	2,500 men
Centre: Poços de Caldas–Guaxupé	Central Brigade	Colonel Amaral	about six FPM Battalions (inc. 5th, 9th, 11th and 14th FPM)	3,000 men
Left flank (south): Ouro Fino–Pouso Alegre	Barcelos	Colonel Cristovão Barcelos	Perhaps the 12th RI, reinforced (18 July) by 4th RCD, 10th RI, 11th RI, 8th RAM, el. 4th BE, el 6th BC	900-3,000 men
Total: 7,200-9,300 men				

second largest and widest river in South America after the Amazon. This detachment was officially created on 22 July in Uberaba, and was made up of Mato Grosso, Goiás and Minas Gerais FP units.[13] At the beginning of its operations, the 6th BC and the 4th Minas FP Battalions were kept at bay by the Paulistas at Igarapava and Jaguará.[14] Shortly after, the detachment separated from the 4th Infantry Division and became an independent unit that would act in Mato Grosso do Sul, as we saw in Chapter 3.[15]

The Paulista Offensive Against Minas Gerais (14-25 July)

Both sides were on the defensive until 14 July, just waiting to see what the next actions of their enemies would be. By this date, the Paulistas covered the whole north-eastern sector of São Paulo with only the 7th BCP, which was greatly strengthened by the calling up of reservists, so it now had 700 soldiers located at Mogi das Cruzes and São Jose dos Campos. The commander of this front, Lieutenant Colonel João Dias de Campos, moved to Campinas and Mogi Mirim, in the south-east of the front, where he set up his command post, distributing the battalion among various centres of population: some of them were in the north at Igarapava, on the railroad that connected Campinas to Uberaba, while others were in the centre at Ribeirão Preto, following the same route (both areas were in the Ribeirão Preto Sector under Joaviano Brandâo). They were also in the main sector of Mogi Mirim, where the troops were concentrated in São João da Boa Vista, to the south-east near the Minas border, protecting a railway branch that ran into that state; in Espírito Santo do Pinhal, where another railway branch was covering the approaches to the north-east of Mogi Mirim; in Itapira, protecting other railway access to Mogi Mirim from the east; and in Socorro, south-east of Mogi Morim.[16] The area to the south-east of Mogi Mirim and Campinas comprised the most important section of the Minas Front, since from there the railway started that ran north more or less parallel to the Minas border. If this railroad was cut by enemy forces, it would isolate all the formations further

Colonel Barcelos' troops providing food to the Minas Gerais population. (Museu da Imagen e do Som de São Paulo)

Cavalry soldiers of the Força Publica de Minas Gerais, marching to the front. (Higuchi)

from Socorro, the soldiers of Captain Castro de Oliveira; and from Bandeirante, those of Captain Cícero Bueno Brandâo.[20] The offensive began around Ribeirão Preto, when a company (perhaps from the 1st BPMC) of about 100 soldiers under the later famous Captain Romão Gomes crossed the border and entered Minas to take Guaxupé, where they were stopped on 19 July by the 11th Minas FP Battalion under Major Lemos de Silva, with probably about 500 troops from the 'Central Brigade'. Lemos urged the rebels to accept an armistice with Minas Gerais' commitment to remain neutral or he would attack them. As Gomes refused, Lemos then attacked the Paulistas. The Minas troops were pushed back in the fighting, causing four opposition killed but suffering just one casualty themselves.

Further south, other elements of the 7th BCP under João Dias began a rapid offensive, moving by truck or train heading to Pouso Alegre, to go from there to Itajubá to strike the rear of the Minas 'South Brigade' located in the Sierra de Mantiqueira. The advance would be supported further south by Captain Cícero's battalion from Bragança Paulista. In the morning, Dias placed his command post at Jacutinga, and moved within an hour to Ouro Fino, following the railroad.

north. In this area, two companies of the 7th BCP had been placed at Itapira and Eleutério since 14 July, reinforced four days later by the volunteers of the Paes de Leme Battalion[17] under Captain Pietscher (allegedly 600 men, according to contemporary press reports).[18] The 7th BCP was led by Major Borges Hygino dos Santos, who assumed command of the Eleutério Sub-Sector.

Seeing the apparent inactivity of the Minas Gerais forces and the government's lack of control in the area, Klinger's staff organised an invasion to force the state to align with the rebels. The attack was accompanied by a propaganda campaign urging support for the rebellion. Consequently, a Paulista aircraft flew over Tres Coraçoes at low altitude to drop leaflets on 16 July.[19] The offensive was arranged as follows: the forces of Captain Romão Gomes would attack from the Casa Branca–Lindòia Sub-Sector; those of Lieutenant Isidoro Rodrigues from São João de Boavista; from Espírito Santo do Pinhal, the troops of Major Francisco Garcia; in Itapira, the soldiers of Hygino; from Mogi Mirim, the Paes de Leme under Pietscher;

This group, called the Piratininga, consisted of the Plinio Prado Battalion, Chico Vieira's 14 de Julho Battalion and the Paes Leme Battalion, reinforced by the 23 de Maio Battalion from Socorro. Its vanguard, comprising perhaps 350 Paulistas (a company of the Paes Leme under Captain Pietscher, two others from the 23 de Maio and a platoon and machine gun team from the 7th BCFP), reached Pouso Alegre, deep in Minas, but after securing an initial victory they found about 900 loyalist soldiers waiting for them. The Federals (the 8th RAM, reinforced by elements of the 11th RI, 4th BE and even the 6th BC), led by Colonel Porto Alegre, were barricaded in the town, and eventually the Constitutionalist troops were repulsed and left totally disorganised.[21] The Paulistas suffered 14 killed (and between 87 and 118 casualties in all, depending on the source), including the commander, Fernão Sales, who would later give his name to his battalion.[22] It seems that the Paes Leme Battalion moved forward to start the attack against the orders of Major Hygino, for this reason being hereafter called the 'Suicide Battalion', forcing

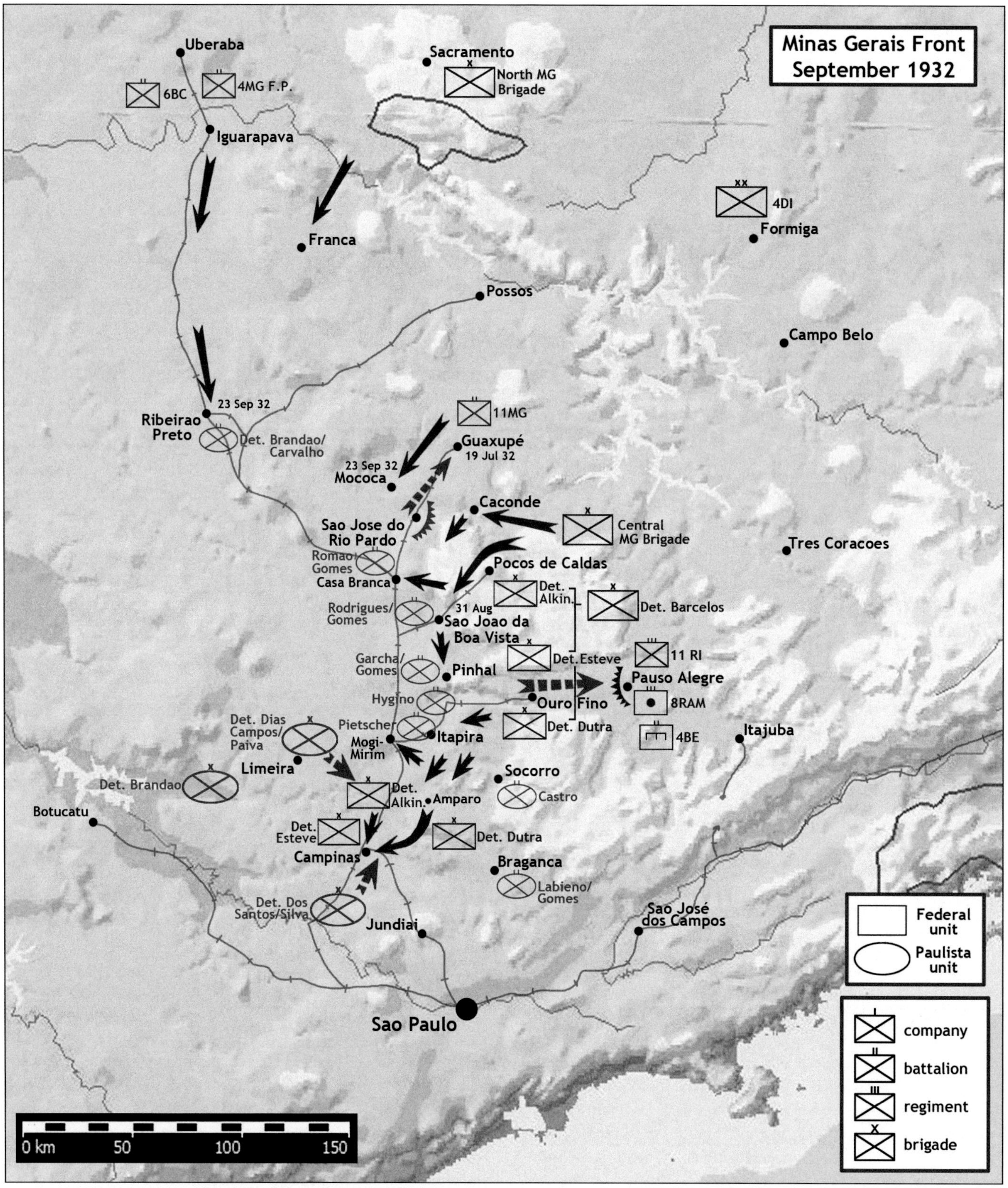

Operations on the Minas Gerais frontline in July-September 1932. (Map by Tom Cooper)

Hygino to send in several sections of the 7th BCP to help them. It appears that the attack was made following a direct order issued by the civilian Governor Toledo, who had subverted the orders of Dias Campos, creating chaos in the chain of command. Apparently, the idea was to destabilise the Federal 8th RAM, as Captain Pietscher had several friends there, but Vargas' secret service discovered the plot and moved to other posts all the officers that sympathised with the rebels.[23]

The Armistice of Guaxupé (22 July-1 August)

On 22 July, a little further to the north, under instruction from Klinger and the commander of the sector, Joviniano Brandâo, Captain Romão Gomes finally accepted the armistice proposed by Lemos, that was signed in Guaxupé, under which all Paulista troops agreed to evacuate Minas territory, in exchange for the promise of the state's neutrality. Gomes initially hesitated because he had been reinforced with a small battalion of volunteers under Captain Ramos, and he realised that by following the railroad he could threaten Tres Coraçoes, but eventually he obeyed the orders and withdrew to an

The Paulista Piratininga Battalion departing to the front. Note the black and white Paulista flags and still the absence of any helmet. (Coleção Paulo Florençiano, Taubaté, via Donato)

Captain Pietscher, the Paulista commander of the Paes Leme Battalion. (Waldemar Martins Ferreira Filho, via Donato)

area near São João de Boa Vista in Prata, changing his sector to that north-east of Mogi Mirim.

Further south, the sector forces under João Dias also retreated to re-enter Paulista territory, setting up his headquarters in Itapira. There, Dias deployed elements of the 7th BCP at various points covering the Mogi Mirim crossroads: Major Garcia was in Espírito Santo do Pinhal, blocking the north-east accesses; Major Hygino was in Eleutério with two companies on the railway that penetrated Minas, also covering the headquarters and Mogi Mirim (where the 'Barreto Leme' Volunteers Battalion was deployed under Captain Tenorio); Captain Pietscher had the Paes Leme Battalion at Barão de Ataliba; and Captain Castro, with the 23 de Maio Battalion – now reduced to only 40 soldiers – was in Socorro, to the south-east, covering the Mogi Mirim–Campinas railway. The Dias Sector, ranging from Prata to Socorro, thus extended for 200km, and he had insufficient troops to defend it.[24] However, these 500 or so soldiers were soon reinforced to create a force of some 1,500-2,000 combatants.[25] The two companies of Hygino's 7th BCP in Eleutério were reinforced by the Esportivo Battalion, while the 3rd BCP arrived to act as a reserve in Mogi Mirim.[26] On 30 July, Dias de Campos issued orders to further reinforce this Hygino Sub-Sector with the Pinhalense Battalion under Major Francisco Garcia, the Rio Grande do Norte Battalion of Colonel Serverino da Costa, the Francisco Glicério Battalion led by Major da Silva Costa and the 3rd Company/1st MMDC Engineer Battalion of Captain Pereira Lima. Finally, the Vila Americana and Limeirense Battalions also arrived in this sector.[27]

In the air, the first action of the Federal Aviation in this theatre was cited on 30 July, when Góis Monteiro (as mentioned in Volume 1, it must be remembered that although he was based in the Paraíba Sector, Minas Gerais also depended on him) ordered 10 recognition flights over the Paulista positions, to help him discover their deployment in detail, in preparation for the next offensive. Because of the distance between the airfield at Resende, in the Paraíba Valley, and that at Dos Afonsos, even further back in Rio, the Federals started using the field at Pouso Alegre, Minas, to refuel. On 31 July, they continued with their exploration flights, this time also bombing the Paulista trenches, dropping 24 10kg bombs.[28]

The Paulistas Resist at Eleutério (2-10 August)

Fearing the worst, Colonel Taborda, commander of the Southern Front (see Chapter 1), requested urgent reinforcements, so Klinger ordered Dias to cede two companies of the 7th BCP from Major Hygino's Sub-Sector, in Eleutério, to be sent to Itapetininga. On 2 August, when some of these troops had just departed, the Federals, breaching the armistice terms, began an offensive in the area between Prata and Eleutério, in the Dias Sector. The government forces in Minas had been progressively reinforced. Among others, the Detachment Barcelos received the 1st Alagoas FP Battalion, along with the troops of the 4th Division that were in the Sierra Mantiqueira (see Volume 1), including the 4th RCD under Gaspar Dutra that arrived at Pouso Alegre on 31 July, and the 10th and 11th RI and the 25th BC. The 4th RCD and 28th BC were placed in Jacutinga. In front of Eleuterio, a vanguard detachment of the 4th Division was created under Colonel Galdino Esteve, comprising the 4th RCD, 6th BC, 29th BC, a heavy machine gun company of the 11th RI, 12th RI and a mounted artillery battery under Ferreira. These forces began attacking São Roque, Fartura and Recreio, in the Eleutério gorge area where the railroad passed, turning to the south-west and ending at Mogi Mirim and Campinas. Several skirmishes began at Fartura, in the Prata area in the north of the sector, just 14km from the command post of the rebel Captain Romão Gomes. Meanwhile, Hygino, in the south of the sector, was not fooled by this secondary attack and kept the bulk of his contingent in Eleutério. He received reinforcements in the shape of the novice Campineiros volunteers of Captain Moura and the Paes Leme Battalion on 4 August.

The Federals started to press forward in the Eleutério area, attacking and bombing with artillery the Paes Leme Battalion, which suffered two injured on 5 August. The assaulting Federals comprised the Alkindar Squadron/4th RCD and a mounted battery, replaced in the evening by a company of the 29th BC. The rebels then sent 146 soldiers from the 3rd Battalion/Regiment 9 de Julho to Hygino as further reinforcements. In the meantime, the government troops began pushing the Constitutionalists from the Sapucaí area on the road to Eleuterio. To make matters worse, soon after two Paulista aircraft arrived (newcomers from the southern theatre, where the bulk of the rebel airframes were now based) and had refuelled at Mogi Mirim, they mistakenly bombed their own positions. Nevertheless, the aircraft took off again and this time hit their targets, clearing the Sapucaí area of enemy forces and silencing the Federal artillery that was forced to fall back, the Paulistas taking some Federal prisoners and war materiel in a local counterattack.[29] The Paes Leme troops of Pietscher completed the victory when attacking with machine guns on 6 August, disbanding the loyal troops of the 29th BC and taking eight prisoners.[30] After being dismissed for this defeat, the unit's commander, Colonel Lucio Ferreira, committed suicide by shooting himself in the head.[31] The Paulistas also used armoured train TB-5 that supported the Esportivo, Paes Leme and 9 de Julho Battalions in a move into Sapucaí, Minas. Other troops moved to the area included the Pinhalense Battalion in Espírito do Pinhal, the Rio Grande do Norte and the 1st Civil Militia (under Romão Gomes) in São João de Boa Vista, the Francisco Glicério in São Jose do Rio Pardo and the Barreto Leme, Esportivo, a company of the 7th BCP and the 3rd Company/1st Engineer Battalions in Mogi Mirim. With the Federal 29th BC withdrawing in Sapucaí, the 6th BC began to depart, so Colonel Pinheiro sent them as reinforcement to Colonel Dutra's 4th RCD, which was able to hold the line.[32]

However, the Federals continued pressing. To coordinate the next offensive, Colonel Pinheiro appointed the aggressive Colonel Gaspar Dutra as commander of the spearhead on 7 August, replacing Colonel Esteves.[33] The Varguistas attacked Eleutério and Pinhal again, trying to envelop the Paulistas at Bento Cunha, in Hacienda Malheiros, using artillery and automatic weapons. To accomplish this, they used the 6th BC and a battalion of the 10th RI. Captain Moura, who was defending the area with just 35 Campinas volunteers, had to fall back to Barão de Ataliba to link up with the Paes Leme Battalion. Meanwhile, further south in Socorro, Captain Castro with Battalion 23 de Maio entered Minas territory to take Monte Sião, on

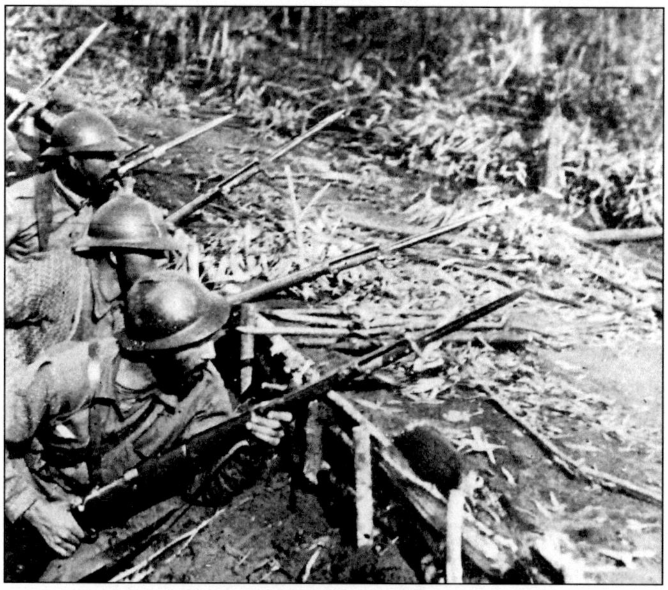

Paulista soldiers defending their positions with bayonets. Note the mixture of civilian dress and uniform, and the omnipresent Adrian helmet, which identifies them as Paulistas due to the absence of helmets among the Federal troopers. Despite there being some discussion that the Paulistas used only cork helmets and the metal ones were just for exhibition, this picture taken on the front line proves the contrary. (Paulo Florençano Collection, Taubaté, via Donato)

The Esportivo Battalion marching to the front through São Paulo's streets. (Coleção Paulo Florençano, Taubaté, via Donato)

The famous football player Luizinho joined the Esportivo Battalion, that held the lines at Eleutério. Note the caps and thick coats worn by the troopers in the middle of the Austral winter. (Museu da Imagen en do Som de São Paulo, via Catalogo)

Table 15: The 1st Battle of Eleutério (3-10 August)		
Federals		
Detachment Barcelos		
Vanguard, Detachment Esteve		
Colonel Colatino Esteve		
Units	Location	Strength
4th RCD	Gorges of Eleutério	500 riders
6th BC	Sapucaí	500 soldiers
29th BC	Sapucaí	500 soldiers
Heavy machine gun company/11th RI		100 soldiers
12th RI		1,500 soldiers
Ferreira Mounted Artillery Battery		100 soldiers, four cannons
Total		**3,200 soldiers, four cannons**
Reinforcements		
Vanguard, Detachment Dutra		
On 7 August, Colonel Eurico Gaspar Dutra took over the vanguard		
Battalion/11st RI		500 soldiers
Total		**3,700 soldiers, four cannons**
Paulistas		
Sector Mogi Mirim		
Colonel João Dias		
Sub-Sector Major Hygino		
Unit	**Location**	**Strength**
III/9 de Julho Regiment	Eleutério	146 soldiers
Paes de Leme Battalion	Barão de Ataliba	200 soldiers
23 de Maio Battalion	Socorro	40 soldiers
El. 7th BCP	Itapira–Mogi crossroads	150 soliers
Esportivo Battalion	Eleutério/Mogi Mirim	200 soldiers
Romão Gomes (1st BPCV)	Fartura, São João de Boa Vista	200 soldiers
Barreto Lemos Battalion	Eleutério/Mogi Mirim	200 soldiers
3rd BCP	Mogi Mirim	200 soldiers
Total		**1,336 men**
Reinforcements		
Pinhalense Battalion	Espírito do Pinhal	200 soldiers
3rd Company/1st MMDC Engineer Battalion	Mogi Mirim	100 soldiers
Rio Grande do Norte Battalion	São João de Boa Vista	200 soldiers
Limeirense Battalion		200 soldiers
Villa Americana Battalion		200 soldiers
Francisco Glicério Battalion	São Jose do Rio Pardo	200 soldiers
Armoured Train		
At least on 5 and 10 August, two Paulista combat aircraft		
Total: 2,436 soldiers, armoured train and two aircraft		

the Federals' left flank. They responded by firing across the line at Eleutério, and north of São Jose de Rio Pardo, in the sector under Commander Joviniano. Out of ammunition, the Dias Sector, which was operating in Eleutério, received 100,000 cartridges, equivalent to all the Paulistas' daily production. Meanwhile, Major Hygino, who was in charge in this area, called for artillery support on 9 August. The Federals tried to infiltrate again through Bento Cunha, threatening Barão de Ataliba, but Hygino's stout defence forced them to retire again, suffering one wounded. The Federals still threatened to envelop him on both flanks, so Hygino requested air support. Although enemy pressure on his left flank increased again, Hygino was again able to withstand it. On 10 August, the government insisted on pressing through the centre of the line at Eleutério, supported by artillery, but were once again halted. Rebel aircraft also strafed the Varguistas, who left behind much materiel when they retreated. That same day, Romão Gomes' troops were sent from São João de Boavista to Eleutério, as a reserve, to support the Esportivo Battalion and replace the Paes Leme, which was in need of a break, being sent to Cruzeiro in the Paraíba Valley.[34]

Concerning the aviation, as we saw in Volume 1 and Chapter 1, all the Paulista aircraft were deployed since 16 July in the south, until the arrival of the Federal devices forced them to return from Itapetininga to Lorena, in the Paraíba Valley, on 12 August.[35] From there, they could attend to both the Minas and Paraíba fronts. However, at least from 5 August, two rebel airframes began operating in Minas, so apparently this redeployment was made gradually. On 12 August, there were five Constitutionalist aircraft (the Wacos C-2, C-3 and C-5, and the Potez A-116 and A-212) at Lorena. On 14 August, to avoid attacks from the Federal aviation in Paraíba and to cross the Sierra de Mantiqueira for each attack on the Minas Front, all the airframes were moved further back, to the Campo de Marte, São Paulo city.[36] From there, they would shortly return to the south again, to Itapetininga.[37]

Tentative Federal Attacks from the South: Socorro and Lindoia (15-25 August)

The loyalists, after a three-day rest, attacked again on 15 August, striking now in the centre at Eleutério, artillery targeting the Paulista right flank during the afternoon. Failing to gain any immediate advantage, the Federals relied on just sporadic gunfire until 24 August. On 16 August, Lieutenant Fonseca of the rebel 2nd BE made a sortie with the bayonet at Grama, to the north, taking eight prisoners, but the loyalist position was recovered that evening.[38] Colonel Dutra prepared to recover Monte Sião in Minas, north of Lindoia, on 15 August with a squadron of the 4th RCD and the 1st Paraíba Police Battalion, but when they moved forward the 150 Paulistas who had been defending the position had already left.[39]

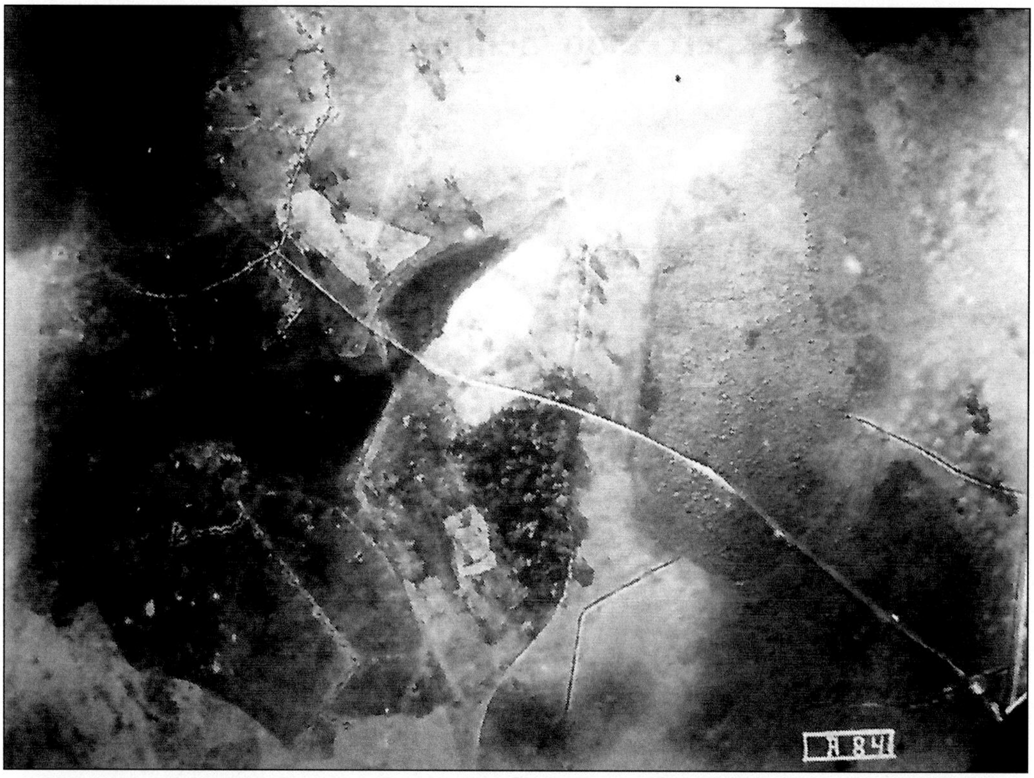

A picture taken from the air by a Federal aircraft on a reconnaissance mission, showing the Paulista positions and trenches in Eleutério. These positions were on the heights that crossed the road. (Daróz)

Paulista soldiers in a shallow improvised trench to get cover from Federal aircraft. Note their Mauser 7mm rifles and their Adrian steel helmets. Paulista soldiers regularly wore these metal helmets, but the Federal ones were usually cloth caps or hats, or even fake leather Adrian helmets, with the exception of their high-ranking officers. (Daróz)

In the meantime, the most aggressive actions were carried out in the north and south of Eleutério, seeking weak spots for a breakthrough. On 18 August, the Federal 1st Paraíba FP Battalion tried to attack in the south from Monte Sião, near Socorro, where 40 soldiers from de Castro´s 23 de Maio Battalion were emplaced. To reinforce them, troops under Captain Souza Filho were moved there from the quiet sector of Bragança Paulista further south. Major Hygino came in person to the area, and the new Chief of Staff of the sector, Captain Romão Gomes, organised reinforcements from Lindoia, somewhat north of Socorro. Gomes sent Captain Domicildes' company, another company from Eleutério and the Jiustiça Battalion from the general reserve in Campinas. In addition, to create new reserves, two companies (one from Prata and the other from São José do Rio Pardo) were moved to the rear in Mogi Mirim, in south-west Eleutério and north-west Socorro.

The Federals, with elements of the 1st Police Paraíba State Regiment of Major Tavora, tried to break the front the same day at Terma Lindoia, where Captain Romão Gomes himself had to lead a counterattack to keep the rebel positions. After suffering three casualties, Gomes managed to force the government forces to retreat. The captain acted brilliantly as Chief of Staff for another 10 days, organising reinforcements, until he was forced to rest up to heal a freshly stitched wound.[40] Meanwhile, Góis Monteiro did not surrender, and the Minas Amaral FP Brigade was ordered to attack again on 19 August.[41]

Meanwhile, at least two aircraft, if not all of the Paulista aviation, had apparently returned from the south at least since 20 August, arriving at Guaratinguetá in the Paraíba Valley, an aerodrome that would operate occasionally in the Minas theatre.[42] They were reinforced by the defection of the Nid-72 number K-423 fighter on 20 or 21 August (see Volume 1). On 23 August, two Wacos and two Potez aircraft were at the air base, although one of them, the A-116, was destroyed on the ground by a Federal airstrike, as was described in Volume 1. Thereafter, the four surviving Paulista aircraft fell back again to São Paulo, and then to the Mogi Mirim airfield, closer to the Mineiro theatre, between 21 and 23 August.[43] These airframes would briefly return south to Itapetininga, at least until 26 August.[44] Once the Paulistas were deprived of any air support, the largest Federal offensive was triggered on the Mineiro front.

Breaking the Front at Eleutério (24-28 August)

In the meantime, on 18 August, Colonel Dutra was preparing his forces in Jacutinga for the final assault of Eleutério. These comprised the 5th Bahia FP, the 14th Corpo Provisório of Rio Grande do Sul (a unit under the brave Benjamin Vargas, brother of the president) and the 4th RCD.[45] Oblivious to what was about to fall upon him, Major Hygino launched a counterattack against the Varguistas flanks on 24 August, retaking the Hacienda Amarela, on his left, and awaiting reinforcements from Major Santino. At the Hacienda Aliança, on the left or north of Eleutério, the Paulistas repulsed an attack by the Federal 11th RI.[46] However, during the afternoon, a government counterattack managed to regain the positions taken by the rebels. A further attack was then prepared with the support of the new commander of Pinhal Sector under Major Romão Gomes, further to the left, to recover Aliança once more.[47]

However, this action was not executed since that same day, 25 August, the Federals launched a massive assault after a heavy artillery bombardment. The units from the 4th Division taking part in the attack comprised some 6,100 men (the 11th RI, 10th BC, 4th RCD, 5th and 6th Batteries of the 8th RAM, pontoon and sapper companies of the 4th BE, 6th BC, 29th BC, 1st Paraíba Police, 5th Bahía Police, 14th Corpo Provisório, 26th BC, Schneider Mounted Battery and Section Krupp Mounted Battery). Part of these troops made up the Galdino Esteves Detachment that would attack Eleutério frontally, in the centre with some 2,200 soldiers (the 11th RI, 14th Corpo, and 5th and 6th Batteries/8th RAM), while the Dutra Detachment would march from the south in an attempt to envelop the Paulistas with some 1,100 combatants (the 4th RCD, 5th Bahia Police and Schneider Mounted Artillery Battery). Attacking Eleutério from the north was the Detachment Alkinder. Behind Esteves were the 1st Company/10th RI and 6th BC as reserve, while backing up Alkinder was the 29th BC and behind Dutra were the 26th BC and 10th BC, with the 1st Paraíba State Police Battalion in Monte Sião. Further north, supporting the main assault, the Amaral Centre Brigade would attack the line Jardim–Espírito Santo do Pinhal–Mogi Guaçu–Mogi Mirim.[48]

Around the Eleutério railway and the bridge over the river of the same name, after the initial assaults the dead bodies of the brave loyalist troops began to pile up in the middle of the two hills that formed a gorge occupied by the rebels. These were the soldiers of the 14th Corpo Provisório/Mixed Brigade Rio Grande do Sul, under Benjamin Vargas, that were left alone as their accompanying and flanking troops failed to move out of their lines, losing 42 men in the valiant assault. The entrenched Paulista defenders were from the 9 July and Rio Grande do Norte Battalions, which were later reinforced by some 200 soldiers from the Osorio Battalion, making about 800 troops in all. On top of that, they had the help of armoured train TB-5, but this soon became a non-factor after its driver was killed. In the meantime, Dutra's 5th Bahía Police Battalion tried to take the enemy position by outflanking it through Barão Ataliba. They first crossed the Eleutério River without opposition, creating a bridgehead that was kept open during the night of 24-25 August. Following behind them, the pontoon company of the 4th BE built a bridge over the river at Fazenda Velha. At 0530 hours on 25 August, the 5th Bahía attacked, followed by the 1st Paraíba and the 4th RCD, then the 10th BC and finally a battalion of the 11th RI, to exploit the success. They managed to expel the rebel Volunteer Company under Captain Elvimerodach that was defending the area, threatening the entire rear of the Paulista position in Eleutério. The attack was completed before the arrival of the Barretos Company that had been sent to support the position. Consequently, the rebels came under fire from the front and the rear, so finally, after about 20 days of resistance, the position began to collapse into panic. Major Hygino, once depleted of ammunition and surrounded by the enemy, ordered a retreat on 26 August, leaving the Barão de Ataliba and Eleutério positions and marching back to hunker down behind the Peixe River. Due to this withdrawal, the rebel forces further north around Pinhal also had to abandon the Hacienda Aliança and Ponte Preta, retreating to the Hacienda Alberto Florencio.[49] Similarly, the fall of São Roque caused the abandonment of Recreio and Fartura.[50] Finally, the 1st Paraíba Battalion, in which served Luthero Vargas, son of the president, reached the Peixe River on 27 August, but it was unable to cross the bridge as the Paulistas blew it up in front of their noses. On the other extreme of the offensive, in the north, the Amaral Central Minas FP Brigade took Caconde, Prata, Jardim and Mococa, and

The Jiustiça Battalion departing for the front. Note the battalion flag with the words *'Ordem e Progresso'*, as on the Brazilian flag, further evidence of the lack of any independent feelings on the Paulista side. (Coleção Paulo Florençano, Taubaté, via Donato)

finally assaulted Espírito Santo do Pinhal.[51]

Federal troops preparing for lunch. As the owner of the picture is Cristavão Barcelos, these troops were probably part of his detachment. Note the dark winter coat and the large Gaúcho hat. (FGV, CPDDC, Cristovão Barcelos, via Catalogo)

The Paulista 7 Setembro Battalion in Mococa, departing for the front. Mococa was taken by the Federals at the end of August. (Unknown author, FGV, CPDDC, Yasuhiko Nakamura Collection, via Catalogo)

The Paulista Aviation Saves the Day (26-30 August)

With the front broken, the Paulista aviation was urgently sent back to the Minas theatre from the south, landing in Mogi Mirim on 26 August. Once there, the pilots were awakened at 0400 hours and taken out of the hotel where they were sleeping, going on to perform one of the most brilliant actions of the war. The 1st Constitutionalist Fighter Group, with at least four aircraft under the command of Captain Adherbal da Costa Oliveira (Major Lysias was on the border with Paraguay waiting for the first batch of Falcon deliveries, see Chapter 3), began to perform support missions, with continuous departures every 15 minutes. The Paulistas bombed and strafed the advancing Federal troops for no less than nine hours, between 0600 hours and 1500 hours, in groups of two or three aircraft, doing this again on the following day. However, this energetic performance was not continued, as orders were sent to suspend it due to the risk of destruction of the aircraft under such intensive use. The aircraft also had to urgently move back to the south. Nevertheless, seven Paulista pilots were cited for distinction for these two days' activities: Captain Adherbal da Costa Oliveira, 1st Lieutenants Arthur da Motta Filho and Sylvio Hoeltz, and 2nd Lieutenants Mario Machado Bittencourt, José Daniel de Camargo, Hugo Gavião de Souza Neves and Eugenio Sodre Borges.[52] No author mentions the specific aircraft involved in this brilliant defensive action, but as we know the Paulista aviation had four aircraft in the region at the time,[53] we may deduct that there were two Wacos, the Potez A-212 and the Nid-72.[54]

Meanwhile, the Federals, almost devoid of any air support except for some sporadic interventions from the Paraíba Valley, decided to allocate for Minas three of the new batch of Waco aircraft that had just arrived from the USA. Góis Monteiro wrote to General Pinheiro, the theatre commander, on 28 August to inform him about the activation of the Pouso Alegre Detachment, which would include the new Wacos C-7, C-8 and C-11. Bad weather forced them to return to the Paraíba Valley on 29 August, but they finally managed to land at their new base on the 30th. This group would remain under the command of 1st Lieutenant Joelmir Campos de Araripe Macedo, accompanied by the pilots Júlio and Nero Moura. Major Eduardo Gomes himself, supreme commander of the Federal aviation, travelled there to organise the group and its operations.[55] The government, unlike the rebels, then finally realised that the Campinas area near Minas Gerais, and also São Paulo city, with its massive railway connections, was the most strategic sector to attack in order to end the war more rapidly.

Disaster in Itapira (28-30 August)

With the Paulista soldiers still fleeing, Sector Commander Dias tried to organise a new line on the left bank of the Peixe River, a tributary of the Guassu, on 27 August. The front would follow the railroad

Despite being described as the famous *'Fantasma da Morte'* ('Death Phantom') train, this is probably armored train TB-4 or TB-5, operating on the Mogiana railway. (Museu da Imagen e do Son de São Paulo, via Catalogo)

that headed south from Eleutério before turning west towards Mogi Mirim, and the sector would still be under the command of the now-promoted Commandant Hygino. The position was strong, with heights controlling the river and railway, some 4km from Itapira. However, the soldiers, after withdrawing about 30km, were badly disorganised, not knowing where the unit to which they belonged was located, and many officers were also in the rear. Consequently, the troops in the new line began to leave their trenches before being attacked. To compensate for this, some 200 soldiers from the Osorio Battalion were sent to reinforce them, while four Paulista aircraft covered the deployment by strafing the attacking Federal troops. However, attempts to blow up the bridges over the Peixe River at São Roque and Rocha (on the railroad), and at Mariano, Cunha and Araújo Cintra, were not carried out in the chaos. Exhausted after 25 days of fighting and unable to control the defection of his men, Hygino was relieved as the sub-sector commander and replaced by Major Santino. Several very unfair testimonies have accused Commandant Hygino of treason for this defeat, and even claim that on one occasion a soldier came close to blowing the commander's brains out with a gun when he paid a visit to a hospital. But the truth is that Hygino was able to hold the Federal troops together for a month despite inferior numbers and weapons. Around about the same

The Nieuport Nid-72 that defected to the rebel side with Captain Adherbal da Costa Oliveira (see Volume 1). Despite this aircraft being commonly described as painted white with black bands, it seems that before September 1932 it kept its original green with a white band hiding the serial number, and with its nose painted white. It probably had these colours when covering the Eleutério withdrawal. (FGV, CPDDC, donation by João Batista Pereira de Almeida, via Catalogo)

Major Eduardo Gomes, pilot and operational commander of the Army Aviation Service, patron of the Brazilian aviation and leader of its air forces during the Second World War. He ended his career with the rank of Marshal, twice became a minister, and was also a presidential candidate on two occasions, being defeated by Dutra (in 1945) and then Vargas (1950). This brave, devout Catholic and reserved officer had several mistresses, but lived with his mother and remained single all his life. (Saito)

Table 16: 2nd Battle of Eleutério (24 August)	
Federals	
4th Division	
Colonel Pinheiro	
Units	**Strength**
Alkinder Detachment (attacking from the North)	
One squadron/4th RCD	100 riders
Reserve	
29th BC	500 soldiers
Esteve Detachment (attacking frontally)	
11th RI	1,500 soldiers
14th Corpo Provisório/Rio Grande do Sul Mixed Brigade	500 riders
5th and 6th Batteries/8th RAM	200 soldiers, eight guns
Reserve	
1st Company/10th RI	100 soldiers
6th BC	500 soldiers
Dutra Detachment (enveloping from the south)	
4th RCD	400 riders
5th Bahía Police Battalion	500 soldiers
Schneider Mounted Artillery Battery	100 soldiers, four guns
Reserve	
26th BC	500 soldiers
10th BC	500 soldiers
1st Paraíba Police Battalion	500 soldiers
Grand reserve	
Pontoon and sapper companies/4th BE	100 soldiers
Section Krupp Mounted Battery	50 soldiers, two guns
Total: 6,150 soldiers, 14 guns	
Paulistas	
Sector Mogi Mirim	
Colonel João Dias	
Sub-Sector Major Hygino	
Rio Grande do Norte Battalion	300 soldiers
9 de Julho Battalion	300 soldiers
Osorio Battalion	200 soldiers
Armoured Train	
Total: 800 soldiers, plus an Armoured Train	

time, Major Romão Gomes also left the General Staff to recover from his wounds.[56]

Santino barely managed to get the the withdrawing troops (including all of the Esportivo Battalion under Captain Ramos) back to the railway station, where they waited to be sent to the front line. In the meantime, only Major Quintino's troops and a platoon of the company under Lieutenant Nogueira and Captain Corrêa – about 250 soldiers in all – stayed in their positions. Corrêa left the line on three occasions with his troops before he was relieved by Lieutenant Cesar Moreira. The situation improved somewhat, but officers were still abandoning the trenches to bring food and ammunition, leaving the soldiers without their commanders. Despite this, Santino finally

Table 17: Aviation on the Minas Gerais Front (26 August-30 September)			
Federals			
Pouso Alegre Air Detachment (Mogi Mirim from 30 August)			
1st Lieutenant Joelmir Campos de Araripe Macedo			
(from 30 August)			
Waco	C-7		
Waco	C-8	Downed by AA fire (11 September)	
Waco	C-11		
21 September: In Transit to the South			
Waco	C-13	Destroyed by bombing (21 September)	
Waco	C-17	Destroyed by bombing (21 September)	
Waco		Damaged by bombing (21 September)	
Waco		Damaged by bombing (21 September)	
Paulistas			
Retreat from Mogi Mirim (26-27 August)			
1st GAvCA			
Acting Commander: Captain Adherbal da Costa Oliveira			
Potez	A-212		
Waco	C-2		
Waco	C-3		
Waco	C-5		
Nid-72	K-423		
Note: only two of these three Wacos were present			
Attack on Mogi Mirim Federal Air Detachment (20-21 September)			
1st GAvCA			
Major Lysias Rodrigues			
Falcon	Kiry-Kiry		
Falcon	Kaburé-Y		
Waco	Verde (C-3)		
Nid-72	K-423		
Other Missions (21 September)			
Potez	Nosso Potez A-212		Crash landed (21 September)

managed to entrench along the Peixe River the General Osorio and Piratininga Battalions, and that of Major Adonis,[57] about 600-800 soldiers in all. All along the line there was chaos, with tiny battalions coming and going, some of them fleeing while others mixed with other battalions. Consequently, it is not easy to create a correct order of battle for the Paulista forces.[58]

On 29 August, the Federals were ready for their next push. Dutra's troops were divided into two groups: that of Costa Netto, made up of the 4th RCD and a company of the 11th RI, would attack Itapira from Fazenda Rocha, while the one under Lieutenant Colonel Porto Alegre, comprising the 1st Paraíba Battalion and the 10th BC, would assault the Tanquinho sector, crossing the Peixe River over the remains of the railway bridge. A battalion of the 11th RI would make up the reserve. An artillery battery would support the assault. During the offensive, the 11th RI would finally join the Porto Alegre column, and the 14th Corpo Provisiório of Benjamin Vargas would

A rare good example of a fully armed, red-painted *vermelinho* Federal Waco (there are more post-war pictures of silver-paintedexamples), taken in Pouso Alegre, Minas. This C-11 aircraft flew directly from the USA and helped the Dutra Detachment to break through the front. It was later moved to Mogi Mirim, where it participated in the bombing of Campinas, and was then badly damaged in the deadliest Paulista attack made on its air base. Note the number '11' on its tail without the typical 'C' letter. (Daróz)

reinforce Costa Netto, coming from Barão de Ataliba.[59] There were some 2,700 soldiers in all. Moreover, the three Federal Wacos – C-7, C-8 and C-11 – departed from Pouso Alegre to machine gun the rebels, causing little damage but creating such a panic[60] that the Paulistas offered little resistance. Their flanks began to retreat, having to withdraw to the heights and then to the town of Itapira, followed by the Varguista troops. Many Paulista soldiers boarded the trains and trucks that were fleeing to Mogi Mirim.[61] The rebel evacuation in the end was only possible because the Provisorios Riograndenses of the 14th Corpo and the 1st FP Paraíba Battalion were distracted sacking the buildings of Itapira.[62] The São Paulo aviation, again in the south at this time, was non-existent.

Volunteer Luis Fausto Junqueirado, of the Newton Prado Cavalry Squadron, in parade uniform with a large Paulista flag. Note the winter coat over one of his shoulders. This squadron fought along the Peixe River (Abril, Nosso Século, Paulo Florençano, via Catalogo)

The Fall of Mogi Mirim (30 August-4 September)

A new defensive position had been built within three days by Sector Commander Colonel Dias, anticipating the imminent withdrawal. This was about 20km further back, in the Morro de Gravi, a height located just outside Mogi Mirim. It was vital that the Paulistas defend this position because all the trains that connected with the rest of the rebel positions (further north, parallel to the border with Minas) departed from the town. The fall of Mogi Mirim would leave all their forces unsupplied. The lines here were occupied by the 9 de Julho Battalion under Major Robillot (or more correctly, the 4th Battalion/Regiment 9 de Julho, as pointed out by some authors) and the 6th RI under Major Marco Antonio (a unit that had been used as a strategic reserve on the Paraíba Front, and was now moved to Minas). However, further back, in Mogi Mirim itself, the Paulistas had up to 1,500 additional soldiers who had fled from Eleutério and Itapira in total disarray, trying to find a train to take them away from the war – the *Esportivo* Battalion of Freinderich. That same evening, some 800 men boarded a convoy to be reorganised into new units in Campinas. As 300 rifles were needed to equip the recently arrived 9 de Julho Battalion, some of the weapons of these escaping units were given to them, but with such disorder that these 300 men eventually received more than 800 weapons.[63]

Following these redeployments, some 1,600 rebels were positioned in Morro de Gravi (including the newly arrived Piratininga Battalion). At the same time, a new commander of the sector (now called the Mogi Mirim Sector) was appointed in the person of Lieutenant Colonel Oscar Saturnino de Paiva, replacing Dias de Campos. The defensive perimeter was mainly in Morro de Gravi, but also extended to the east of Macuco, north-west of the Haciendas of Calungo and Pinheiros and south-east of Capela. Armoured train TB-5 was sent to Itapira, further east, and made contact with Federal forces just 10km outside the city. Even in front of the Morro de Gravi, the loyalists were barely 2km away. As has been stated, the fall of Mogi Mirim, isolating the troops further north, would have forced the retreat of all such forces from the Pinhal–Boa Vista–Rio Pardo line to a new Palmeiras–Pirasunungа–Ararás line further west. Klinger ordered Paiva to prepare another defensive line along the Jaguarí River, 60km further back to the south, north of Campinas, using the previously disbanded forces. He clearly had little confidence in the resistance of Paiva's troops.[64]

A Federal *vermelinho* Waco flying over Pouso Alegre, Minas Gerais, where a government Air Detachment was created between 28 August and 5 September. Later, when moved to Mogi Mirim, the Pouso Alegre aerodrome was still used as a base to refuel aircraft flying to or from the Paraíba Valley. (Daróz)

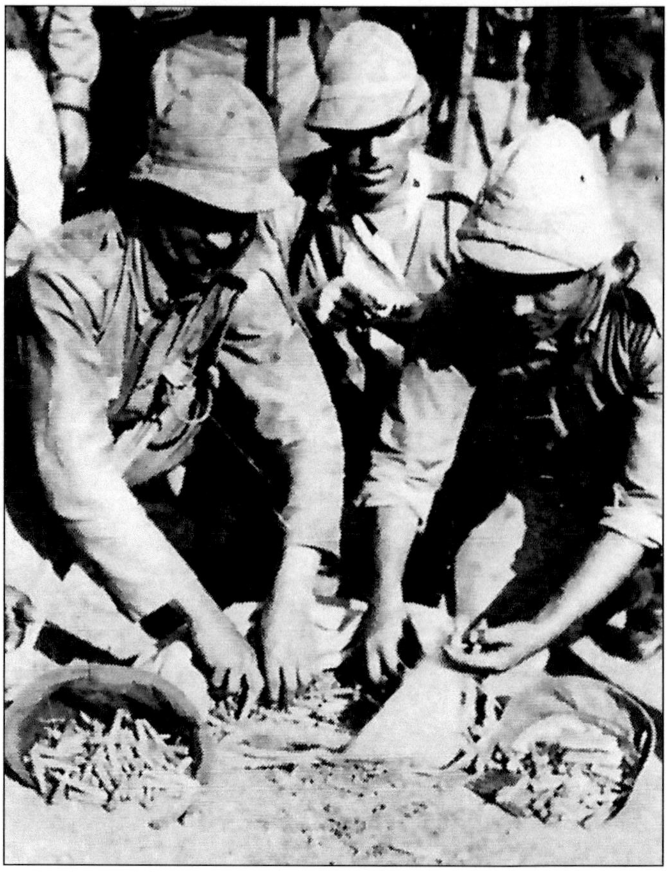

Paulista soldiers counting cartridges in the front line at Jaguarí. The abundance or lack of ammunition became an increasingly key factor for the success or failure of the rebel resistance. (Museu da Imagem e do Som de São Paulo, via Donato)

On 1 September, the Federals started preparations for their next move with two or three reconnaissance flights over Mogi Mirim made by their Wacos, also bombing and strafing enemy positions. That day also saw the start of a false rumour that Borges Medeiro had rebelled in Rio Grande do Sul with a reported 10,000 troops, but this was quickly denied. On 3 September, 300 of the retreating Paulista troops were reorganised, and after forming the Adonais Battalion under the major of the same name, they were sent to the left wing at Gravi, in Macuco. They arrived just in time, as the Federal assault finally began on 4 September, preceded by an aerial and artillery bombardment. The cavalry advanced in the vanguard, followed by the infantry. The assault was again led by Eurico Gaspar Dutra's detachment, along with the Porto Alegre Group, consisting of, among others, the just arrived 1st Ceará Provisional Battalion, the provincial 5th Bahía and Alagoas Battalions and the 14th Corpo Provisório/Rio Grande do Sul Military Brigade, under the brother of President Vargas. Lacking any artillery or air support, the rebels were unable to even lift their heads out of their trenches as a storm of bullets and bombs fell upon them. Panicked, the new Adonais Battalion, on the left in Macuco, fled from their positions, followed by the 14 de Julho, allowing the Federals to occupy their trenches. As a result, the Paulistas' 6th RI and Piratininga Battalion began to be fired at from the rear, so Paiva ordered the abandonment of Gravi and Mogi Mirim

Constitutionalist prisoners being held at Manacá, near Passa-Quatro in Minas Gerais. (FGV, CPDDC, Gustavo Capanema, via Catalogo)

Table 18: Battle of Itapira-Mori Morim (28 August-4 September)	
Paulistas	
Sub-Sector Mogi Mirim	
Colonel Santino	
Itapira Deployment (28-30 August):	
Units	**Strength**
Osorio Battalion	200 men
Deportivo Battalion	300 men
Piratininga Battalion	200 men
Adonis Battalion	200 men
Total	**900 men**
Morro de Gravi (Gravi Gorge). Deployment at Mogi Mirim (1-4 September)	
Sector Mogi Mirim	
Lieutenant Colonel Oscar Saturnino de Paiva	
Units	**Strength**
4th/9 de Julho Regiment	300 men
6th RI	900 men
Piratininga Battalion	200 men
Adonais Battalion	300 men
14 de Julho Battalion	200 men
Armoured train	
Total	**1,900 men**
Federals	
Detachment Dutra	
Colonel Eurico Gaspar Dutra	
Costa Netto Group	
4th RCD	500 riders
Company/11th RI	100 soldiers
Reinforcements	
4th Corpo Provisiório	500 riders
Porto Alegre Group	
1st Paraíba Battalion	500 soldiers
10th BC	500 soldiers
Reinforcements	
11th RI	1,500 soldiers
Reserve	
Battalion/11th RI	500 soldiers
Artillery Battery	100 soldiers, four guns
Total	4,200 soldiers, four guns
Pouso Alegre Air Detachment	
Waco C-7	
Wacp C-8	
Waco C-11	

to avoid his forces being enveloped. Mogi Guassu, his northernmost position defended by 300 soldiers under Captain Pinto de Melo, also had to be abandoned at full speed. Subsequently, five trains full of retreating rebel troops departed 60km south to Jaguaría, north of the river there. During the Federal offensive, Dutra took some 445 rebel prisoners. Góis Monteiro, cleverly recognising the importance of this front once a breakthrough was achieved, proposed to the Minister of War on 5 September that all reinforcements should be sent to the sector.[65]

The Legend of Romão Gomes Is Forged in the North (31 August-4 September)

The fall of Mogi Mirim was a huge disaster for the Paulistas, as it meant the railroad that connected the town with the northern areas, especially Ribeirão Preto, was now cut. With the loss of Mogi Mirim, any supplies could only be provided after a further delay caused by going by road or rail to the west from Campinas, 60 miles south of Mogi, and then turning to the east.

Major Romão Gomes, in charge of defending the São João de Boavista Sub-Sector, to the north-east of the main Mogi Mirim Sector, was being heavily pressed by the Minas FP Central Brigade on 31 August, and urgently requested ammunition for his troops. Paiva ordered the withdrawal of his units and the abandonment of São João, despite the sub-sector having stabilised. Thus, Gomes gave up the city to the enemy without a fight, falling back on Cascavel, to the south, and then Casa Branca, to the northeast, following the railway that split to São Jose de Rio Pardo and to the north-west to Ribeirão Preto, thus protecting both cities from the south.[66] Consequently, Amaral's Central FPM Brigade began to occupy the villages in the Mogiana region.[67] Shortly thereafter, on 1 September, the 5th, 9th and 14th Minas FP Battalions, and many armed civilians – some 2,000 soldiers in all – attacked Romão Gomes' 1st BMCP in Prata, slightly north-east of São João de Boavista. The next day, Gomes was reinforced by the Bombardas Company (an improvised unit armed with a kind of mortar created by Jacobino, a rebel naval engineer). Later, armoured train TB-4 appeared and caused panic among the government troops even before opening fire. However, finding themselves enveloped, the Paulistas had to leave their positions again at nightfall.[68]

On 2 September, Major Joviniano Brandâo, commander of the Ribeirão Preto and Barretos Sector, appointed Romão Gomes as Sub-Sector Commander of the former town. This appointment was made because of a previous confrontation between the front commander, Jose Dias dos Santos, and the sub-sector commander, João Leal Ferreira. Ferreira had ended up in prison for refusing to obey orders received from Santos, so Gomes was chosen to replace him. At that time, the Federal Minas FP Central Brigade was attacking the bridge over the Rio Pardo on the road to Mococa, about 30km north of Gomes' position. On 4 September, the Federals, after occupying Cascavel and Vargem Grande, south of Gomes, advanced on Lagôa. Gomes was thus being enveloped on both flanks. Nevertheless, Gomes asked for 250 soldiers to stop them and executed a successful counterattack the same day. In a theatre in which after the fall of Eleutério there was nothing but defeats and setbacks for the rebels, this minor local success cemented the legend, somewhat exaggerated but based on actual facts, of the Column Romão Gomes and its commander. Gomes attacked the government left flank at Lagôa station, near Casa Branca, killing many loyalist troops and taking between four and 13 prisoners, according to different sources. The most important consequence was that the 5th, 9th and 14th Battalions of Minas FP were pushed back. The Paulista armoured train TB-4 pursued them but came to halt when the driver was shot and seriously wounded. Nevertheless, several days later the Federals were able to retake the position, despite a renewed intervention by the armoured train. On the same day, 4 September, about 120km further north but still in the Gomes Sub-Sector near São Jose de Rio Pardo, in Santo Antonio, Lieutenant Figueira's 2nd BE managed to outflank a Federal advance and repulse it, causing several dead and one wounded, while also taking five prisoners and two machine guns. Gomes sent in support the Rio Preto Battalion, made up of local volunteers, that night.[69] It seemed that Gomes was the only commander able to achieve any victories, albeit minor defensive ones, but still victories, so on 12 September he was promoted to lieutenant colonel.[70]

No Help for Socorro and Amparo (31 August-10 September)

Further south of the main Mogi Mirim Sector, in the Lindoia-Socorro Sub-Sector (14km in length), there were also fighting. Captain Castro Oliveira was in charge there for the rebels, being responsible for protecting the south-east approaches to Mogi Mirim and those to Campinas from the north-east. When Itapira, further north, fell on 31 August, Castro's position was threatened by a road from there that cut the rebel rear. Paiva thus ordered Castro to fall back west to Sierra Negra and to base his command post in Socorro. Shortly thereafter, on 6 September, Captain Alceu moved with some reservists to defend Brumado, Hacienda Santa Helena and Santo Aleixo, positions located just north of Amparo.[71]

Two days later, on 8 September, the Federal Dutra attacked these three positions aggressively with artillery and aviation, probably using the three Wacos C-7, C-8 and C-11 from Pouso Alegre. Dutra's detachment, departing from Mogi Mirim and then Itapira, was to attack in the direction of Amparo. Dutra's forces comprised the 14th Corpo Provisório, 1st Paraíba Police, 1st Ceará, 4th RCD and the Schneider Mounted Artillery Battery. Dutra first launched his cavalry, followed by the infantry. Paiva then sent a 100-man rebel company to Amparo under Captain Silvio Lopes from the Justiça Battalion (located on the Jaguari River at Pedreira, to the south-west), along with another company led by Captain Isidoro. Alceu's troops (that were retreating from Brumado) also went to Amparo, while 108 soldiers under Captain Freire occupied Duas Pontes to the rear, near Coqueiros, to cover an eventual withdrawal. At the same time, the Commander of the Central Staff, Julio Cesar Alfieri, who had been coordinating all combat on the Minas border from São Paulo, appeared in the area and asked Major Mario Rangel, commander at Campinas, to send a mortar company to Amparo in trucks, as well as the company of Lieutenant Mario Bueno, the HQ Company of the sector, and 40 soldiers to replace the exhausted combatants of the Rio Grande do Norte Battalion.[72]

On 9 September, with the Federals at the door of Amparo – defended by the Justiça Company – the Paulistas hesitated whether reinforce them with the 108 soldiers of the reserve in Duas Pontes, while the government *vermelinhos* Wacos were bombing the village, wounding three troops. Castro, commander of the sub-sector, tried desperately to counterattack on 10 September to relieve the pressure on Amparo, using two recently received mortars (which could only reach up to 1,300 metres from the Paulista front) and the 1st Santos Volunteer Battalion, which fell on the 1st Ceará Battalion. However, the government troops of Dutra and Benjamin Vargas advanced their mountain artillery to shell this sub-sector, and the rebel counterstroke was repulsed. The exhausted rebels evacuated their trenches at 1100 hours, embarking west on five trains to Coqueiros.[73] Amparo (which in English means 'Help')

The able Captain Romão Gomes, one of the legends of the Paulista forces. (Diários Associados, via Donato)

A Paulista Bombarda Company of the Guardia Civil under Pedro Kauffman on 9 July 1932. Note the locally made mortar, below in the centre left. Due to the lack of artillery, this mortar unit was used on the Minas Front. (A Gazeta São Paulo, via Donato)

was indeed helpless, and fell. With the loss of the position, the entire right flank of the new Paulista line in Jaguarí, north of the river of the same name, was in the air and threatened with encirclement from the direction of Pedreira. The bright and aggressive Eurico Gaspar Dutra was promoted again, and at least from 10 September he commanded not only the vanguard, but his own detachment in the Northern Sector of São Paulo.[74] All these successes were made without the help of the 11th RI and the 10th BC (which apparently formed the Esteve Detachment), that were still in Mogi Mirim instead of advancing against Comanducaia, as desperately requested of his brother the president by Benjamin Vargas.[75]

The Paulista Artillery Downs a Federal Aircraft (5-11 September)

Meanwhile, the situation improved even further for the Federals. With the fall of Mogi Mirim on 5 September, and once the surrounding area was cleared with the taking of Amparo, the government decided to transfer the three Wacos – C-7, C-8 and C-11 – from Detachment Pouso Alegre to Mogi Mirim on 11 September. By so doing, the loyalist aircraft would only have to fly 60km instead of 200km in order to attack Campinas, their next target. On the same day, the government *vermelinhos* began attacking the Mogiana railway line that ran from Mogi Mirim to the north and south of the front. Also on that day, the Waco C-8 piloted by 2nd Lieutenant Lauro Aguirre Horta Barbosa flew low to attack a railway convoy in Casa Branca but was shot down by anti-aircraft fire from troops under Romão Gomes (or from the train itself). The testimony of the *Folha da Note* newspaper about this event is full of mistakes. The newspaper reports that the pilot jumped by parachute from 4,000 metres, but at such a height it is unlikely that the aircraft could be reached by the Paulistas' machine guns. The aircraft ended up partially buried into the ground, upside down. In the report, it first states that the pilot who fell from the airframe was badly burned, but then it mentions that there were two occupants. However, the Wacos only had a crew of one, as the front seat was taken up by the installation of machine guns; furthermore, the daily flight report records that only Horta was travelling in the Waco. Whatever the case, the downing of the Waco further contributed to the growing aura of Romão Gomes.[76]

Meanwhile, the Paulista aviation was being reinforced to act on the Minas Front. On 6 September, two partially armed Falcons (*Kyri-Kyri* and *Kavuré-Y*), escorted by the Nid.72 *Negrinho*, arrived at Campo de Marte, in São Paulo city, joining the *Taguató* that had already been there for some days. Once there, the three Falcons could install and adjust their weapons. Nevertheless, soon after, only two of them were operational as the *Taguató* was damaged when trying to synchronise its guns with the propeller. Probably the only part of the aircraft damaged was the propeller itself, so the machine remained in the Paulista records when delivered to the government after the surrender. However, it probably never fought again in the war as it was damaged, except for a final action in Mato Grosso at the end of the war, as narrated in Chapter 3.[77]

These aircraft were not able to operate in Minas, as we have no information about them until 19 September. They probably had to depart to the south, as we know of some interventions by the Paulista aviation there on 10 and 16 September. It is only on 19 September that we hear about the three Falcons being present on the Minas Front again in Campinas.[78]

The Withdrawal to the Jaguarí River (13-15 September)

Back on the ground, the Paulistas, leaving Amparo by train, continued until they reached Pedreira. A force was sent to Coqueiros, a little further to the east, to contain the enemy. In Pedreira, Major José Francisco replaced Castro as commander of the defeated troops, intending to hold positions there and at Ingatuba, Entre Montes and Alto de Arèa Branca. Francisco asked for the North-west São Paulo Battalion, with some 150 soldiers, to occupy Morungaba and the line between Arêa Branca and Pantano. In Coqueiros, the Federals already had (according to rebel estimations) some 800 infantry of the 1st Ceará Provisional Battalion and other units, some 300 riders, a 75mm cannon and 14 heavy machine guns, with another four 75mm pieces in the rear at Amparo. To oppose them, Francisco had only 450 Paulistas, which were reinforced with two mortars, 300 more soldiers and some sappers. Francisco consequently blew up the bridges over the Jaguarí River and fortified his positions. [79]

An improvised Paulista trench along the Jaguarí River. Note the light machine gun. (FGV, CPDDC, Yasuhiko Nekamura Collection, via Catalogo)

On 12 September, further to the north, the Paulistas attacked the west of Mogi Mirim. The rebel assault was repulsed, the defeated troops escaping to Arhur Nogueira. The Federal units in Mogi Mirim (the 6th BC and 11th RI under Lieutenant Colonel Pyrineus) then finally moved forward, some 5km to the west to the village of Sobradinho, expelling the Paulistas and taking 85 prisoners.[80]

Returning to the south, the Federal attack – again made by the ever-present Detachment Dutra, began on 13 September. Dutra expelled the Paulistas at Duas Pontes, to the west of Pedreira. The government's objective was to join up with

Segunda edição

A GAZETA

O BOMBARDEIO DE CIDADES ABERTAS

Os "ossos" de um avião dictatorial

Combate aereo sob os céos do sector da Mogyana!

O coronel João Cabanas

A população de Queluz "soccorrida" pela dictadura

A desaggregação outubrista

COMMUNICADO DO SERVIÇO DE PUBLICIDADE, A'S 11 HORAS DE HOJE

As operações de guerra proseguiram, durante a noite, em todos os sectores, sem grandes combates.

Sómente na região do Norte houve um poderoso ataque de artilharia por parte das tropas dictatoriaes, cujo resultado foi nullo, porquanto as nossas tropas não recuaram de posição alguma.

O sr. João Alberto deixa a chefia de policia e abandona o governo da Dictadura

A "charge" que motivou a suspensão do "Diario da Noite", do Rio

As excellencias do phonographo-acta

AMNISTIA FISCAL

O NOVO PREFEITO DE NOVA YORK E' ENERGICO

UM ARTIGO DE MAXIMO GORKI

DECRETOS E LEIS NA "GAZETA DE MADRID"

Abastecimento de leite á Capital

The *A Gazeta* newspaper reporting the downing by rebel anti-aircraft artillery of the Federal Waco C-8 flown by Horta Barbosa. (Daróz)

the Federal Alkindar Detachment in Posse to alleviate the pressure it was feeling from a local counterattack in Ressaca (nowadays Santo Antonio de Posse). The rebels managed to regain Duas Pontes in a counterstroke. However, a subsequent loyalist attack was brutal, with strong artillery forces, and the Paulistas eventually had to abandon the line and all of the sub-sector. The Ingatuba line could not be maintained, the forces of Captain Isidoro being reduced to just 60 men. At the end of 14 September, the rebels had retreated to Pedreira, where telephone communications with Campinas were cut, so the Constitutionalists had to leave due to the risk of being surrounded by the Federals. This further retreat was forced upon them by the manoeuvre made by Dutra, according to the instructions of the new Chief of Staff of the 4th Division, Colonel Paes de Andrade. Dutra – with the 4th RCD, a company of the 1st Ceará and a mounted artillery section – was to attack Pedreira frontally, while a sub-detachment under Captain Moreira, with a company of the 1st Ceará and the 14th Corpo Provisório, crossed the Camanducaia River in Duas Pontes, attacking the flank or rear of the Paulistas that were pressing the Alkindar Detachment. However, Moreira's troops lost their way, so they moved west to Pedreira, contributing to the fall of the village. The loss of Pedreira led to the fall of the whole Paulista Jaguarí line along the Camanducaia River, located further west, due to the risk of being outflanked from Pedreira. Thus, on 15 September, all the rebel forces withdrew to the south bank of the Jaguarí River, protecting the roads in the north and north-east of Campinas. While Dutra's men were doing all the hard work on the Minas Front, the other Federal units were acting less brilliantly. For example, it was only on 20 September – five days after it being abandoned – that the 10th RI of Pedra's detachment moved to occupy Jaguari (probably modern Jaguariúna).[81]

The Situation on the Front (15 September)

At this time, on 15 September, the Paulista forces on the Mineiro Front were organised in various sectors. Major Junqueira was at the northern end of the line, with some troops armed with only outdated Winchester rifles, to defend the banks of the Rio Grande River, opposite the Minas 'triangle', with his command post in Barretos. The sector under Lieutenant Colonel Martiniano de Carvalho was located about 200km further to the south-east in Ribeirão Preto, defending the approaches to the city. Sub-Sector 'Romão Gomes' was in Casa Branca, another 200km south-east, with orders to retake Grama and even Pinhal, threatening the rear of the main Federal attack in the northern part of the main front of the theatre. The Joviniano Brandão Sector, based at Limeira about 50km north-west of Campinas, was defending a large bulge produced by

A machine gun team handling a Hotchkiss weapon, locally adapted as an anti-aircraft gun. Note that none of them wear the Adrian helmets, but the cloth hats, so perhaps these troops are Federals and not rebels. (O Cruceiro Magazine, via Daróz)

the Federal advance. It consisted of two sub-sectors: one under Major Musa in Artur Nogueira and the other commanded by Lieutenant Colonel Faria in Ararás, north of Limeira, facing Mogi Mirim, and later in Conchal. The sector under Lieutenant Colonel Virgilio Ribeiro dos Santos, defending Campinas, was to take the offensive from Morungaba to stop the Federals coming from Amparo. Finally, the sector of Major Labieno Gomes in Bragança Paulista, to the south-east of Campinas, was intended to send reinforcements to the most threatened sectors along the front.[82] In all, there were between 5,000 and 6,000 Paulista troops along the front, but they were very weak in artillery, with only a single Krupp gun.[83]

The Campinas Sector was the strongest of these units, with 2,199 men in mid-September, divided into five groups: the 1st Group (580 men) under Captain Pinto de Melo, made up of two companies of the 6th BCP (260 men), the 9 de Julho Battalion (120), Diocesano Battalion (130) and São Paulo Civil Guard (70); the 2nd Group (480) commanded by Captain Benedito dos Santos, comprising the Catanduvas (120), Rio Preto (110), Misto (100) and Serra Negra (150) Battalions; the 3rd Group (500) under Captain Trita, with the N. Sra. Aparecida Battalion(180), a company of the 7th BCP (90), the Pinahalense Battalion (80) and Liga de Defesa Paulista Battalion (150); the 4th Group (389) of Captain Nunes da Costa, with the Noroeste (110), General Ossorio (83) and Legião Paulista (146) Battalions and a company of the 3rd BCP (50); and finally the 5th Group (250) under Major Leonidas, with the Justiça de Estado (80), Novo Horizonte (100) and Legião Negra (70) Battalions.[84]

Opposing them, the Federals had the Minas Gerais forces of the Brigade North (part of Detachment Rabelo) in the Minas 'triangle', to attack Barreiro; the Brigade Centre facing Ribeirão Preto and Casa Branca; and further south the three detachments of the 4th Division made up of regulars, provisional soldiers and police units from other states. One of these detachments' mission was to march from Mogi Mirim against Limeira; the southernmost detachment was also advancing from Mogi Mirim against northern Campinas; and to the south-east, the third detachment, once having taken Amparo, was to attack Campinas from the north-east. They were commanded by Dutra, supported by Barcelos (who arrived once the Mantiqueira Tunnel on the Paraíba Front was taken, as related in Volume 1) and Paes de Andrade. These three detachments, according to information gathered by the Paulista intelligence service, were composed of elements of the 4th Division (10th RI, 10th BC, 4th RCD and 8th RAM), the 3rd Division (9th RI), other regular and state troops of the 23rd BC, 29th BC, 6th BC, 22nd BC, 21st BC, 2nd BE (probably actually the 4th BE), Alagoas and Pernambuco FPs units and troops of the Military Brigade of Rio Grande do Sul, totalling some 12,000 soldiers, with 16 pieces of artillery and three Waco aircraft (the Paulistas exaggeratedly talk about 12 aircraft). Also in the Dutra Detachment were the 11th RI (from 28 September), 1st Ceará, 14th Corpo Provisório, 1st Paraíba, 28th BC, 2nd Rio Grande do Sul and 6th BC. Apolinário states that rather than Andrade leading a detachment, he was the 4th Division Chief of Staff. The deployment or even existence of these detachments is far from clear. Even Silva mentions a totally different deployment.[85] If we add to these troops

A Paulista Curtiss O-1E Falcon, the best aircraft available for the rebels, along with the Nid.72. Four of these aircraft – the *Taguató*, *Kyri-Kyri*, *Kaburé-Y* and *José Mario* – flew combat missions, but never all at the same time. Mistakenly, most sources claim that only two or three of these aircraft performed in the war. Note that strangely, the Paulista black bands of this machine are only painted below, on its belly. (Daróz)

A sapper battalion before departing for the front. Note the spades and the absence of rifles. (Coleção Paulo Florençano, Taubaté, via Donato)

Paulista recruits from the Liga de Defesa Paulista marching to the front. Note the use of civilian belts. This unit formed part of the Campinas defences. (Abril, Nosso Século, Paulo Florençano collection, via Catalogo)

the Minas Brigades in the north, perhaps there could have been 18,000 men in this sector, in which case the Federals enjoyed a three-to-one superiority.

The Paulista Counteroffensives (11-16 September)

As we have seen, the chances of success of any counteroffensive were remote, but still the Paulistas tried it, and more than once. First, a diversionary attack was attempted by Joviniano Brandâo's units in the Limeira Sector, in the northern part of the main theatre. The attack was planned and executed 24 hours later, to try to stop the advance of the Federal detachment attacking in the south, which at that time had not yet taken Amparo, but was moving dangerously towards it. The attack itself would be carried out indirectly, not against the southern detachment but against the northern one, to the west of Mogi Mirim, with the aim of forcing the southern force to retreat to Itapira after seeing the Federal northern flank threatened. Due to lack of ammunition, rebel front commander Colonel Saturnino Paiva had to postpone the attack, and when it was finally launched on 12 September, Amparo had fallen. The attack was still made against the 9th RI, but Brandâo only managed to take 12 prisoners, 10 rifles and two heavy machine guns, his forces failing dramatically in their bid to impel the loyalists to halt their offensive and having to go back to their initial positions. Brandâo then called for the Romão Gomes Column, located to the north-east, to support his attack on 14 September, but Gomes delayed his departure because it would involve leaving their positions in the sub-sector, precisely when the Minas FP Central Brigade was giving the impression of leaving Grama.[86] But on the contrary, these Federal troops had been reinforced with the Minas FP Brigade under Colonel Lery, after the fall of the Mantiquiera Tunnel on 13 September (see Volume 1).[87] In desperation, Gomes proposed the bombing of Poços de Caldas, in Minas Gerais, to force the Federals to withdraw, but without result.[88]

A second Paulista counterattack was then arranged. General Klinger ordered the 1st BCP under Lieutenant Colonel Virgilio Ribeiro dos Santos (who had severely defeated the Federals in Cunha, on the coast, as related in Volume 1) to be moved to the under-threat Campinas, the third largest city of São Paulo State. Virgilio set out with his 300 soldiers for Itatiba, south-east of Campinas, as the sector's reserve. Shortly after, on 15 September, Virgilio proposed a counterattack on the left flank or southern sector of the government detachments, in cooperation with Commander Abrantes. Colonel Paiva replied that such a move was "a mere fantasy" and offered his post to anyone who would dare to lead the attack. Klinger then gave the sector to Colonel Eduardo Lejeune, and the detachment

Table 19: Minas Gerais Front Detachments (15 September)		
Paulistas		
Location	**Detachment**	**Strength/Units**
North/left flank (Barretos, Rio Grande, facing Minas 'triangle')	Junqueira	Some 800
Ribeirão Preto	Carvalho	Some 800
Casa Branca, facing Grama/Pinhal	Romão Gomes	Some 800
Limeira	Brandâo	Some 800 (in two sub-sectors)
Sub-Sector (Artur Nogueira)	Brandâo/Musa	(Some 400)
Sub-Sector (Ararás)	Brandâo/Faria	(Some 400)
Campinas	Ribeiro dos Santos	2,199 men in five groups, comprising 19 battalions/companies
South-east/right flank (Bragança Paulista)	Labieno Gomes	Some 800
Total: Some 6,000 soldiers		
Federals		
4th Division/East Army Detachment		
Colonel Pinheiro		
Location	**Detachments**	**Units**
North/right flank: Minas 'triangle', facing Barreiro	Brigade North	Minas FPs Battalions
Facing Ribeirão Preto/Casa Branca	Brigades Centre & South	10th BC, 8th RAM, 9th RI, 11th RI (until 28 September), 23rd BC, 29th BC, 22nd BC, 21st BC, 4th BE, Alagoas, Pernambuco and Rio Grande do Sul FPs, Minas FP Battalions. (Of these units, some were also in the Barcelos Detachment)
Mogi Mirim facing Limeira	Andrade	
Mogi Mirim facing Campinas	Barcelos	10th RI and others (see above)
South/left flank: Amparo facing Campinas	Dutra	4th RCD, 4th BE, 6th BC, 11th RI (from 28 September), 1st Ceará, 1st Paraíba, 2nd Rio Grande do Sul, 14th Corpo Provisório, 28th BC, 6th Battery/8th RAM
Total: 18,000 soldiers		
Federal Reinforcements		
	Detachment Guedes Fontoura	3,000 soldiers
	Detachment Heitor Borges	3,000 soldiers
Total Federals, 20 September 24,000 soldiers		

defending Campinas to Colonel Herculano Carvalho e Silva, author of one of the main sources of this work.[89]

Lejeune requested and received several mortar companies and additional aircraft, that had arrived on the 14th, to perform this counteroffensive. He also asked for support from the Romão Gomes Column further to the north, but Gomes was once again unable to cooperate. The redeployment of Captain Ferreira's 8th BCP to help in the attack thus had to be postponed again. When Ferreira had arrived at Limeira, in the central sub-sector, he had to be diverted to São Jose and Caconde to contain the Minas FP Central Brigade, that was attacking again in Grama, feinting to São Jose and Caconde on 16 September. It would be nine or 10 days before Ferreira's troops would be available, which was too late to join Virgilio's attack. Nevertheless, despite being deprived of this support, Virgilio's offensive with his 1st BCP started from Itatiba, south-east of Campinas, the troops advancing along the road north-east towards Morungaba, trying to destroy the Federal left flank of the southern detachment and to retake Amparo. Two companies of the 23 Maio Battalion, from Bragança Paulista, were to join them. However, the attack only began three days after it was conceived, on 18 September, and the opposing government commander, witnessing the preparations, guessed the sector that would be attacked and duly reinforced it, meaning there were now 800 troops there against the mere 300 of Virgilio's attacking Paulistas. The Federals placed two squadrons of the 14th Corpo Provisório in Fazenda São Rafael, the 1st Paraíba on the road at Tres Pontes (further to the east), the 28th BC at Coqueiros and the 1st Ceará in Pedreira. Furthermore, Captain Ulderico's company of the rebel 1st BCP did not stop at Haciendas São Bento and São Rafael in order to cover the flank of the attack, as expected, so the loyalist troops moving along the road

Federal troops defending the Mantiqueira Tunnel Front (see Volume 1). These soldiers were later sent to the Minas Gerais Front under Barcelos, to support Dutra's offensive against Campinas. Despite being in high mountains and in the middle of the Austral winter, these troops strangely appear without shirts. (FGV, CPDDC, Yasuhiko Nakamura, via Catalogo)

In the centre, Medical Captain and future President of Brazil Juscelino Kubistscheck, who fought with the Minas Gerais Força Publica, talking with a Paulista prisoner (note his white scarf). (FGV, CPDDC, Gustavo Capanema, via Catalogo)

The Paulista Aviation's Swansong (19-30 September)

Meanwhile, the Federals resumed their concentric offensive against Campinas, marching one detachment from the north and another from the north-east. By 19 September, the central lines of the front had been broken, the Varguistas overpowering the flank around the railway station at Carlos Gomes. Almost simultaneously, at the other end of the front in Pupos, the loyalists pressed forward over the Alto Cafezal heights and Entre Montes, defended by troops under Castro, the commander of the sub-sector. Forced to retreat, the Paulistas formed a new defensive line on the road to Tanquinho, with Major Musa in Roseira to help with an attack against the enemy's right flank. At that time, the Federal detachment under Major Pedra, with the 29th BC in the vanguard, took Vila de Jaguarí, and marching to the south occupied Carlos Gomes on 24 September. The fall of Carlos Gomes forced the Paulistas to also abandon their positions in Pupos. A new line of defence was hastily organised on the left bank of the Jaguarí and on the Cabras heights. For the moment, the Federals were held behind the Jaguarí River. All the bridges over this 50-metre-wide natural obstacle had been destroyed.

On 25 September, the Federals marshalled their forces for their next offensive. The 2nd Battalion/Rio Grande do Sul Brigade was placed in Pupos, with the 1st Ceará in Ingatuba. The Ppontoon company of the 4th BE rebuilt the bridge at Pupos, and the troops prepared for the assault. The Federal Western Detachment was in the line running through Atibaia, Fazenda Taquinho Velho and Desembragador Furtado on 24 September. The Eastern Detachment was formed under Dutra, comprising the 28th BC, 2nd Battalion Riograndense, 14th Corpo Provisório Riograndense, 1st Ceará, 1st Paraíba, 4th RCD (less the 9th Squadron), 6th Battery/8th RAM and the Schneider Mounted Battery. They were to move to the line Pedreira–Ingatuba–Arraial dos Souzas (south of Campinas), enveloping any resistance encountered by the Western Detachment and cutting the road with Jundiaí.[91]

from Amparo to Barrio das Onças surprised and pocketed half of the Paulista right wing, taking 50 rebels as prisoners. This Paulista offensive also ended disastrously, with between 265 and 290 losses according to Federal sources. Another attack was made against Pedreira on 19 September, but that too was seen off by the 1st Ceará, after being reinforced by the 28th BC. The 23 Maio also attacked at Termas de Lindòia, but without effect. On 20 September, the Paulistas attacked Pedreira once more, but were again repulsed. On the same day, the Federal 2nd Battalion/Rio Grande do Sul Mixed Brigade arrived at Amparo, moving then to Coqueiros and being incorporated in Dutra's detachment.[90]

Federal troops in São Bento, which was taken by the loyalists after one of the last Paulista counteroffensives. (FGV, CPDDC, Yasuhiko Nakamura Collection, via Catalogo)

over Campinas for the other Paulista aircraft, the *Kavuré-Y* and Motta Lima's 'Green' Waco. These first two aircraft then climbed to 1,500 metres and moved north, when one of the Federal Wacos appeared at 2,500 metres. The *vermelinho*, which was intending to bomb Fazenda Ataíba, only saw one Paulista Falcon due to the cloudy and foggy conditions. As it was the first appearance of the Falcons in this theatre, the government pilot likely did not know whose aircraft this was, and perhaps even took it to be a silver-painted Moth. Whatever the case, he launched into a dive for the attack. However, Lysias' Falcon turned and fired at him three times while the Federal Waco was closing in. Lysias then dived to his left and came back to his right, appearing on the tail of the Waco and firing at it again several times. At this moment, the Paulista Nid also appeared above the Federal Waco, launching into an attack. The Waco reacted by diving to tree-top level, returning to his lines while under the protection of Varguista anti-aircraft fire that forced the Paulista *Negrinho* Nid to pull back. The other two Paulista aircraft then arrived, but having lost the element of surprise, Lysias decided to cancel the attack against Mogi Mirim.[95]

At the same time, in preparation for the final assault, the two surviving Federal Wacos based in Mogi Mirim, the C-7 and C-11, began to make a series of attacks on Campinas. On 18 September, one *vermelinho* in the morning and the other in the afternoon dropped three bombs to destroy the railway station of the Mogyana Company in Campinas, hitting a station garage but also some civilian buildings, leaving 12 people injured and killing a 10-year-old child, Aldo Chioratto, who was acting as a messenger for the Paulista troops. That same afternoon, the two Wacos bombed the Campinas railway station of the Paulista Company, missing their target but causing seven civilian wounded, including a grandmother with her four daughters and granddaughter. On 20 September, the Federal Wacos dropped 12 bombs over the aviation field of the Campineiro Jockey Club in the town, five bombs hitting the target but the rest again falling on civil buildings, leaving one more person injured. On the morning of 21 September, another Federal *vermelinho* targeted Campina's Mogiana railway station, hitting it with two bombs. Paradoxically, that same day the government published several complaints regarding the shelling by the Paulistas of cities occupied by the Federals, threatening to do the same in retaliation. The rebels were apparently using a train-mounted 150mm Schneider cannon called *Catarina* to carry out such attacks against Lorena on the Paraíba Front (see Volume 1).[92]

With so many Federal bombing raids against Campinas, the rebel aviation was forced to act, performing its largest aerial action of the war. On 20 September, Major Borges moved to São Paulo all the available Constitutionalist Aviation Group, which then moved on to Viracopos in Campinas. There, Borges organised a squadron under Major Lysias Rodrigues, accompanied by Captain Jose Ângelo Gomes Ribeiro. This unit consisted of two Falcons (the *Kyri-Kyri* and *Kavuré-Y*), the C-3 Waco *Verde* ('Green')[93] and the Nid-72 K-423 called *Negrinho* under Captain Adherbal Costa Oliveira. Major Lysias wanted to surprise the entire Federal Aviation based in Mogi Mirim while still on the ground. When he launched the attack, the Paulistas discovered two Federal Wacos, probably the C-7 and C-11, that had just taken off for another attack.[94] It seems that at 1045 hours, the *Kyri-Kyri* under Lysias and Abílio, and the Nid *Negrinho* flown by Adherbal, took off, waiting at low level

The final attack against Mogi Mirim airfield was carried out the next day, 21 September,[96] by the same four Paulista aircraft. The *Kyri-Kyri* Falcon was flown by Lysias Rodrigues and Abílio Pereira de Almeida, with the *Kavuré-Y* under Gomes Riberio and Mario Machado Bittencourt. Adherbal da Costa piloted the Nid-72 *Negrinho*, while the 'Green' Waco (C-3) was flown by Motta Lima and Hugo Neves. The group departed at 0830 hours. This time the 1st Fighter Group of Lysias Rodrigues managed to surprise the two Federal Wacos C-7 and C-11 of the Mogi Mirim Air Detachment on the ground, along with four other newcomers. These were a group of Wacos which were on a stopover at the airfield before flying on to the Southern Front. The Paulistas' attack thus fell upon an over-occupied aerodrome with six aircraft. During the subsequent bombing attack, one Varguista aircraft was able to take off, but the remaining airframes were hit by the diving rebel aircraft. This mission was followed by another attack that was launched that evening. According to Lysias' report, all six Federal aircraft were left in flames after being bombed and strafed. However, Góis Monteiro only reported two Wacos destroyed, the C-13 and C-17 of Lieutenants França and Guilherme,[97] although several more were probably damaged, at least two of them so severely that they had to be sent away to be rebuilt.[98] Whatever the truth, the result of the rebel mission was sensational, and certainly the most successful of the whole air war.

Yet the Paulista joy was somewhat muted, since that same morning (or the previous day according to some reports), the Potez A-212 (called *Nosso Potez*, 'Our Potez', as it was the only active Paulista Potez), after being repaired at Itapetininga in the south, crash landed on the airfield at Viracopos, in Campinas, turning over and being destroyed. Its crew – 1st Lieutenant Daniel Camargo and 2nd

A rebel naval cannon installed on a train platform, perhaps the 150mm Schneider gun operating on the Paraíba Front. Note the naval uniforms and the anti-aircraft machine gun on the left. (Unknown author, Abril, Nosso Século, courtesy Museu do Telefone, via Catalogo)

A view of the destroyed Federal Wacos C-13 and C-17 after the rebel air attack against Mogi Mirim, the most successful of the war. (Daróz)

Lieutenant José Ferraz Leite, civilian pilots who had transferred to the army – were both wounded, the former with the loss of an eye.[99]

Surprisingly, despite their losses, the Federal bombing over Campinas continued. On 23 September, two Federal Wacos (probably C-7 and C-11) dropped four bombs on the Campineiro Jockey Club airfield, causing little damage. In addition, the loyalists attacked Rio Claro, Jundiaí and Bragança Paulista. The rebel aircraft had most likely already left this sector at the time, since at least on 23 or maybe 24 September they were on the coast, trying to lift the naval blockade of Santos (see Volume 1), thus once again leaving control of the skies to the government. On 26 September, a Federal attack over Bragança involved three aircraft, so we may deduct that the Mogi Mirim Air Detachment had by then been reinforced or had received temporary help from the Paraíba Valley. The Federals attacked the station and a railway convoy in Bragança. However, both the bombs and strafing with machine guns missed their target, and one civilian was injured. In Rio Claro, on 29 September, a further attack also missed its objectives, but this time there were no civilian casualties. The Paulista population mistakenly believed that the government's aerial forces were committing terror bombing against civilians to force them to abandon the war, but the reality was more simple: bombing was not an easy task.[100]

The Last Paulista Offensive ... and the Surrender (23 September-1 October)

Klinger, having no available reserves along the entire Minas Front, immediately ordered the withdrawal of Romão Gomes' Column in the north-east of the Southern Sector. The conquest of Campinas would mean the definitive isolation of its sub-sector, so it was pointless to continue defending the positions at Branca. At the same time, further north, the troops of General Rabelo[101] (maybe the North and Central Minas FP Brigades) had taken Ribeirão Preto and França, in the north-east of the front against the troops of Carvalho's Sector, so Gomes could now also be attacked from the north. Thus, to avoid being enveloped, Gomes was forced to abandon his sector on 23 September, despite having been trying to reconquer Grama at the time.[102]

Once Gomes arrived at Campinas, a plan was established by Herculano e Silva and Lejeune for an attack to distract the Federals from the city. Gomes, with 1,600 troops – the largest contingent ever used in a Paulista offensive – was to advance towards Hacienda Iracema, facing Pedreira, to the east, attacking the southern Federal detachment. On 26 September, these troops went by truck towards the three bridges over the Atibaia River. This offensive was the last great hope of saving Campinas, and somewhat optimistically it was believed it might change the course of the war. The fighting began in the Hacienda Iracema heights, but the offensive – which continued until 28 September – lacked much spirit because of the rumours that an armistice was being negotiated. On the 29th, General Klinger asked Vargas for a cessation of hostilities. The next day, the Federal Wacos flew across all sectors, while the column of Gomes was strongly harassed. With rebel morale sinking, Klinger ordered Gomes to abandon the offensive and to withdraw to Jundiaí, south of Campinas.[103]

This city of about 130,000 inhabitants, besides being one of the largest in São Paulo State – maybe the third in size – was a vital communications centre from which railroads linked with the capital to the south, as well as throughout the north and north-west of the state. Its fall would thus be an irreparable catastrophe

The Paulista Nid-72, ironically known as *Negrinho* ('Little Black') after being painted in white or silver in September 1932. This aircraft deserted from the Federals in the hands of Captain Adherbal da Costa, who is also in the picture, and took part in the Mogi Mirim attack. (Daróz)

A view of the destroyed Potez A-212 *Nosso Potez* ('Our Potez', as there were no more such aircraft available to the rebels at the time) after suffering an accident when landing at Campinas. It was also the only aircraft in the war to down an enemy machine (the Potez A-117) during air combat. Note the white Paulista band on the fuselage. (Daróz)

for the Paulista cause. In addition, Campinas was just 60km from São Paulo city, so its capture would threaten the nerve-centre of the whole rebellion. Seeing Campinas threatened and about to fall, the rebel will to fight disappeared completely. In the end, the front at Minas, with its proximity to Campinas and the capital, was the key theatre of the war, a fact only realised late on by the Federals, but even later by the Paulistas, who still had huge resources deployed in the Paraíba Valley.

When the Federals, belatedly, did realise the importance of this theatre, they sent units from the Southern Front to Minas, such as the Riograndenses or the 9th RI, while from Paraíba Valley they sent the 1st RI, the Minas FP Lery Brigade and the Guedes Fontoura Detachment (this unit was sent to Itapira, and headed towards Limeira–Ararás–Rio Claro). The new Heitor Borges Detachment, which was created in September, three artillery batteries and the Bahia FP were also sent to the Minas Front. Indeed, towards the end of the war, of the 10 detachments of the Army of the East, six of them were fighting in Minas, where between 20,000 and 24,000 Federal soldiers were facing some 6,000 Paulistas.[104]

On 28 September, the 1st Ceará Battalion crossed the Jaguarí River, supported by fire from the 6th Battery/8th RAM, and was then replaced by Vargas' 14th Corpo Provisório. All the 11th RI was placed under Dutra to protect his rearguard in Amparo. The 14th Corpo marched to Pedreira and Entre Montes, the sapper company of the 4th BE improved the Entre Montes–Coqueiros road and the 1st Ceará attacked the Paulistas in Fazenda Retiro, who were already fighting with the 6th BC. The Paulistas then began negotiations for an armistice as the front was collapsing everywhere, so the 4th Division halted its march. Nevertheless, the Barcelos Detachment crossed the Atibaia River and, marching to the South, took the station at Tanquinho, 12km from Campinas, on the Mogi Mirim–Campinas railroad. Then, on 30 September, orders were given for the 4th Division to continue its march, so the 1st Paraíba moved near Entre Montes, the 28th BC occupied Pedreira, the 14th Corpo Provisório went to the central power building, the 4th RCD marched to Areia Branca, near Morungaba, and the 2nd Battalion Riograndense went to Arraial das Souzas. The Paulistas reacted by retiring behind the Atibaia River and destroying the bridges, although the Federals then sent the 4th BE to repair them.

Rebel forces were collapsing everywhere. Nearly all of the Catanduva Battalion left the front. The Federal Fontoura Detachment did nothing, but the Detachment Gwyer took Conchal (north-west of Mogi Mirim), capturing 72 rebels. On the same day, the Paulistas abandoned Campinas, but Paes de Andrade, terrified about what Dutra's fearsome troops might do upon entering such a large city, ordered his detachment to remain, so Campinas was eventually entered by the more peaceful soldiers of the 10th RI of the Barcelos Detachment on 1 October, who marched in from the north without a fight.[105]

The rebel commander of the sector, Colonel Herculano de Carvalho e Silva, on behalf of the Paulista Public Force (or FPP), signed a separate peace with the Vargas government. Consequently, the FPP forces were put under Góis Monteiro's control, with all FPP units on any front ordered to retire to São Paulo city. The war, although in theory continuing until 2 October, had for all practical purposes already ended.

5
THE VARGAS AGE

In the last days of September, the Constitutionalists tottered from disaster to disaster on all fronts, except in Mato Grosso. Resistance to the Federal concentric advance was collapsing. On the Paraíba Front, the 2nd DIO was about to be enveloped and completely surrounded from the south (see Volume 1). On the Minas Front, several concentric columns were preparing to storm Campinas, isolating the entire north-east of the state from its capital. Finally, in the south, government troops had overcome the barrier of the Paranapanema River and had isolated the entire state to the north-west of São Paulo city.

Nearly a month-and-a-half earlier, on 12 August, predicting the imminent debacle, Bertoldo Klinger, the São Paulo State supreme commander, had already contacted President Getúlio Vargas to ask for a negotiated surrender, but the suggested conditions were so harsh that the fighting continued. On 27 September, Klinger again raised the issue of an armistice, and in a meeting that continued all night and into the next day, the Paulistas decided to continue fighting before contacting the Federal government again. However, around 2200 hours, rumours began circulating that the Paulista FP was thinking about the possibility of signing an armistice on their own. Klinger then stepped forward and, without even consulting with the São Paulo State government led by Pedro de Toledo, prepared a telegram to send to the national government about the possibility of an armistice. FP Colonel Herculano de Carvalho e Silva, commander of the Campinas Front (and the author of one of the best works about the war), General Basilio Taborda, commander of the Southern Front, and Major Ivo Borges, the head of the rebel aviation, supported this decision. However, Pedro de Toledo, humiliated because they had not consulted him, refused to sign the telegram. Nevertheless, Klinger sent the telegram on 29 September, at 0100 hours, simply proposing to suspend hostilities on all fronts. President Vargas then delegated any contact with the Paulistas to General Góis Monteiro, and the imminent final offensive on the Paraíba Front was postponed so that the envoys of the rebels could be received.[1]

Downfall (29 September-1 October)

Aware of the negotiations, rebel hardliners, including the aviator Major Lysias Rodrigues, tried to overthrow Klinger to continue the struggle, and also to replace Colonel Herculano e Silva with Romão Gomes. However, Gomes, the hero of the Paulistas, declined, saying that the war was already lost. Colonel Figueiredo, the rebel commander in the Paraíba Valley, then decided that if São Paulo surrendered, then the struggle should continue in Mato Grosso. Consequently, he prepared the organisation of a column from the 2nd DIO to be moved to Campo Grande, sending his Chief of Staff, the brilliant mulatto Colonel Palimércio de Resende, by train to Mato Grosso to coordinate the preparations. Meanwhile, Klinger's envoys, Colonel Ilhabela and Major Ivo Borges, meeting Góis Monteiro in Cruzeiro on 29 September, received the conditions of the armistice,

Colonel Figueiredo, commander of all the rebel forces in the Paraíba Valley, with his son Guilherme and his relative José de Figueiredo Lobo, in Cruzeiro. (FGV, CPDDC, Guilherme Figueiredo Collection, via Catalogo)

Cartoon from 1932 of General Góis Monteiro at the front, behind the trenches, ironically commenting about the consequences of being too soft with the Paulistas during recent years. (Biblioteca Municipal Mario Andrade, via Donato)

that would also cover Mato Grosso with a delay of eight days: the Constitutionalists had 48 hours to leave all their positions, which would be occupied by the South and East Federal Armies. During the same period, the rebels would deliver any Federal Army weapon taken during the revolt, as well as all São Paulo FPP automatic weapons, 70 percent of their railway engines and 20 percent of all motor vehicles. Finally, it was expressly stated that there would be no political concessions of any kind, the only thing granted to the Paulistas being to recognise their bravery and noble sentiments. In short, it was not an armistice; it was a surrender.[2]

Humiliated, the rebel envoys refused to sign the document. President Vargas then issued a proclamation "for a Brazil of the future, nationalist and heroic, and against the Brazil of the past, regionalist and medieval", and gradually began to restart the fighting in all sectors. The Paulistas no longer had sufficient ammunition, and there were trenches where their soldiers, having exhausted their cartridges, took their knives and even their helmets to fend off the impending offensive. However, most of these positions were simply abandoned or else the rebel soldiers fraternised with the enemy, so the Federal offensive came up against no material resistance on 29 and 30 September. The rumour that an armistice was being negotiated was in the air, and nobody wanted to be the last to die for a lost cause. Seeing the widespread collapse, General Klinger asked Colonel Figueiredo to send him two companies of the 6th RI to São Paulo city to contain any internal revolt. The colonel sent the 2nd FP BCP under Major Otaviano Gonçales. On 1 October, Colonel Basilio Taborda from the Southern Front was appointed by General Klinger as the commander of the city, while in the Paraíba theatre, dozens of soldiers and civilian volunteers were trying to embark on the trains being organised by Palimércio Resende for a retreat to Mato Grosso do Sul. At noon, Resende departed on his mission, encountering along the way Paulistas soldiers returning home. After a few hours, the Federal thrust cut the railroad, so the last Paulista strategic redeployment of the war came to nothing. However, Resende did not dare say anything to spoil the plans of his peers. Klinger then once again sent emissaries to try to gain some concessions from Góis Monteiro, but they returned empty-handed at 2300 hours. Klinger issued orders to try to hold a final defensive line along the Guaratinguetá River, while the other fronts collapsed. The Federals, meanwhile, were prepared on 2 October to launch "at 0800, the final offensive".[3]

The 'Treason' of the Paulista FP (2-4 October)

However, this final attack was not going to be necessary. At 0100 hours on 2 October, rumours began that all FP units were instructed to stop fighting and to leave the front. At 0200 hours, a volunteer battalion with a brilliant record left their trenches, leaving a 6km gap in Figueiredo's lines. What had happened was that the Paulista FP, seeing everything was lost and that it made no sense to continue giving their lives for nothing, had during the night of 1-2 October signed an agreement of surrender in Cruzeiro, under which 10,000 soldiers of the Paulista Police distributed along all fronts under the rebel flags were to be put under the orders of Vargas' Provisional Government. This contingent was to leave the front and fall back to the capital, keeping order there until the entry of Federal troops. In

Colonel Palimércio Resende, the brilliant 2nd DIO Chief of Staff, who tried to organise the last resistance from Paraíba to Mato Grosso do Sul. (Museu da Imagen e do Som de São Paullo, via Donato)

Paulista FP Colonel Herculano da Carvalho e Silva, the last commander of the Campinas Sector and author of one of the best works about the 1932 war, was accused of betraying the Paulistas when he arranged a separate peace treaty with Góis Monteiro to end the conflict. (Coleção Paulo Florençano, Taubaté, via Donato)

return, the grades obtained by the officers of the Public Police Force during the Paulista War would be respected. Paradoxically, one of the signatories of this agreement was Major Gonçalves himself, sent by Figueiredo to defend the capital and one of the paladins of continuing the war. The instigator of this manoeuvre had been the commander of the Campinas Sector, Colonel Herculano de Carvalho e Silva of the Paulista FP, who had maintained contacts since at least 30 September with General Góis Monteiro.[4]

On the Paraíba Front, the police troops withdrew before 0800 hours, opening a 6km gap in Figueiredo's defensive lines. With the departure of other soldiers who were tired of the war, shortly before the start of the final Federal offensive, only the 4th BC, the Freitas Borges and Saldanha da Gama Battalions and a company under Captain Sandi (who had started the war as a mere sergeant) were left on the right flank of the rebels. Defeated before the fighting started, a convoy of 33 wagons – soon followed by another 22 – began to evacuate the largest possible number of troops that could continue the fight in Mato Grosso, as organised by Figueiredo. However, this was impossible to do, as Resende's vanguard discovered, but he dared not report this. They departed at 0900 hours, followed by the Federals, covered in the rear by armoured train TB-6 *Phantasma da Morte*. Nevertheless, when they reached Jacareí they received a telegram informing them that if they did not surrender, they would be attacked by their former FP compatriots when passing through São Paulo. Furthermore, as we have seen, the rail communications were cut as the Federals, marching from Botucatu against Baurú, had taken Itú and the Sorocabana railway line. Thus, finally, Figueiredo's convoy had to stop.[5]

In São Paulo, the last act of the drama was played out. At 1500 hours, General Góis Monteiro ordered Colonel Herculano e Silva to take control of the Constitutionalist revolutionary government and maintain order until his arrival. Aware of this fact, Pedro de Toledo, governor of the rebel state, declared the end of the São Paulo government at 1530 hours at the Champs Elysees Palace. His words were simple: "We go home to wait for prison." At dawn the next day, 3 October, the convoy of 55 wagons waiting in Jacareí to march for Mato Grosso were finally dissolved. Its organiser, Colonel Palimércio Resende, was still able to reach Três Lagoas, only to find that the state Constitutionalist commander, Colonel Horta Barbosa, had also accepted Góis Monteiro's authority and had orders to put him in jail. The confusing situation in Campo Grande was finally resolved on 4 October when some of the Constitutionalist troops rebelled in favour of President Vargas. The war was over.[6]

The Consequences

The war, although a huge conflict by the scale of Latin America (the biggest in Brazil's history, being surpassed only by the Chaco War and the Mexican Revolution), because of its short duration and the civility of its fighters, was relatively bloodless. Paradoxically, many textbooks on the history of Brazil tread very carefully when talking about the war, or even do not mention it at all. Perhaps this trend is due to a wish to minimise the remembrance of a recent civil war that could weaken the ties between Brazilians. Indeed, today in São Paulo, some people selfishly tell the story of this conflict as if it was a war for independence. This is a false approach that has permeated broad sectors of the population, as also happened recently in countries such as Spain, with the manipulated history of an alleged Catalan independence war during the 1936-39 Civil War, and even in the War of the Spanish Succession (1701-14).

Concerning the butcher´s bill, as always, the death toll varies depending on the author. For some, the war caused 1,050 Federal dead versus 2,200 for the rebels. Others reduce the number of Paulista casualties to figures between 601 and 1,000, even breaking

2ª FOLHA DA NOITE 2ª

Director-Superintendente: OCTAVIANO ALVES DE LIMA — PROPRIEDADE DA EMPRESA "FOLHA DA MANHÃ" LTDA. — Director-Gerente: DIOGENES DE LEMOS AZEVEDO

ANNO XII — RUA DO CARMO, 7 e 7-A TEL. 2-7181 (RÊDE INTERNA) — S. PAULO — SEXTA-FEIRA, 30 DE SETEMBRO DE 1932 — END. TELEGR. — "FOLHA" CAIXA POSTAL, 2.900 — N. 3.606

São Paulo fará uma paz honrosa!

AFFIRMA O GENERAL BERTHOLDO KLINGER RECEBENDO UMA MANIFESTAÇÃO POPULAR

Durante as manifestações que hoje se verificaram na cidade, numerosa multidão, a cuja frente se erguiam as bandeiras nacional e paulista, dirigiu-se ao Quartel General das Forças Constitucionalistas.

Assomando, então, a uma das janellas o general Klinger pediu ao povo que tivesse confiança. São Paulo faria uma paz honrosa. E se assim não fosse, até a ultima gotta de seu proprio sangue estava disposto a derramar por São Paulo.

A multidão acclamou largamente o general Klinger.

(Esta noticia foi visada pelo general Klinger)

*

TAMBEM O GOVERNADOR PEDRO DE TOLEDO CONFIA QUE SE FARA' UMA PAZ HONROSA

Esteve hoje á tarde no palacio dos Campos Elyseos um grande grupo de voluntarios das trincheiras, acompanhados de enorme massa popular, manifestando desejos de se entender com o governador Pedro de Toledo.

Após os necessarios entendimentos com o pessoal de palacio, os manifestantes organizaram uma commissão composta dos srs. Rufino Alves, tenentes Paulo Waldemar, Raymundo Pereira, Alaerte Frugoli e do sargento Francisco Gentil Guzzi, que subiu para trocar impressões com o Governador, tendo falado em nome de todos o sr. Rufino Alves, que disse da deliberação em que estavam os combatentes todos de proseguir na guerra, a não ser que o accôrdo em tentativa seja honroso para S. Paulo.

Respondendo, o sr. Pedro de Toledo disse estar S. Paulo convencido da grandeza de sua causa, pelo que só acceitaria uma paz por todos os motivos honrosa.

GOVERNADOR PEDRO DE TOLEDO

GENERAL BERTHOLDO KLINGER

CARTAS SEMANAES DE LONDRES

CORRIDA AEREA "PELA TAÇA DO REI" — A SAUDE NACIONAL — EQUILIBRIO DO ORÇAMENTO — A CONVERSÃO DO EMPRESTIMO DE GUERRA

LONDRES, agosto — (Andrew Blackmore) — O desenvolvimento da aviação civil na Grã-Bretanha tem tido resultados bastante satisfactorios; uma das caracteristicas mais notaveis deste desenvolvimento é a excellencia dos pequenos apparelhos que o publico póde com- grandes diminuições nos obitos devidos a muitas doenças. No anno passado houve menos casos de adulteração de materias alimenticias do que em qualquer anno anterior desde que começaram a ser compilados os factos — apenas 4,6 por cento do total exami- em pratica para levar a cabo a conversão. Em resultado do bom trabalho do Governo, augmentou enormemente o espirito de confiança da nação, e nota-se em toda a parte um optimismo muito mais pronunciado do que ha um anno.

OS "BONUS" PRÓ-CONSTITUIÇÃO NÃO PODEM SER RECUSADOS

Têm-nos chegado queixas contra pessoas que se recusam a acceitar os "bonus" pró-Constituição, emittidos pelo governo de S. Paulo. Entretanto, em absoluto não se justifica essa attitude, pois se trata de emissão lastreada, não havendo ainda determinação alguma legal,

A CIRCULAÇÃO DE BONDES NO CENTRO DA CIDADE

Em virtude de entendimentos entre a Chefia de Policia e a Superintendencia da S. Paulo Light Power Co., os bondes não circularão no centro da cidade de 21 horas em diante, voltan-

The front page of the *Folha da Noite* newspaper of 30 September 1932, optimistically calling the surrender an honourable peace (*"paz honrosa"*). On the left is Toledo, President of São Paulo, and on the right General Klinger, supreme commander of the rebels. (Folha de Sào Paulo, via Donato)

Paulista leaders going to exile. Isolated in the fourth row is Euclides Figuereido, commander of the 2nd Division on the Paraíba Valley Front, with his son below; also, just below him, is the poet Guilherme de Almeida. Third from the left in the first row, seated, is General Vasconcelos, who was sent by Vargas to control São Paulo but who turned to the rebels. Next to him, looking at the camera, is General Dias Lopes, political leader of the revolution, who had already led the previous failed uprising of 1924-25. At the end, also seated, is the commander of the rebel forces, General Klinger. (FGV, CPDDC, Yasuhiko Nakamura Collection, via Catalogo)

President Getúlio Vargas making a speech on the radio.

down the numbers to 353 volunteers, 249 regulars and 150 from other states.[7] Authors such as Daróz speak of 850 Paulistas officially killed, while concerning the Federals, as no official statistics were ever released, he reports that the military attaché of the United States, William Sackville, after touring the battlefields between 12 and 22 October estimated the government casualties as 1,050 dead and 3,800 wounded.[8] The author of this work estimates that the number of rebels wounded probably amounted to between 2,500 and 3,500, and that the Federals maybe also took some 2,000 to 3,000 Paulistas prisoner during the military operations.[9]

Nevertheless, in the end there was no further pain after the war, as President Vargas, in a generous gesture to help bury the divisions created by the conflict, humanely sent just 200 rebels into exile, but did not execute any of them.

Under President Vargas' Rule

Surprisingly, once the conflict ended, President Vargas assumed some of the proposals of the rebels, keeping his word in calling for democratic elections and approving a new constitution. Nevertheless, his attempt to govern democratically in 1934 caused him many problems, with an escalation of violence from both the far left and right. Vargas finally launched another coup in 1937 to implement a regime inspired by the fascism of Mussolini. He thus created the *Estado Novo*, a corporatism regime with no freedoms, but very progressive in the social sphere, which paradoxically led him into confrontation with both the Integralista Party (a purely fascist group) and the Communists.

Getúlio Vargas was a political giant in Brazil, probably the most prominent leader in the contemporary history of the country. However, as a military strongman, he distrusted the liberal democratic system, which he considered weak, preferring a strong regime (a euphemism for having no opposition) that let him do what he honestly thought was the best for his country. He had no problem with imposing harsh measures if needed, such as when he deftly controlled the effect of the Great Depression on the country with the much-criticised system of destroying crops to maintain their high prices. Vargas was deposed when democracy was reinstated in 1945, but was back in power when he won the 1950 elections, ruling again until his suicide in 1954. In that year, it is believed his brother Benjamin may have been involved in the attempted assassination of a journalist, a scandal that had even reached Getúlio; the president, in the middle of a severe depression affecting the country, did not have the willpower to withstand the shame. Before ending his life, he wrote his political testament, a document that is still considered a touchstone of Brazilian politics.[10]

In the end, although São Paulo had lost the conflict and Getúlio Vargas ruled for another couple of decades, the Constitutionalist Revolution acquired a romantic halo for its defence of the democratic

Coffee crops being burned under Vargas' orders in Santos in 1931 to keep the prices high following the 1929 Great Depression. (Familia Pires do Rio, via Donato)

Table 20: Fate of Combat aircraft during the War					
Paulistas					
Type	**N. Plate**	**Role**	**Arrival**	**Fate**	**Notes**
Waco	C-2	Bomber	9 July		Improperly armed
Waco	C-3	Fighter-Bomber	14 July		Defected from Federals. *Waco Verde*. Armed with synchronised machine gun
Waco	C-5	Bomber	9 July		Unproperly armed
Potez	A-116	Bomber	9 July	Destroyed by bombing, 21-23 August	*Potez do Comandante*
Potez	A-212	Bomber	9 July	Destroyed by accident, 21 September	*Nosso Potez*. Made the only air kill of the war.
Nid-72	K-423	Fighter	20 August		Deserted from Federals
Falcon	*Taguató*	Bomber	25 August – 1 September		
Falcon	*Kyri-Kyri*	Bomber	25 August – 1 September		
Falcon	*Kaburé-Y*	Bomber	25 August – 1 September	Downed by anti-aircraft fire or accident, 24 September	
Falcon	*José Mario*	Bomber	24 September		
Federals					
Type	**N. Plate**	**Role**	**Arrival**	**Fate**	**Notes**
Potez	A-111	Bomber	9 July	Useless	Under repair
Potez	A-114	Bomber	9 July		
Potez	A-115	Bomber	9 July		
Potez	A-117	Bomber	9 July	Downed 8 August	Later repaired
Potez	A-119	Bomber	9 July	Useless	Under repair
Potez	A-211	Bomber	9 July		
Potez	A-214	Bomber	9 July	Useless	Under repair
Potez	A-216	Bomber	9 July		Crashed 27 July, later repaired
Potez	A-217	Bomber	9 July		
Waco	M	Fighter-Bomber	9 July		'M' for Military (armed version)
Waco	C-1	Fighter-Bomber	9 July	Crash landed, 5 August	Armed with synchronised machine gun
Waco	C-3	Fighter-Bomber	9 July	Defected to the Paulistas, 14 July	Armed with synchronised machine gun
Waco	C-4	Fighter-Bomber	9 July		Armed with synchronised machine gun
Waco	C-7	Fighter-Bomber	24 August		
Waco	C-8	Fighter-Bomber	24 August	Downed by anti-aircraft fire, 8 September	
Waco	C-9	Fighter-Bomber	24 August		
Waco	C-10	Fighter-Bomber	24 August		
Waco	C-11	Fighter-Bomber	24 August		
Waco	C-12	Fighter-Bomber	4-8 September		
Waco	C-13	Fighter-Bomber	4-8 September	Destroyed by bombing, 21 September	

(continued on page 84

(continued from page 83)

Since then, all Paulista citizens are proud of the involvement of

Table 20: Fate of Combat aircraft during the War

Waco	C-14	Fighter-Bomber	4-8 September		
Waco	C-15	Fighter-Bomber	4-8 September		
Waco	C-16	Fighter-Bomber	4-8 September		
Waco	C-17	Fighter-Bomber	13 September	Destroyed by bombing, 21 September	
Waco	C-18	Recce	13 September		Equipped with radio and camera
Waco	C-19	Fighter-Bomber	13 September		
Waco	C-20	Recce	13 September		Equipped with radio and camera
Waco	C-21	Recce	13 September		Equipped with radio and camera
Nid-72	K-422	Fighter	9 July		
Nid-72	K-423	Fighter	9 July	Defected to the Paulistas, 20 August	
Amiot 122	K-621	Bomber	9 July		Not cited in the sources. Perhaps under repair
Amiot 122	K-624	Bomber	9 July		Scarcely used
Martin PM-1	111	Recce, bomber	9 July		Seaplane
Martin PM-1	112	Recce, bomber	9 July	Sunk by accident, 12 September	Seaplane
SM. 55	1	Heavy bomber	9 July		Seaplane
SM. 55	4	Heavy bomber	9 July		Seaplane
SM. 55	8	Heavy bomber	9 July		Seaplane
SM. 55	6	Heavy bomber	9 July		Seaplane. Under repair
SM. 55	10	Heavy bomber	9 July		Under repair
SM. 55	11	Heavy bomber	9 July		Seaplane. Under repair
Corsair	1-0-2	Fighter	9 July	This (or 1-0-3) destroyed by accident, 20 August	
Corsair	1-0-3	Fighter	9 July	This (or 1-0-2) destroyed by accident, 20 August	
Corsair	1-0-4	Fighter	9 July		
Corsair	1-0-6	Fighter	9 July		

their grandparents in this war, the last Brazilian civil war and the last struggle which tried to preserve freedoms in Brazil.

This anonymous poster shows a Gaucho (note his hat and long boots, perhaps a call for rebellion to Rio Grande do Sul) handling Getulio Vargas, with a navy officer behind (in the white uniform) and with the Paulista flag. It has the legend: "Down with the Dictatorship". (Courtesy Eric Apolinario)

This is an anonymous MMDC Militia poster with the legend: "Paulista! I already honoured my duty, and you?" (Courtesy Eric Apolinario)

Another anonymous version of the famous US Army recruitment poster for the MMDC Milita with the legend: "You have a duty to honor. Consult with your conscience!" (Courtesy Eric Apolinario)

BIBLIOGRAPHY

(All in Brazilian, unless other language as noted)

Books

Anon., *Historia do Exercito Brasileiro* (Brasília: Estado Maior do Exercito, 1972)

Apolinário, Eric Lucian, *Inverno Escarlate* (São Paulo: Editora Gregory, 2018)

Caminha Giorgis, Luiz Eduardo, *Historia de la III Region Militar, Volume II* (Porto Alegre: Unknown Publisher)

Catalogo, *Revolução de 32, a Fotografía e a Política* (Funarte, 1982)

Coutinho, Lourival, *O General Goes Depoe* (Rio de Janeiro: Coelho Branco, 1956)

Daróz, Carlos Roberto Carvalho, (I) *Un Céu Cinzento* (Rio de Janeiero: Biblioteca do Exercito, 2017)

Donato, Hernani, (I) *A Revolução de 32* (São Paulo: Circulo do Livro, 1982)

Donato, Hernani, (II) *Dicionário das Batalhas Brasileiras* (São Paulo: Ibrasa, 1996)

Flores Jr, Jackson, *Aeronaves Militares Brasileiras* (Rio de Janeiro: Action Editora, 2016)

Garcia da Silveira, Ronan, *Historia de Coxim* (Coxim: Prefeitura de Coxim, 1995)

Hagedorn, Dan, *Latin American Air Wars 1912–1969* (Crowborough: Hikoki Publications, 2006) (English)

Hilton, Stanley, *1932, A Guerra Civil Brasileira* (Rio de Janeiro: NovaFronteira, 1982)

Ibanhes, Brígido, *Selvino Jacques, o último dosbandoleiros* (S. Paulo: Scortecci Editora, 1995)

Iglesias, Francisco, *Historia Contemporánea de Brasil* (Mexico: Fondo de Cultura Económica, 1999) (Spanish)

Jowett, Philip, *Latin American Wars 1900–1941* (Oxford: Osprey, 2018) (English)

McCann, Frank, *Soldiers of the Pátria* (Stanford: Stanford University Press, 2003) (English)

Paraná do Brasil, Irany, *1932, a Guerra de São Paulo* (São Paulo: Factash Editoria, 2006)

Passos, Rodolpho Emiliano, *Goiás de ontem* (Goiana: Author's edition, 1987)

Pereira Leite Neto, Luiz, *As Operaçoes Militares na Revolução de 1932* (Rio de Janeiro: Monografia Escola de Comando e Estado Maior do Exercito, ECEME, 1991)

Peres Zanetti, Sandro, *Intervenção do Exército no proceso político Brasileiro* (Rio de Janeiro: Escola de Comando e Estado Maior do Exercito Mareschal Castello Branco, 2009)

Puigari, Umberto, *Nas Fronteiras de Mato Grosso, Terra Abandonada* (São Paulo: Umberto Puigari, 1933)

Ramos, Antonio, *As Operaçoes Militares na Revolução de 1932* (Rio de Janeiro: Monografia ECEME, 1989)

Rodrigues, Jose Wasth and Barroso, Gustavo, *Uniformes do Exercito Brasileiro, 1730–1922* (Rio de Janeiro: Ministerio de Guerra, 1922)

Rodrigues, Lysias, *Gavioes de Penacho* (São Paulo: Tipografía Rossolillo, 1934)

Silva, Herculano de Carvalho, *A Revolução Constitucionalista* (São Paulo: Civilização Brasileira, 1932)

Articles

Camazano Alamino, Aparecido, 'Cores da Aviação Militar Brasileira', *Asas Magazine*, no. 70 (2012) <https.//issuu.com/revistaasas/docs/asas_70_virtual/3?ff>, accessed 2020.

Cotta, Francis Albert, 'As Trincheras da Mantiqueira', Policia Militar de Minas Gerais (2017) <https://revista.policiamilitar.mg.gov.br/index.php/alferes/article/view/120>, accessed 2017.

Daróz, Carlos Roberto Carvalho, (II) 'Aviação de caça e pesca?', *ll Seminario de Estudos: Poder Aeroespacial e Estudis Estrategicos* (Programa de Pos-graduacão em Ciencias Aeroespaciales – UNIFA, 2009).

Daróz, Carlos Roberyo Carvalho, (III) 'O Fantasma Da Morte – O Trem Blindado Paulista de 1932', (2010) <https://darozhistoriamilitar.blogspot.com/2010/05/o-fantasma-da-morte-o-trem-blindado.html?_sm_au_=iVV61S07NsGGnJWFj1q0vKscFs0qW>, accessed 2018.

Della Rosa, Ricardo, 'A Frente do Vale do Paraíba na Revolução de 1932', *Jornal o Lince* (2010), <http://www.jornalolince.com.br/2010/arquivos/panopticum-frente-vale-paraiba-revolucão-1932-www.jornãolince.com.br-edicão033.pdf>, accessed 2018.

García de Gabiola, Javier, 'São Paulo en armas', *Historia y Vida no 535* (Barcelona: Prisma, 2012) (Spanish).

Helio Lopes, Raimundo, 'Entre Militares e voluntarios: Os Batalhoes Provisorios cearenses', *Revista Brasileira de Historia Militar*, Year 1, no. 2 (August 2010), RBHMh.

Higuchi, Helio and Bastos Junior, Paulo Roberto, '1932 Combates entre Brasileiros'.

Juncal, Fabriciano, 'Batalhoes de Araçatuba', Museu Araça (2017) <http://museuaraca.blogspot.de/p/ata-e-revolucão-de-32.html>, accessed 2017.

Lintz Geraldo, Alcyr, 'Aviação no Conflito Constitucionalista de 1932', *Reservaer* (2008), <http://reservaer.com.br>, accessed 2017.

Maranhão, Ricardo, 'São Paulo 1932, Tecnología a Serviço da Revolução', *Netleland* (2008) <http://netleland.net/hasampa/epopeia1932/rev32tech.html>, accessed 2017.

Moreira Bento, Claudio (I), 'Operaçoes da Aviação do Exercito a partir de Resende, no combate a Revolução de 1932 no Vale de Paraíba e frente Mineira', *Docplayer* (2018), <https://docplayer.com.br/51398963-Operacoes-da-aviacão-do-exercito-a-partir-de-resende-no-combate-a-revolucão-de-1932-no-vale-do-Paraíba-e-frente-mineira.html>, accessed 2018.

Moreira Bento, Claudio (II), 'Os 70 Anos da Revolução Paulista de 1932', *O Guararapes*. CGC 10.149.526/0001-09 (2009), no. 35, Oct–Dec.

Oliveira Melo, Edilberto de, 'Historia da aviação da Força Pública Paulista – Parte 2', https://www.pilotopolicial.com.br/historia-da-aviacão-da-forca-publica-paulista-parte-2/>, accessed 2020.

Ribeiro, Arnor da Silva, 'Mundos de Silvino Jacques', Thesis and Dissertation, São Paulo University (2011) <https://teses.usp.br>, accessed 2018.

Ribeiro, Cassio, 'A Revolução Constitucionalista de 1932', *O Rebate* (2008), <http://orebate-cassioribeiro.blogspot.

com/2008/07/revoluo-constitucionalista-de-1932.html?_sm_au_=iVV61S07NsGGnJWFj1q0vKscFs0qW>, accessed 2016.

Righi, Sérgio, 'O Estado de Maracajú e o Movimento Constitucionalista de 1932', *Ultima Trincheira* (2018) <http://www.ultimatrincheira.com.br/maracaju.htm>, accessed 2018.

Silva Parreira, Luiz Eduardo (I), 'E o Sul do Mato Grosso foi às Armas!', *Polemologia* (2012) <https://polemologia.blogspot.com>, accessed 2019.

Silva Parreira (II), 'Tres Lagoas: O front esquecido da Revolução de 32 no sul do Mato Grosso', unpublished (2019).

Soares, Fidelis Julio Cesar, 'Calibre 32. Resende em Armas', Universidad Foral Ruiz de Fora, ECSB Defesa (2010) <http://www.ecsbdefesa.com.br/defesa/fts/CALIBRE32.pdf>, accessed 2017.

Walsh, Paul P., 'The Paulista War: An Example of Conventional Warfare in Latin America in the Inter-War Period', Conference held at the Military History Society (Calgary: unpublished, 2002) (English).

Web Pages

Arruda, Lucas, <https://www.campograndenews.com.br/lado-b/artes-23-08-2011-08/na-historia-desses-lados-do-brasil-o-estado-ja-teve-seu-proprio-lampião>, accessed 2021.

Dell Rosa, Ricardo, <www.tudoporSãopaulo.com.br>, collectable web page, now moved to Facebook, accessed 2016.

<www.desastresaeroes.net>.

<Jusbrasil.com.br>.

LAAHS: Latin American Aviation Historical Society, <http://laahs.com>.

<Naval.com.br>.

<www.revolvy.com>.

<www.rudnei.cunha.nom.br>.

Saito, Juniti, <https://www.revistãoperacional.com.br/ordem-do-dia-aniversario-marechal-do-ar-eduardo-gomes/>, accessed 2021.

Stephani Bastos, Expedito Carlos, <http://netleland.net/hsampa/epopeia1932/blindados1932.html/>, accessed 2020–21.

Vieira Pereira, Fernanda Cristina, Pires, Gilberto and Rodrigues Araújo, Cleia, <https://en.calameo.com/read/0040487225c2c91273761>, accessed 2020–21.

NOTES

Introduction and Errata

1 Oliveira Melo. See the fifth picture of a Nid, in the block of photos reproduced in Chapter 1, below the text. Consulted in April 2020 and February 2021.

2 Oliveira Melo. See the photo of a Falcon, below the text, reproduced in Chapter 1. Consulted in April 2020 and February 2021.

3 Rodrigues, p.16. It seems that the Paulistas could confuse the Federal Potez A-117 with the Paulista A-116, hence the plate number was visible at least on 8 August. Rodrigues, p.37, for the colours of the destroyed Potez.

4 Camazano Alamino, pp.30-31. Consulted on 9 April 2020.

5 Stephani Bastos. Accessed in 2020 and 2021.

Chapter 1

1 Silva, pp.149-150. Hilton, p.122.

2 Calculations made by the author of this work. Volunteer battalions used to have only some 200-300 soldiers, but we know that this one had 500 rifles, plus 200 troopers sent by the 8th BCP to the area, along with 100 for the riders of a cavalry squadron, and 50 men and four pieces for the artillery battery.

3 Hagedorn, Ch.12, p.18.

4 Daróz, pp.123, 127. Hilton, p.194. Rodrigues, p.7, for Lysias assuming the command of the group.

5 Hagedorn, Ch.12, p.18. Hilton, p.209.

6 Ramos, Annex E, p.A VIII.

7 Calculations made by the author of this work. Some 1,500 soldiers for the infantry regiment (three battalions), 500 per infantry battalion, and 200 soldiers and eight pieces per artillery group.

8 Ramos mentions here the 2nd BC, but we do not know if this information is correct: this unit belonged to the 1st Federal Division, based in Rio de Janeiro, and although it is possible that this battalion was sent by sea to Paraná, we consider it unlikely. Perhaps this is a wrong reference for the 7th, 8th or 9th BC of the 3rd Infantry Division, or perhaps it refers to the 2nd RCI or the 12th RCI that were part of the 1st or 3rd Cavalry Divisions. More probably, it could refer to the 2nd RC/Mixed Brigade of Rio Grande do Sul, cited on 22 July in the taking of Faxina.

9 Ramos, Annex E, p.E VIII.

10 Hilton, pp.121-122.

11 Silva, pp.150-154. Ramos, Annex E, p.E VIII and Map 10, p.33. Hilton, pp.121-123. General Lima constantly complained that his riders were operating without horses.

12 Silva, pp.150-154. Ramos, Annex E, p.E VIII and Map 10, p.33.

13 The presence of both units is somewhat puzzling. The 2nd RC/Rio Grande Brigade is not cited in any order of battle before. Maybe this is the mysterious 2nd BC mentioned before. Regarding the 3rd Battalion, the mystery is even greater. We do not know to which unit this battalion belonged. Perhaps it was part of the 13th RI, or maybe one of the battalions of the Military Brigade of Rio Grande do Sul.

14 Silva, pp.154-155. Ramos, p.34. Hilton, p.126.

15 Hilton, p.125.

16 Silva, p.155.

17 Ramos, Map 11, p.35.

18 Silva, pp.155-156. Silva, somewhat mischievously, insinuates that Moraes was being incompetent or lethargic with the absence of any counterattack, but from Ramos we know that he was being threatened by the forces of Boanerges, as we shall see later. Hilton, pp.125-126, 194.

19 Donato, p.136.

20 Ramos, pp.3-4.

21 Calculations made by this author: about 500 soldiers per Federal battalion, 300 per Paulistas unit, 100 per company and artillery battery and 50 per artillery section.

22 Ramos, p.34.
23 Silva, pp.157-158. Ramos, p.31, for the Pinhalzinho action. Hilton, p.126.
24 Silva, pp.159-160, 162, for the issues of Detachment Tenorio and Colonel Barbosa. Silva also for the deployment of Federal troops in the siege and for the rescue attempt from Guapiara. For Boanerges' actions, see Ramos, p.36 and Map 12.
25 Donato, p.136.
26 Silva, pp.160-161.
27 Silva, pp.160-161. Hilton, p.127.
28 Silva, p.199. Ramos, Map 16.
29 Silva, pp.200-202.
30 Ramos, p.30, says in early July, but Silva says that it was in late July. We follow him due to his detailed explanation.
31 Silva, pp.202-203.
32 Hilton, p.127. The author of this work estimates about 2,000 soldiers, a similar figure to the official one.
33 Donato, Map, p.139.
34 Ramos, pp.30-31.
35 Silva, p.203.
36 Donato, Map, p.139.
37 Ramos, pp.34, 37 and Map 16. See Hilton, p.127, for the Catupera action, and p.311 for the revolt of the 3rd RC. Paraná do Brasil, p.128, nevertheless states that the rebellion was on 13 September.
38 Silva, p.203. Hilton, p.127, for Itaporanga.
39 Paraná do Brasil, pp.126-128.
40 Paraná do Brasil, p.133.
41 Hilton, p.127, citing Lima. According to my calculations, there could be about 2,000 men, a lower figure.
42 Paraná do Brasil, pp.134-136.
43 Ramos, pp.40, 43, 44 and Map 16.
44 Paraná do Brasil, p.138.
45 Silva, p.203.
46 Ramos, p.44 and Map 16.
47 Hilton, p.127. In my view there were about 2,000 men, a similar figure.
48 Donato, map of Jorge Mancini, p.139. For Playsant, see Silva, p.203. Troop calculations made by me.
49 Hilton, p.127.
50 Daróz, p.136, Hagedorn, Ch.12, p.12. Hilton, p.198, but he states that the pilot was França. Lintz Geraldo, p.2.
51 Rodrigues, pp.8-11. Daróz, pp.136-137. Hagedorn, Ch.12, p.19. Hilton, pp.208, 218. Donato, p.140. Rodrigues mentions the Potez A-212 attacking the Federal Potez A-117, on 28 July. Daróz does not mention the missions of 26 and 27 July, but directly places the Paulista airfield attack on 26 July. Hagedorn, however, does mention these missions, and places the attack on the 28th. Donato is not very reliable for air actions, but he mentions a Paulista attack on Faxina with the same pilot and observer as mentioned by the other authors in a Potez A-212 that damaged the Potez A-116 on the ground (instead of the Potez A-211), on 28 September. It seems that Donato was wrong with the number of the Potez damaged, and mistakenly mentions September instead of July, but it seems to refer to this 28 July attack, thus giving perhaps the reason indirectly to Rodrigues and Hagedorn, whom we follow. On the other hand, here Hagedorn speaks of two Paulista Potez aircraft attacking, but Dároz and Major Lysias only talk about one Potez. So, it seems that both authors are right here. Related to the attacked Potez, Rodrigues is wrong, as it was not the A-117, but the A-211. Later, Daróz speaks of the second Federal mission when the landing gear broke, while according to Hagedorn it would be the fourth. Finally, the damage of the Federal Potez when landing is omitted by Hagedorn. Lintz Geraldo, pp.2, 6, says erroneously that on 28 July, the Federal Potez was destroyed on the ground.
52 Hilton, p.209. Lintz Geraldo, p.6, for the reconnaissance missions.
53 Daróz, pp.139, 141-142. See Hilton, p.198, for the complaints from Vadomiro Lima. Hagedorn, Ch.12, p.22. However, for the A-211, Hagedorn states that it was still under repair, so according to him the support missions were carried out by the Potez A-117. See Hilton, p.209, for the Buri train and the Potez A-211.
54 Rodrigues, p.13. Daróz, p.143. Hagedorn, Ch, 12, p.22.
55 Rodrigues, pp.15-16. Daróz, pp.143, 145. Daróz II, p.255, does not clarify whether the aircraft was destroyed or not. Hagedorn, Ch, 12, p.22; Lintz Geraldo, pp.2, 6; Lintz Geraldo, p.2, and Garcia de Gabiola, p.66, claim that the aircraft was not destroyed. Moreira Bento, p.6, says that the aircraft was destroyed. Concerning the action, Lysias Rodrigues, cited also by Daróz, does not clarify who was the author of the downing, he or his gunner, something that we know from Hagedorn. Also, Lysias mentions the Potez A-212, but then changes it to the A-116, that according to him was not present as it was having its engine cleaned. Also, with the distance, he meant that it was not easy to distinguish between the Federal and the Paulista Potez due to their near equal plates (A-116 and A-117). This implies that at least until the beginning of August, the Paulista aircrafts still had not got their white bands covering their plate numbers.
56 Hilton, pp.209, 210. It's not clear whether Lysias (Rodrigues, pp.19-21) refers also to this action when he narrates that three Wacos and a Nid, under Adherbal, strafed the enemy infantry and cavalry columns. Probably he is mixing this action with another one made at the end of August, as we will see, as the Nid and Adherbal only arrived at the Paulista lines later, and as Lysias says that he was in Mato Grosso waiting for the new Paulista Falcons, something that also happened at the end of August.
57 Daróz, p.142, says that the Potez A-114 arrived on 5 August, but it seems that there were no more Federal aircraft in the skies at the time of the downing of the Potez A-117, except perhaps for the A-211, which was damaged, so it was not in the combat on 8 August. Consequently, we rely on Hagedorn, Ch.12, p.23, which talks about the Potez's arrival on 11 August. Another possibility is that both authors are right about the Potez A-114, and it arrived on 5 August, but that it was operating only on 11 August. Hagerdorn, concerning the downed Potez A-117, says contradictorily and wrongly that it arrived later. Lintz Geraldo, p.2, says that two Corsairs arrived. Then, between 5 and 11 August, two more Potez aircraft came, followed by a third Potez on 24 August, two Wacos on 1 September, and throughout September another two Corsairs. Hilton, p.209, states that Petit was in the south with three aircraft on 12 August.
58 Daróz says that the two Corsairs arrived in the first week of August, but again we rely here more on Hagedorn, Ch.12, p.23, because as we have said, these fighters, with a speed of 269km/h, if present, would had been escorting the Potez that was shot down on 8 August. Perhaps they arrived earlier but were only operating on 12 August.
59 Daróz, pp.142-143. Hagedorn, Ch.12, p.23.
60 Daróz, pp.145-146. According to Hilton, p.198, these were one Corsair followed by two more, following Cardoso's instructions dated 31 July and 6 August.
61 Hilton, pp.209, 218.
62 Ramos, p.47, and Annex J, p.A XXI.
63 Silva, p.163.

64 We have a report a few days later, on 15 August, that give between 930 and 1,030 soldiers for five battalions and a squadron.
65 Donato, p.136, mentions Mascarenhas' artillery and fixes the date of the attack on 13 August. Ramos, pp.37, 47, states the combat was on 12-13 August and mentions Jardim Squadron. As the Federal counteroffensive was on the 15th and 16th, it is probable that Silva mistakenly mentioned 15 August for the Paulista attack.
66 Silva, p.163.
67 Ramos, p.39, Map 13.
68 Hilton, p.140.
69 Ramos, Appendix F, pp.A X, A XI.
70 Donato, pp.136, 146, for the figure of 6,000 Federal soldiers.
71 Donato, p.147.
72 Donato, p.136, surprisingly mentions battalions which are not listed in the order of battle from Ramos. Donato mentions the 16th BC Santa Catarina, but this unit was based in Mato Grosso, so perhaps he refers to the Police Battalion of Santa Catarina that is mentioned in the order of battle from Ramos, Annex F. See Silva, pp.163-164. For the aviation, see Hilton, p.204.
73 Donato, p.137.
74 Ramos, p.48.
75 Silva, pp.163-164. Ramos, p.48.
76 Ramos, p.37.
77 Ramos, Annex F, pp.A XII, XIII. Ramos cites the II/13th and II/8th Battalions at full strength, but they should each be only perhaps half or one-third strength, as these units are cited again in two and three other detachments respectively. Hilton, pp.127-128, for the casualties.
78 Ramos, Annex L, p.A XXII.
79 Hagedorn, Ch.12, p.24. Daróz, p.147, 14 August in Campo de Marte.
80 Daróz, p.149.
81 Daróz, p.149.
82 Lintz Geraldo, p.2.
83 Daróz, p.148. Hagedorn, Ch.12, p.24.
84 Hagedorn, Ch.12, p.25.
85 Lintz Geraldo, p.6. Rodrigues, pp.19-21, seems to place this action on 9 August, but that is wrong, as he mentions that Lysias and Gomes Ribeiro received the Falcons near Paraguay at the end of the month. Also, he mentions the Nid, that also defected in late August and whose pilot, Adherbal, was acting as commander of the aviation. He goes on to mention, apart from the Nid, three Wacos flown by Motta and Mario, Camargo and Leite, and Silvio and Hugo Neves. The strange issue is that these aircraft used the first pilot seat to mount their machine guns, so with two pilots per aircraft they could not fire at enemy troops due to their lack of weapons. Perhaps they were bombing rather than firing at these troops, or they were using hand weapons. Rodrigues mentions several attacks on cavalry or infantry, but he probably confused the objective, as Lintz Geraldo instead mentions bombing actions in Buri that are compatible with using two pilots per aircraft.
86 Lintz Geraldo, p.6, mentions that three Wacos departed from Resende for Minas to take part in the battle. He adds that they retreated to Itapetininga. From Hagedorn, Ch.12, p.25, we know that they stayed in Itapira at least until 26 August. Finally, from Donato, p.139, we know that there were three Paulista aircraft which bombed the area of Fundão in the south, which were probably the three Wacos who had fought in Itapira, Minas.
87 Donato, p.139, mentions only three aircraft without naming the type. Perhaps this was the action commented on by Rodrigues, pp.19-21, as he mentions three Wacos with six pilots, one of them being Silvio Hoeltz, covered by Adherbal in his Nid-72.
88 Lintz Geraldo, p.6.
89 Daróz, pp.153, 155. Daróz II, p.250, says in late August. Lintz Geraldo, p.2, says on 1 September.
90 Hilton, p.210.
91 Hilton, p.199. Rodrigues, pp.25-29, for the details of the fighting.
92 Daróz, p.165.
93 Hilton, p.210.
94 Daróz, p.168.
95 Lintz Geraldo, p.2, mentions the arrival of two Corsairs, but there were only four in total: two had already arrived, and we know that one of them was destroyed in an accident, so we have reduced it to just one more.
96 Hilton, p.209.
97 Donato, p.139, for the figures.
98 Ramos, pp.41, 48-49, Maps 14 and 16.
99 Donato, pp.136, 139. Lintz Geraldo, pp.2, 6, for the types.
100 Silva, p.164. Ramos, pp.41, 48-49, Maps 14 and 16.
101 Hilton, p.127, for the date.
102 Ramos, Annex F, cites the II Battalion/8th RI, but it should be just part of it, perhaps a third, as it is also cited in two other detachments.
103 Silva, pp.165-166. Ramos, pp.50-51, Maps 14 and 18.
104 The 1st, 2nd and 3rd BC belonged to the 1st Division, which fought in the Paraíba, so it is unlikely that these units were on the Southern Front. On the other hand, in other orders of battle from Ramos, he mentions two battalions of Cazadores of the Pernambuco Police. The 3rd Pernambuco and 1st Rio Grande do Sul were probably received as reinforcements in September, as they are not mentioned in the order of battle but are on the Map.
105 pp.40, 42, Map 15; also pp.50, 51 and Annex G.
106 Ramos, p.52, Map 18 and Annex M.
107 Due to the attrition and fragmentation of the units, here we have calculated them on 200 men per battalion and 100 per company. These numbers are consistent with the available data for the second and third battles of Buri.
108 For the three paragraphs, see Ramos, p.52, Map 19 and Annexes G and M.
109 Hilton, pp.121, 109.
110 Ramos, pp.43, 53.
111 Silva, p.168.
112 Ramos, pp.43, 53.
113 Donato, p.137, cites Captain Gomes' action erroneously in the Battle of Buri, but no unit from Paraná participated in this battle, and the Damião Ferreira bridge is in the area of the Das Almas River, far to the south-east, so we have placed this later, in the Das Almas River action.
114 Donato, p.143, Jorge Mancini's Map.
115 Ramos, pp.43, 53 and Annex H.
116 Donato, p.142.
117 Silva, p.167.
118 Ramos, pp.43, 53 and Annex I. Silva, p.167. Donato, p.143, Jorge Mancini's Map.
119 Ramos, pp.43, 53.
120 Donato, pp.144, 142.
121 Ramos, pp.44, 45, Map 17, and p.53.
122 Hilton, p.121. Maranhão, p.3, talks also of 18,000 Federals and about 8,000 rebels.

Chapter 2

1 Hilton, pp.312-315.
2 http://www.naval.com.br/ngb/F/F022/F022.htm.

3 Hilton, pp.308-309.
4 Donato, p.150.
5 Donato, p.140. Hilton, p.309.
6 Donato, p.151. Hilton, p.310.
7 Giorgis, pp.208-211.
8 Hilton, p.310.
9 Giorgis, Vol. II, p.243.
10 Hilton, p.310. Giorgis, pp.232, 243. Donato, p.146.
11 Donato, p.148.
12 Hilton, p.311.
13 Hilton, p.311.
14 Donato, p.150.
15 Giorgis, p.245.
16 Donato, pp.148, 150.
17 Hilton, p.312. Donato, p.148.
18 Hagedorn, Ch.12, p.22.
19 Ramos, p.59.
20 Wikipedia, article about Sylvio Van Erven.

Chapter 3

1 Juncal, p.1.
2 Juncal, p.1.
3 Decree 21,953, 13 October 1932 (www.jusbrasil.com.br.). In this decree, the 6th BE was dissolved at the end of the war, hence it had revolted.
4 Garcia da Silveira, p.171.
5 Juncal, p.1.
6 Righi, p.1.
7 Donato, p.148. Ramos, p.57.
8 Silva, pp.313, 119-122. Righi, p.1. For the Matogrossenses reinforcements, Silva Parreira (II).
9 Ramos, p.25. According to Silva Parreira (II), Carvalinho commanded a group of thieves, and not any military unit.
10 Hilton, pp.116-117, and n.48, p.344. Ramos, p.25.
11 Silva, p.119.
12 Righi, p.1.
13 Silva Parreira (II).
14 Silva, pp.119-122. Passos, p.96.
15 Passos, p.96.
16 Passos, pp.105, 112. Barbosa, p.174. Righi, p.1. Silva Parreira (II) for the number of soldiers and Noronha.
17 Ramos, p.56.
18 Daróz, p.159.
19 Donato, p.150.
20 Silva Ribeiro, p.91. Donato, p.148. Pereira Leite Neto, p.39, and Ramos, p.56. Interestingly, none of these authors cite the 6th Engineers Battalion (BE), but the 6th BC, which is wrong. The 6th BE was based in Aquidauana (where Donato mentions wrongly the barracks of the 6th BC, which was actually located in Uberaba, in Minas Gerais; it was the only unit of the 2nd Division which did not rebel against the government). Therefore, we understand that this is the BE instead of the BC.
21 Silva Ribeiro, pp.82, 85.
22 Ramos, p.59. Donato, p.148. The origin of the 'Bronze Column' is not clear. Although it seemed in principle to be composed of local elements, both Ramos and Donato agree that it came from Campo Grande. Pereira Leite Neto instead says that it was made up of forces coming from Campo Grande, Tres Lagoas and even Baurú, in São Paulo (presumably referring in the latter case to the Paulista troops sent from Baurú to Campo Grande and Tres Lagoas). On the other hand, in *Historia do Exercito Brasileiro*, p.944, it is said that the 'Bronze Column' had been created with local troops from Dourados and Ponta Porã. See also Moreira Bento II. Probably all these are correct.
23 State Public Archives, Bulletin No. 2 of the Commission of Ponta Porã in Mato Grosso do Sul, A 30 Years Path, p.50.
24 Silva Ribeiro, pp.87, 90–91. For the 6th BCP and the commander of the 11th RCI, see Silva, p.122. However, according to Silva Parreira, p.1, both the 11th RCI and the 'Taunay' Battalion were sent to the Paulistas, reinforcing the Southern Front.
25 Ramos, p.56.
26 Do not confuse this Kiki Barbosa Martins with Henrique Barbosa Martins, who brought the 'Gato Preto' Battalion to the Tres Lagoas Sector.
27 Silva Ribeiro, pp.86–88. Silva Parreira, p.1.
28 Silva Ribeiro, pp.83, 86–87, 92.
29 Moreira Bento, p.10, Lintz Geraldo, p.4, and Hilton, Ch.12, p.10, talk about just nine aircrafts, but if we take into account that one aircraft crashed before the delivery (Hilton, p.10, and Moreira, p.10), another was kept in Paraguayan hands, another was destroyed in combat and eventually the Federal government recovered seven aircrafts, the final number should be 10 machines. Flores Jr, p.456, also speaks of 10 aircraft. Daróz, pp.72, 155, only speaks about the three aircraft that entered into action.
30 Moreira Bento, p.10, and Hagedorn, Ch.12, p.10. This fact is not mentioned by any other author.
31 Moreira Bento, p.10, changes the order and states that two Falcons arrived at Encarnación, but a third one crashed en route and a fourth was held by Paraguay. Nevertheless, Hilton, p.267, gives us the date of the Paraguayan incident, 25 August, so it had to be before the arrival of the other aircrafts.
32 Hilton, p.267. Flores Jr, p.456, indirectly seems to refer also to one aircraft. Moreira Bento, p.10, talks about two aircraft arriving at Encarnación, and not one, as does Hagedorn, Ch.12, p.10, also adding that they arrived on 1 September.
33 We know of this accident from Moreira Bento, p.10, and Linz Geraldo, p.5, but the name of the aircraft is omitted. Della Rosa on his web page states in a generic way that the *Taguató* was lost on land, so it could be to a bombing, but we do not have any record about this, so perhaps this was the aircraft damaged when synchronizing its weapons. Lysias also mentions the *Taguató* as destroyed, not giving any explanation about this (Rodrigues, p.59).
34 Moreira Bento, p.10, and Linz Geraldo, p.5. Hilton, for the retention in Mato Grosso.
35 Hilton, pp.264-268. Hagerdorn, Ch 12, pp.10-11.
36 Hagedorn, Ch.12, p.25. Donato, p.150. Flores Jr, p.456, is not clear whether this was on 2 or 3 September.
37 Lintz Geraldo, p.6, mentions that the Paulistas were waiting until 5 September. He confuses the *Negrinho* with one of the Falcons. Hagedorn, Ch 12, p.25.
38 Hagedorn, Ch.12, pp.5, 10-11, for the four Falcons received on 28 September, and for the seven available after the war. Flores Jr, p.456, for the names of the aircraft.
39 Hagedorn, Ch.12, p.25. Daróz, pp.158-159, for the deployment of the Avro. For the performance of the aircraft, Daróz, pp.89, 93.
40 Daróz, p.159.
41 Ramos, p.57.
42 Ibanhes, pp.84, 86. Donato, p.148, says that there was even combat with bayonets and knives.
43 Donato, p.148.
44 Ramos, p.57, and Puigari, p.190.

45 Ramos, p.57, Puigari, p.190. Silva Parreira, p.1, speaks of 1,200 Federal soldiers.
46 Puigari, p.190.
47 Donato, p.150. Ramos, p.57. Silva Ribeiro, pp.88-91. Hilton, p.142. Puigari, p.190.
48 Hilton, p.303.
49 Silva Ribeiro, p.91. Donato, p.150.
50 Daróz, pp.159-160, says that these were the same three initial Paulista Falcons, but the *Taguató* was destroyed when trying to synchronise its machine guns and the *Kaburé-Y* exploded on 24 September when attacking the cruiser *Rio Grande do Sul*. Therefore, these aircraft could only be the *Kyri-Kyri* and two new specimens, perhaps the *José Mario* and *Taguató* (if it was repaired). See also naval.br.com for the same facts and the October date. Also Moreira Bento, p.10.

Chapter 4

1 Ramos, p.25.
2 Daróz, p.110.
3 Silva, p.313. Maranaho, p.3, talks about 8,000 Paulistas.
4 Ramos, p.25.
5 Hilton, pp.117, 118. See Donato, p.126, for Ribeirão Preto.
6 Cotta, p.2.
7 Silva, p.253.
8 Apolinário, p.48. This author mentions a report made by Lieutenant Stênio to his superiors, Colonel Pinheiro and Major Pedro, but he does not mention any General Esteve who gave the name to the detachment, a general would not be under the control of a colonel and a major, so perhaps this data is wrong or 'General Esteve' was only an honorary name.
9 Cotta, p.2.
10 Coutinho, p.196.
11 Cotta, pp.4, 9. Taking into account that Minas Gerais had 20 battalions equipped during the war (Hilton, p.174), and that seven of them would be deployed in the South Brigade, with 3,289 troops (Cotta, pp.4, 9), we can assume that the other 13 units, once divided by half between the North and Central Brigades, would have about 3,000 more troops in each formation.
12 Silva, p.313. Despite this author assuming that the 6th BC was based in Uberaba, Apolinário, p.75 and in the rest of his work constantly mentions this unit as being deployed in Goiás.
13 Ramos, p.25, and Hilton, p.113.
14 Silva, p.313.
15 Hilton, p.117, Ramos, p.25.
16 Silva, p.251.
17 Paraná do Brasil, pp.95, 98-99, 101.
18 Apolinário, pp.48-50.
19 Hilton, p.199.
20 Apolinário, p.64.
21 Silva, pp.174-175, 252-253. The 1st Romão Battalion, the 11th Mineiro Battalion and the dead are quoted by Donato, p.148. See Apolinário, pp.54-55, for the composition of the vanguard attacking Pouso Alegre. The Federals, exaggerating, talked about 1,000 Paulistas attacking. Silva says that the defenders were the 12th RI, but this information is contradicted by Apolinário, pp.51-52, 59-63, which mention the other units stated in the text. Here we trust Apolinário rather than Silva, as the latter, being a Paulista combatant, has less trustworthy information about the Federals, as we will see several times. Also, the RAM unit was already based in Pouso Alegre, but not the 12th RI.
22 Donato, p.150. Apolinário, pp.63, 66, for the total losses.
23 Paraná do Brasil, pp.100, 107, 112. Apolinário, pp.51-52, 59-63.
24 Silva, pp.176-177, 254-255.
25 At least 1,500 soldiers are cited by Silva, as we shall see, as fugitives from the front after the loss of Itapira, a month later.
26 Paraná do Brasil, p.112. Apolinário, p.68, for the Barretos Leme Battalion.
27 Apolinário, pp.70, 74.
28 Daróz, pp.138-139.
29 Silva, pp.256-260. Also, Federal reinforcements to Barcelos in Hilton, p.159, and the Esteve Detachment in Apolinário, p.75.
30 Donato, p.139. Hilton p.149.
31 Hilton, p.149.
32 Apolinário, pp.77-78, 81-82.
33 Hilton, p.149. Apolinário, p.83.
34 Silva, pp.260-261, 177-178. Paraná do Brasil, p.112. Apolinário, pp.88-89.
35 Hagedorn, Ch.12, p.22.
36 Daróz, p.147.
37 Hagedorn, Ch.12, p.24.
38 Silva, pp.170-181. Donato, p.140.
39 Apolinário, p.93.
40 Silva, pp.170-181, 262. Apolinário, p.95.
41 Hilton, p.140.
42 Hagedorn, Ch.12, pp.24-25. Daróz, pp.151-152.
43 According to Hilton, p.211, since 21 August, although this author also antedates the air actions at Itapira in late August.
44 Hagedorn, Ch.12, pp.24-25. Daróz, pp.148, 151-152. Some authors say that on 24 August, a newcomer rebel Falcon was strafed at Guaratinguetá, but this probably refers to the destroyed Potez A-116 on 23 August, as the Falcons did not arrive until September.
45 Apolinário, p.97.
46 Silva, p.262, cites the II RI, but he must refer to the 11th and not the 2nd with Roman numerals.
47 Silva, p.262.
48 Apolinário, pp.99-101, 134.
49 See the entire battle in Silva, pp.263-264. Hilton, pp.140-141. For the Federal troops, Apolinário, pp.109-118.
50 Donato, p.145.
51 Apolinário, pp.121, 134.
52 Daróz, pp.234-35. Hagedorn, Ch.12, p.25, says that these brilliant Paulista air actions were made to prevent the fall of Itapira, when in fact this action happened a little earlier, on the Eleutério front. Silva, p.264. Lintz Geraldo, p.6. Hilton, pp.211, 197, perhaps is wrong to say on 21 August, but he confirms the actions on 27 August.
53 Hagedorn, Ch.12, p.25.
54 Captain Adherbal used to handle the Nid-72 fighter, so we may include it in the list. The other six pilots could be in three double-seater aircrafts. We have only the three available Wacos (C-2, C-3 and C-5) and a Potez (A-212, as the A-116 was destroyed on 23 August). As on 21 August we have seen deployed in Mogi Mirim two Wacos, the Potez A-212 and the Nid-72, probably these were the acting aircrafts. If the Wacos had two pilots each, probably they were bombing rather than machine gunning the Federals, as their front seat had to be used to install the machine gun (unless they were using hand weapons).
55 Especially Daróz, pp.152-153. Moreira Bento, p.6. Hilton, p.198, says erroneously that in Pouso Alegre all available Wacos were concentrated.
56 Silva, pp.265-267. Apolinário, pp.130-132, for the allegations of treason made against Hygino.
57 Silva, p.268.

58 Apolinário, p.152, mentions, for example, the Piratininga, the Volunteers of Piratininga, Legiao Negra, Rio Grande do Norte, 9 de Julho, General Osorio, Guarda Civil, Esportivo, Voluntarios Professores, sapper company, the 6th RI, Anhanguera, Americana, Pinhalense, Rio Claro Volunteers Battalions, Chico Vieira and Newton Prado Cavalry Squadrons, but they were all near depleted and probably mixed with other units, creating ad hoc task forces.

59 Apolinário, pp.145-149.

60 Hilton, pp.140, 159. Helio Lopes, p.17, for the Ceará units.

61 Silva, p.268.

62 Hilton, p.159.

63 Silva, pp.268-270. Hilton, pp.141-142, 159.

64 Silva, pp.271-172.

65 Silva, pp.273-276, and Apolinário, p.180, state that this day a Federal aircraft was was shot down, data not mentioned in any specialized source about the air battles of this war: the only anti-aircraft downing occurred later, on 13 September. Helio Lopes, p.18, and Apolinário, pp.160, 183, for the Ceará unit. Hilton, pp.141-142.

66 Silva, pp.185-187.

67 Hilton, p.141.

68 Donato, p.142.

69 Silva, pp.188-190. See Donato, p.140, for the Federal troops and the final fall of the position.

70 Silva, p.195.

71 Silva, pp.280-281.

72 Silva, pp.282-283. See Apolinário for the troops of the Dutra Detachment.

73 Silva, pp.284-286. See Donato, p.136, for the Santos, Dutra and Vargas Battalions. The Ceará Provisional Battalion is quoted by Helio Lopes, p.18.

74 Hilton, pp.149, 350.

75 Apolinário, p.194.

76 Daróz, pp.161-162. Daróz II states that the date was 13 September and that it was the anti-aircraft artillery deployed on the train which produced the downing. However, the website desastreasaereos.net says that it was an accident and not a downing. Maybe the aircraft exploded when it went into a dive, which would explain the 4,000 metres affirmed by the press, as perhaps happened to one of the Falcons later when it attacked a Federal cruiser (see Volume 1). Donato, p.138, states the date wrongly as 17 August.

77 Moreira Bento, p.10. The name of this aircraft is not mentioned, but we may deduct it was the *Taguató*, which is not mentioned in the sources in any action, and that cryptically is only mentioned as destroyed on the ground (Della Rosa, www.tudoporSãopaulo.com, retrieved 9 August 2016).

78 Daróz, p.165.

79 Silva, p.278. Helio Lopes, p.18, for Ceará.

80 Apolinário, pp.201-202.

81 Silva, pp.279-280. Apolinário, pp.202-206, 217, for Dutra manoeuvre, Alkindar and Pedra Detachments.

82 Silva, p.329.

83 Hilton, p.145.

84 Vieira, slides 16–18.

85 Silva, pp.330-331, wrongly mentions the Esteve, Dutra and Dornelles Detachments. Silva based his work exclusively from Paulista sources, and this data comes from information received about the Federal forces from the Paulista Sector commander, with very limited and puzzling information about the forces of his enemies. Lourival Coutinho, pp.210-212, instead, cites Góis Monteiro, the Federal commander, who speaks of the Dutra, Cristovão (Barcelos) and Paes de Andrade Detachments, so this information deserves more confidence. Surprisingly, a large number of authors seem to follow the faulty feedback from Silva instead of that from Countinho. Unfortunately, the latter author does not clarify the exact place of deployment of each unit, so we lack the information to properly track the movements of the Federal units in the Minas sector. Apolinário, p.202, states that Andrade was the 4th Division Chief of Staff, so perhaps this detachment did not exist in the end, or it was formed even later.

86 Silva, pp.330-332.

87 Cotta, p.9.

88 Hilton, p.210.

89 Silva, pp.326-328.

90 Silva, pp.332-334, 287-288. Apolinário, pp.208, 213-214, 217, for the Federal troops and the 23 Maio troops.

91 Silva, pp.337-338. Apolinário, pp.221, 228, 230, for the Federal troops.

92 Daróz, pp.165-166. Donato, p.137. Hagedorn, Ch.12, p.27, cites reports from the US Consul about the bombing of Campinas on 15 and 18 September. Hilton, p.216, says that the bombing was on 19 instead of 18 September, and on 20 September he mentions an attack made by five Wacos, but we know that there were only three aircrafts operating in Minas, unless they had received reinforcements from the Paraíba Front. Hilton, p.218, speaks of the bombing of Lorena. For the name and model of the cannon, see Fidelis Soares, p.5.

93 Concerning the Green Waco, we do not know its number plate, nor the fate of the other two Paulista Wacos. Related to these last two, they were probably out of service or not destined for armed missions, as they had no machine guns installed and we have no reference of any mission with them for weeks previously. The only Waco active was the one identified by its green colour. This was probably the Waco C-3, which defected from the government and was the only correctly armed Waco on the Paulista side.

94 Hagedorn, Ch.12, p.26, and Hilton, p.221, are the only ones to cite this previous mission. Lintz Geraldo, p.6, reverses the order and states that the main attack was on 20 September, and on the 21st a second attack was made.

95 Rodrigues, pp.46-47, says that this dogfight happened on 21 September, but as he states that this occurred one day before the final attack over Mogi Mirim, this probably happened on 20 September. Lintz Geraldo, p.7, also refers to this combat, probably following Rodrigues, but again confuses the *Negrinho* with a Falcon. Daróz, p.243, also mentions the combat, following Rodrigues, but gives no date. Daróz, p.218, mentions this dogfight as being a different one, based on an edition of *A Gazeta* dated 22 September (hence the dogfight happened before, on the 20th or 21st). So Daróz clearly refers with these two dogfights to the same action narrated by Rodrigues. As the dogfighting narrated in *A Gazeta* was seen from ground level, the details are slightly different to Rodrigues' report, something that perhaps confused Daróz. The *A Gazeta* reproduced by Daróz states that the Federal Waco was going to bomb Fazenda Ataíba, Campinas, when the São Paulo aviation emerged from the clouds and attacked him. A rebel device began climbing, and with his speed being lost in the effort, the Federal aircraft tried to escape by diving, so the Paulista aircraft also dived to strafe him, climbed, and then returned to strafe him again, in what looks like the description of a bounce. The Federal aircraft then suffered a violent fall and the engine failed, perhaps damaged by the enemy fire, but after descending, he managed to balance his device and escape.

96 Daróz, p.168, mentions the attack to Mogi Mirim as made on 21 September. Rodrigues, p.48, says it was on 22 September, but he is wrong, as Daróz, p.294, note 177, also mentions a telegram sent by Góis Monteiro reporting the attack that is dated 21 September. Daróz, p.218, also mentions that a dogfight happened the day before the attack, and the *A Gazeta*, the newspaper that talked about it, was edited on the 22nd. Nevertheless, this dogfight could have happened the day before, but also several days before the newspaper's date, so in the end it does not contradict the date of Góis' telegram.

97 Rodrigues, pp.48-50. Daróz, p.168, Daróz II, p.203. Lintz, p.6, who follows Rodrigues, puts Silvio with Abílio in the Nid (in reality a Falcon), but it seems he confused Silvio with Lysias. Moreira Bento, p.7, reports the names of the lieutenants handling the two destroyed aircraft. Lintz, p.6, says instead that five aircraft were destroyed and again confuses the Nid-72 *Negrinho* with one of the Falcons. Donato, p.140, wrongly says that the date was 20 September, mentioning only three Paulistas aircraft that destroyed up to five Federal ones. Hilton, p.221, says that three aircraft were destroyed and two damaged. García de Gabiola, p.65, in a previous work, generically talked about five aircraft damaged or destroyed, following Hilton. Hilton, p.212, and Rodrigues, pp.49–50, say that a Federal Waco was able to take off during the massive attack.

98 Hagedorn, Ch.12, pp.26-27. Hilton, p.221.

99 Daróz, p.168. Moreira Bento, p.7, states wrongly that *Nosso Potez* was destroyed in a bombing of Guaratinguetá on 23 September. Rodrigues, p.10, clarifies that the Potez A-212 was later called *Nosso Potez*. Rodrigues, pp.45-46, clarifies that the accident happened in the morning before the Mogi Mirim attack, and also mentions the departing aerodrome of this aircraft. He states that this happened on 21 September, but as he puts the Mogi Mirim attack wrongly on the 22nd, perhaps his 21 September date is also wrong and it should be one day before.

100 Daróz, p.167.

101 General Rabelo, even though he had turned over Mato Grosso do Sul, still had his headquarters in Uberaba, in the Mineiro Triangle, in August and September (Hilton, p.197).

102 Silva, p.341.

103 Silva, pp.341-42.

104 Ramos, p.26. Lourival Coutinho, pp.211-212. Helio Lopes. p.18.

105 Apolinário, pp.231-243.

Chapter 5

1 Donato, pp.154-156. Hilton, pp.319-321.

2 Donato, p.157-160. Hilton, p.322.

3 Donato, pp.160-164. Hilton, p.323.

4 Donato, pp.164-165. Hilton, p.323.

5 Donato, pp.166-167.

6 Donato, pp.167–71. Hilton, p.324.

7 Jowett, p.34. Cassio Ribeiro, p.28. Donato, p.172.

8 Daróz, p.262.

9 Calculation made at a ratio of about four wounded for each dead.

10 Hilton, pp.325-330. Iglesias, pp.51-68. García de Gabiola, p.65.

ABOUT THE AUTHOR

Javier Garcia de Gabiola, from Spain, works as a lawyer and has published numerous articles and books related to legal issues. Always interested in military history, he also regularly contributes to various Spanish military history magazines, for which he has written more than 50 articles. He has also published multiple pieces with the Universidad Autónoma de México. This is his first instalment for Helion's @War series.